WOMEN CREATING
PATRILYNY

WOMEN CREATING PATRILYNY

Gender and Environment in West Africa

AUDREY SMEDLEY

ALTAMIRA
PRESS

A Division of
ROWMAN & LITTLEFIELD PUBLISHERS, INC.
Walnut Creek • Lanham • New York • Toronto • Oxford

ALTAMIRA PRESS
A division of Rowman & Littlefield Publishers, Inc.
1630 North Main Street, #367
Walnut Creek, CA 94596
www.altamirapress.com

Rowman & Littlefield Publishers, Inc.
A wholly owned subsidiary of The Rowman & Littlefield Publishing Group
4501 Forbes Boulevard, Suite 200
Lanham, MD 20706

PO Box 317
Oxford
OX2 9RU, UK

British Library Cataloguing in Publication Information Available

Library of Congress Cataloging-in-Publication Data

Smedley, Audrey.
    Women creating patriliny : gender and environment in West Africa /
Audrey Smedley.
        p.   cm.
    Includes bibliographical references and index.
    ISBN 0-7591-0317-8 (hardcover : alk. paper)—ISBN 0-7591-0318-6
(pbk. : alk. paper)
    1. Women, Birom—Kinship.   2. Women, Birom—Social conditions.   3.
Women, Birom—Psychology.   4. Patrilineal kinship—Nigeria—Jos Plateau.
5. Sex role—Nigeria—Jos Plateau.   6. Jos Plateau (Nigeria)—Social
life and customs.   I. Title.
    DT515.45.B58S64   2003
    305.48'89636—dc21   2003011061

Printed in the United States of America

♾ ™ The paper used in this publication meets the minimum requirements of American National
Standard for Information Sciences—Permanence of Paper for Printed Library Materials, ANSI/
NISO Z39.48–1992.

CONTENTS

Preface   vii

Introduction   I

CHAPTER 1
The Birom People and Their History   15

CHAPTER 2
Ecological Features of the Precolonial Past   31

CHAPTER 3
Du Village: Organization of Space and People   49

CHAPTER 4
The Ecological Basis of the Kin Group   65

CHAPTER 5
The Life Cycle of the Kin Group   83

CHAPTER 6
Ritual and the Distribution of Public Power   101

CHAPTER 7
Village Wards and Other Forms of Social Control   113

CHAPTER 8
Gender, Marriage, and the Establishment of the Domestic Unit   129

CHAPTER 9
Internal Relationships within the Domestic Unit   163

CHAPTER 10
Social Networks: Webs of Kinship and Friendship   195

CHAPTER 11
Summary and Theoretical Implications   227

APPENDIX A
Economic Realities of the Colonial Era   237

APPENDIX B
Genealogies   259

References   265

Index   273

About the Author   275

PREFACE

EW EXPERIENCES HAVE BEEN as rewarding to me as the opportunity to do field research in anthropology. I was attracted to this field because it allowed me to travel and live in Africa, and during the two years that I was there, a whole new world opened up to me. It was marvelous and transfiguring; it brought insights that could not have been experienced anywhere else. While I cannot speak for others in this ambiguous field, the enlightenment that I received from my stay in West Africa has forever enriched my life and taught me powerful lessons on the human condition. I hope I have passed some of these on to my students and my children.

For their genial hospitality during my stay in Nigeria, I am extremely grateful to the then chief of Jos, the Honorable Rwang Pam, M.B.E., and the Da Gwom Du, Mallam Dung Rwang. Mallam Abubakar Mashegu, A.D.O., kindly took me on tour of many villages and was most helpful in introducing me to the plateau peoples. To Pam Choji, Nyam Pwajok, Dauda Chuang, Paul Rwang, Deme Rwang, Saratu Dung, and Anna Williams go my greatest gratitude for their friendship and ever-willing assistance in collecting information. To Kaneng, Chundung, Honghei, Honghonong; to my "mother" Kaneng; to Davou and Musa; and to all the others who let me share their lives for a time, I owe very special thanks. And with unceasing love and affection, I thank most of all the children of Du village, especially little Choji, for helping to teach me their language and the ways of their people. I only wish that I could have done more for them.

From the time of my arrival in Jos, my life was nourished by the friendship and kindness of many other people. Caroline and Hamo Sassoon invited me into their home with much warmth and cheerfulness; they were a great source of strength and comfort through illness. One can never fully repay such generosity. Major John Vitoria was a gold mine of information on the early years of mining and of relationships with the Birom and other people. I shall never forget him, nor shall I ever forget the unpretentious human warmth of Sister Thomas-Moore and her colleagues at the Roman Catholic Mission at Zawang. They have my warmest thanks. With deep appreciation for their friendship and hospitality, I must also thank Mr. and Mrs. Kayode Eso, Mr. and Mrs. John Lazari, Mr. and Mrs. Bernard Fagg, and Mallam Liman Ciroma, who helped make my stay so pleasant. Some of these friends, alas, are no longer with us, but I shall always cherish the times I spent with them.

Several of my colleagues read various versions or sections of the manuscript and offered helpful recommendations. I am very grateful for the help of Professor Sylvanus S. J. Cookey, who read an earlier version, and Professor Michael Horowitz at Binghamton University, who offered fruitful suggestions on several chapters. Dr. Tanya Baker, who completed the first field research among the Birom people, has graciously allowed me to use materials from her thesis. I thank them all. I also warmly thank Dr. Paul Baxter of Manchester University for the first critical review of the materials that appeared in my original dissertation and especially the late Professor Max Gluckman, who was able to review the original much larger manuscript before his death and was always a source of encouragement. Dr. and Mrs. Emrys Peters were my special friends at Manchester; a stay at their home was always delightful, and I only regret that Emrys left us too soon.

At Virginia Commonwealth University (VCU), where I revised and revamped the materials to focus on women, Michael Stern, my teaching assistant, helped with numerous tasks, such as checking references. Ken Hopson of the VCU Media Resource Center translated the genealogies into the computer, a formidable task that I could not have done myself. I thank them both. The original research was funded by a Ford Foundation Foreign Area Fellowship and a grant from the University of Manchester. The original manuscript from which this book emerged was prepared while I was a Fellow of the Radcliffe Institute in 1971–1973.

INTRODUCTION

ONE OF THE STRONGEST DEVELOPMENTS in anthropology over the past three decades has been the rise of studies that concentrate on women's positions, activities, and roles in society. By the 1970s, it had become apparent that descriptions and analyses of women's lives have been underdeveloped in most anthropological research.[1] Moreover, women had often been ignored by researchers, even in other fields, who failed to view women as agents of social change or as innovators. Scholars argued that women have been made invisible both by their low status in human societies and by researchers conditioned to androcentric (male-centered) perspectives on social systems (Milton 1979). Perhaps this is also a consequence of the reality that most anthropologists, especially those working in Africa, have been men. Given the nature of most human societies with their taboos on sexual interaction, few men, if any, can have the kind of intimate interactions with women that female researchers can have. It is an often unacknowledged reality that male scholars have been restricted in their access to women's private lives by the conventions of the societies they studied. Even many women anthropologists might not be able to collect the kind of information that would give them full access to the emic realities of the women's world.

As a result of the rise of a new feminist consciousness, there was a rush of publications, mostly by women scholars, designed to correct the inadequacy of older ethnographic materials. The theoretical postulates of this era posed the view that women everywhere held subordinate positions in society and were limited in their ability to influence social, political, and religious structures and processes. A model of a universal gender hierarchy in all societies appeared as axiomatic in much of the literature, and many published studies had the objective of describing and elucidating women's oppression in different societies.[2] The concerns of women scholars particularly were expressed in terms of women's inequality in access to positions of power, the ability to exercise power, access to and control over strategic resources, and decision making. Scholars focused on analyzing the sexual division of labor, the cultural construction of gender and its relationship to kinship patterns, and how inequality is manifest in practice and in symbolic forms.

In developing their analyses, some scholars rediscovered the nineteenth-century evolutionists, such as Friedrich Engels, J. J. Bachofen, Edward B. Tylor, and Lewis H. Morgan, who had speculated on the origin of the family and its development over time. These evolutionists had posited that early in the history of the human species, an era of promiscuity had given way to a period of matrilineal development when children were identified only with the mother, a connection that the birth process affirmed. Although the specifics of their theories vary, all saw this stage as being replaced subsequently by the stage of patrilineal identity and organization. For some social theorists, patrilyny was established only after men revolted against rule by women. Patrilyny itself was associated with the rise of property rights and the need to protect property and to transmit property in an orderly fashion from one generation to another. It was seen as a superior form of organization and soon became the dominant principle of social structure in most human societies. This is especially so in Africa. Several years ago, a student and I collected data on descent systems in Africa from the Human Relations Area Files and estimated that in some 80 to 85 percent of all African societies, the ideology of patrilyny is the main organizing principle.

Patrilyny is a mechanism by which children are identified with the father's kin group, that is, a rule of membership and descent. It also strongly correlates with the ownership of property in the male line and male leadership positions in the household and polity. Theoretically, all positions of authority are held by males, and these are transmitted directly to the next generations of males. Patrilineal societies in Africa (and most everywhere else) are also virilocal, with young women leaving their natal homes (of their fathers) at marriage to live in the households of their husband's kin group. It is essentially these facts that gave rise, for example, to Claude Lévi-Strauss's (1960, 1971) "alliance theory" and the wide panoply of beliefs about inequality between the sexes we have seen in the literature. These facts appear to be at the core of "male domination." Women seemed to have no "civic" personality but were moved around like pawns between groups of male kinsmen.

In the 1970s, assumptions were made, particularly by some feminists, that under matrilyny women had greater freedom and higher status with greater control over resources and their children. When men revolted and established patrilyny, male authority over women and children was guaranteed. Thus, matrilyny, in the minds of perhaps most contemporary scholars, became associated with positive benefits for women, while patrilyny was connected with patriarchy and women's oppression.³ Though it was discovered that males also held the leadership positions in matrilineal societies, the ethnographic data seemed to suggest that women experienced less subordination and oppression under matrilyny.

This model of evolutionary change from matrilyny to patrilyny contains assumptions and biases, inherent in Western cosmology, that suffuse all discussions about gender. First, if men had to establish patrilyny by force, one can speculate that there must be perpetual resentment by women and "natural" antagonism between the sexes. Second, women would clearly prefer matrilyny, and therefore they must only tolerate patrilyny wherever it is found in the world. Third, women would not support patrilyny unless it continued to be maintained by male force, or, fourth, women have been brainwashed (by men) into its preservation.

When we look at the ethnographic realities from around the world, we see considerable contradictions between the assumptions of this model and the realities of women's lives. African women in particular are known to be independent, strong, assertive, and self-assured.⁴ There is little or no objective evidence of "natural" conflict between men and women, except in Western industrial societies and in those societies impacted by Western cultural values of gender behavior. It might be argued that women do not *know* that they are oppressed by men in these patrilineal systems until they have been exposed to a wider experience of freedom. However, ideas about women's freedoms do not exist in a vacuum. They must be compared not only to the experiences of women in other societies but also, more appropriately, to the experiences of freedom or lack of freedom of the men in their own societies. In most Third World societies, ordinary men have no more freedom or control over their lives than do their women. Even where men and women can vote, the choices that they have are extremely limited. Economic and political options for all people are constrained by colonialism, Western domination, dictatorships, and the "global market." Few ordinary men (if any) are capable of imposing their will on social systems long dictated by military, economic, and political elites. So I think it important to question whether the men of any Third World community have any rights, powers, or resources much greater than those of women. Both men and women are impoverished and impotent to effect change in their lives.

Even as the paradigm of women's universal oppression was embraced in anthropological publications, some scholars were already beginning to question the uniformity and ethnocentrism with which such assumptions were made. For example, Eleanor Leacock (1978) raised questions about the universality of women's low positions by demonstrating that in egalitarian societies such as foraging groups (hunters and gatherers), women were essentially the equals of men and that gender hierarchy did not exist. She and other researchers warned that scholars in the West were using concepts and imposing categories of reality on Third World women derived from the experiences of Western societies. The very notions of "power," "freedom," and "autonomy" are clearly Western conceptualizations interconnected with Western ideals of "individualism" and "democracy." Research revealed that Third World women did not perceive their world in terms comparable to such concepts in the West. Moreover, the gauges by which we have measured women's status (such as property ownership, control over the means of production, access to public office, and the exercise of public forms of power) clearly reflect Western cultural values and emphases on power and control.

Throughout this period, we have seen the appearance of a number of different theoretical perspectives on women, including psychoanalysis, biological determinism, structuralism, culturalism, and symbolic analysis. Publications have challenged older models of the sexual division of labor in hunting-and-gathering and simple horticultural societies (see, among others, Peacock 1991; Slocum 1975; Weiner 1976). Others have contested the widely held argument that biological differences are the bases for women's subordinate positions. There is, however, widespread acceptance of evidence that gender differences in all societies are greatly determined by cultural factors. This position allows us to comprehend the variety of gender roles found around the world without precluding or ignoring those features of women's lives, such as menstruation, childbearing, and child rearing, that is, biologically based realties that all women have in common that are different from the experiences of men.

This study of a patrilineal society in West Africa does not attempt to contradict all facts concerning widespread subordination of women in human societies, but it brings into question the nature of patrilyny itself and the notion that all patrilineal systems are patriarchal and thus uniformly oppressive to women. "Male dominance," however defined, may well be widespread and is assumed to be so especially in patrilineal societies, but it is important to specify its content and the ways in which patrilineal ideology is manifest. What constitutes patrilineal customs and beliefs differs from one society to another, and the degree to which women can acquire respect and status, autonomy, and even social power may vary widely in different patrilineal societies.

The situation of Birom women ostensibly and superficially appears to be consonant with conventional portrayals of African women. As in many other patrilineal and "patriarchal" societies, they were traditionally barred from holding what high political and ritual offices existed, from owning or inheriting property, and from what appeared to be major decision-making roles in both public and private domains. Other overt manifestations of women's subordinate status can be found in the deference shown to their husbands and fathers. On public walkways and paths, women walk behind their fathers and husbands, and most women take care to cast their eyes downward and assume a humble demeanor while traveling together or engaging in any public situation. They are generally held to be subservient to men and are seen by men as dependent and weak.

Such was their ideology as I noted during two years of field research. Yet like other African women, they did not usually display the behavioral attributes of persons in subordinate positions except in certain specific circumstances. They appeared to have a strong sense of self-identity, autonomy, and pride in their sexual beings. They perceived themselves as having peculiar rights as women, and they had effective means of defending these rights when necessary. When deference and obedience were shown to men, it was primarily to their fathers and husbands, not to men at large (compare Oboler 1985, especially chap. 4) and based on custom rather than personal inclination. This is a phenomenon rarely recognized in much of the literature that seems to describe women as subordinate to all men. While it appears anomalous, incongruous, or inconsistent in Western eyes, Birom women were also the chief supporters of the main ideological ingredients of their patrilineal system.

The Birom people inhabit the northernmost spur of the Jos plateau of Nigeria. This is a rugged, sparse land intermittently dotted with immense rock outcroppings that form clustered hills. The plateau is geographically sandwiched between two distinct ecological zones: the rain forest to the south and the dry savanna grasslands of the western Sudan to the north and surrounding areas. The Birom were one of many indigenous peoples grouped together by colonial administrators and anthropological writers under the term "Plateau Pagans" in part to distinguish them from the Muslim Hausa in the north and surrounding areas and the largely Christian peoples of the south.

Until the mid-twentieth century, not a great deal was known ethnographically about the various peoples who occupied this region. Aside from ethnographic notes in the colonial government files and some brief published descriptions by travelers and colonial government officials (Ames 1934; Gunn 1953, 1956; Meek 1925, 1950; Temple and Temple 1919), little has been written on the cultures of the plateau area. The only professional ethnographic descriptions of the Birom are Tanya Baker's (1954) unpublished study of Bachit and my own articles on the village of Udu (Smedley 1974, 1980).

Like other peoples of the north, the Birom first had contact with Europeans during the early decades of the twentieth century, when the discovery of tin deposits by European mining interests brought outsiders to the plateau. British commercial penetration into other areas of northern Nigeria had begun in the closing years of the nineteenth century. One of the last areas to be brought under British colonial control was the plateau region, where some forty-five different ethnic groups made their homes. In certain locales, mining camps and market towns were soon established, bringing a variety of foreign elements to the plateau. There soon developed in the midst of indigenous lands a complex urbanized society composed almost entirely of foreigners. The forced proximity of these culturally different peoples produced a harvest of myths, misunderstandings, and friction between the indigenous people and the outsiders, a fact that is hardly novel to any colonial situation. By the end of the colonial period (1960), missionaries, older colonial agents, miners, commercial traders, and others who were familiar with the area generally believed that the "pagans" were basically conservative and had been little affected by several decades of contact with the outside world. It was claimed that they had stubbornly refused all efforts to modify their way of life and had declined to mingle with other Nigerian peoples. Contrasts between the plateau people and the more urban Africans, many of whom were ambitious Yoruba and Igbo peoples from the south, were often pointed out as if to demonstrate and prove this rigid adherence to a "primitive" way of life. Many plateau peoples remained in their hill villages, remote from the centers of political and commercial activities, and, like most indigenous peoples, resisted attempts to alter their behavior and their institutions.

The fieldwork on which this study is based took place during the final year of colonial rule and the first year of independence in Nigeria (1959–1961), when the full thrust of the colonial experience with all its ramifications had perhaps reached its zenith. My general objective was to record as much information as possible about the traditional history and culture of the Birom peoples and to examine the ways in which the people and culture were changing as a result of the mining activities and their influences.

It soon became obvious that the indigenous economic pursuits—horticulture, supplemented by hunting and gathering—were no longer sufficient to provide subsistence for the Birom people. On the high plateau, mining and its ancillary activities (labor camps, shops, bars, markets, money lenders, banks, and so forth) had created a severe shortage of arable land and had heavily contributed to deforestation. The result was disturbance to the preexisting ecological balances and to the infinitely complex interlinking of human, animal, and floral relationships that had been the Birom ecosystem. Despite superficial appearances of a rigid separation between village and town lifestyles, investigations disclosed the increasing dependence of the Birom on the products and services of the urban centers and local markets and particularly their necessity to participate in the money economy. Consequently, this study explores in part how the Birom confronted and grappled with the alien forces, both material and nonmaterial, that impinged on their lives as a result of the colonial experience. Of particular importance was the effect on the lives of women.

Birom culture before colonialism (roughly beginning 1910–1930) was a product of adaptive processes that had been taking place on the plateau for at least several hundred years. Since adaptation is a dynamic process of both temporal and functional dimensions, part of this study projects back in time and attempts to assess and analyze the continuity of adaptive changes over time as well as responses to the disruptions of colonialism. This study thus reflects a cultural ecological perspective, one that was determined largely by the data and the fieldwork experience itself (Baker 1962; Bates 1998; Hardesty 1972; Vayda 1969). An ecological perspective has greater explanatory force because it enables us to seek out and to recognize historical (diachronic) events, the constraints of environmental realities, as well as functional and causal linkages among social institutions and the processes that are described.

The Birom data suggest that there were stabilizing elements in the precontact cultures that permitted the retention of basic features of the sociocultural system and yet facilitated their adjustments to change. At the same time, some features of Birom culture and social organization appear to provide sufficient flexibility so that external influences were absorbed or contained without major disturbances in the social system or dramatic modifications in their lifestyles. Moreover, the circumstances of the contact situation itself stimulated or exacerbated certain processes of change and conflict that were already intrinsic to the sociocultural system.

This study begins, then, with an examination of the historical and ecological circumstances under which the Birom people came to settle on and adapt to the harsh lands of the high plateau. This sets the wider context for the investigation of how gender was constructed in the process of dealing with the problems posed by the environment. Earlier writers and travelers had hypothesized that these peoples began moving on to the plateau, beginning in the seventeenth century, while fleeing from slave raiding and warfare of the previous four centuries (Ames 1934; Davies 1944, 1949; Gunn 1953; Temple and Temple 1919). Oral histories from many and varied sources confirmed this, but the specifics differ from region to region. As will be shown, the plateau provided an unusual location for protecting women and children and for defensive actions against slave raiders.

Chapter 1 briefly examines the experience of colonialism and the myriad consequences of not only colonial policies but also the increasing immigration of foreign peoples onto the plateau and the impact this had on indigenous people and natural resources. In this connection, I suggest that the real issues that women everywhere faced and still confront in the colonial and postcolonial worlds have little to do with conflict with or opposition to their men but rather with how to function within societies impacted by the forces of the world market, the exploitative policies of overseas companies, food shortages (often due to the overproduction of cash crops), development programs, unstable currencies, intractable diseases, lack of clean water, lack of schools, inadequate health care, and a host of other problems that they daily confront.

In addition to environmental constraints, the many ethnic groups on the plateau were compelled to develop varying relationships among themselves. In this book, I identify certain features of interethnic interaction that characterized the area and describe intervillage marriages, the Birom custom of sending girls to "Pyomo" lands, and the flexibility of ethnic identity that permitted individuals to migrate and settle among other ethnic groups and assume new ethnic characteristics. This kind of fluidity of ethnic identity and the porous nature of ethnic boundaries seem to characterize many other parts of the African continent. These facts provide a different model of "ethnicity" than the rigid, singular, and inflexible ones too often associated with Western concepts of identity.

In chapter 2, I go back in time and examine the ecology—those aspects of the natural and social environments that historically were critical to the survival of the Birom and other ethnic groups over the past several hundred years. Two major features are identified. The first was the general low fertility of the land and the need to develop cultigens that could survive in the desiccated soils of the plateau. One strategy of adapting to this reality was to divide the land into distinct cultivating zones each with different carrying capacities or capabilities for producing varied crops. This allowed the Birom to cultivate a wide variety of food crops under highly adverse conditions. The pattern of cultivation was also a crucial basis for the sexual division of labor—for the development of gender specific tasks around which evolved an elaborate ideology about gender differences.

The second factor was the fear of warfare and slave raiding that plagued the plateau peoples until well into the twentieth century. As late as 1960, older people still spoke of the hostilities that wracked some of the villages and the constancy of their fears. Real or not, men and women made numerous decisions on the basis of perceived fears. As I will show, these decisions led to certain practices, customs, and ways of organizing that were still intact more than a half century after the British imposed the "pax Britannica" (1902) that made slavery, warfare, and slave trading illegal. How they adapted to these fears was a major contributor to the construction of gender roles.

Chapters 3 to 7 describe and analyze the traditional social organization and examine the ways in which social units, processes, principles, and institutions adjusted to certain realities of the plateau environment. I emphasize a fundamental aspect of adaptive interaction: the relationships of men to property in land and to one another. This perspective isolates a field of social interaction identified as the "politicojural domain" in which the key figures are men and the relationships among them. The idea of a distinct politicojural domain in which men are thought to function and a domestic domain developed around the activities and interests of women was first introduced by Meyer Fortes (1959, 1969), who defined "jural" as "denoting certain aspects or elements of right and duty, privilege and responsibility, laid down in the rules that govern social relations" (1969, 89). These rules "have the backing of the whole society" and "derive their sanction from the political framework of society." Fortes contrasts this with the "moral authority" that governs individual relations at a more private and personal level that relates to norms of conduct. Moral and affective norms and customs derive from the organization of the family and ultimately reflect an analytically discrete domain in which women and kinship relationships constitute major components. This distinction has been extremely useful for analyzing many traditional African societies where complex laws and customs have evolved and there is commonly a strict and highly visible gender division of labor. The concept of separate domains centering on the activities and perspectives of women and men is a flexible one that can be calibrated for a wide variety of social systems; in this, the Birom are not exceptional.

This approach focuses on the structures and processes that preserve the continuity of human groups in relation to the divisions of land. At the level of the patrilineal kin group, the basic unit of society, the linkages among men provide essential structure and stability to the social system but only a limited range of flexibility. It is important to delineate this, as, I will argue later, the most significant findings of this study demonstrate that the relationships among men are more rigidly structured than those that women have with either men or other women.

Chapter 3 describes the village setting and the spatial and social relationships of people as they are organized into kinship units. Chapter 4 looks at some of the ways in which the kin groups derive many of their features from their need to cope with environmental realities. The size and friability of kin groups and many other features all relate directly to the strategies by which land is held and exploited. Chapter 5 explores the life cycles of kin groups as they relate to strategic resources in cultivable land and analyzes in detail the various stages through which each kin group must pass. Restrictions on the flexibility of male-centered units are clearly demonstrated; they provide the necessary and important background for examining the roles of women.

Chapters 6 and 7 describe the indigenous Birom organization of what we would interpret as public power and political processes. The manifestation and exercise of social and political authority is shown as highly dispersed. Much overt power is exercised through ritual leaders who conduct certain ceremonies connected to the annual activities of the farming cycle. There is no form of power, secular or ritual, that is concentrated in a single position, but generalized social power is distributed among a number of individuals and institutions. One of the most important institutions is the internal village division of the ward (*manjei*) and its headman, where many forms of social control and adjudication of complaints occur.

Knowing the structure of male relationships provides only partial knowledge about the social system. In order to fully investigate and to comprehend how this system works, we must look at the activities and roles of women. I demonstrate that women in Birom society function in arenas that are very different from those of men. Chapters 8 to 10 concentrate with more detail on the lives of women, the roles they play within the structure of male relationships, and their interactions with other men and women. These chapters explore the nature of gender distinctions, how they evolved over historical time, and how they relate to adaptive processes. The analysis demonstrates particularly how women's decision making, their activities, and the values they promote contribute to the successful exploitation of this habitat. In the analysis, I emphasize the domain of domestic life and examine the household or domestic unit as it functioned in the closing years of colonial rule. Women are at the center of the household and are seemingly excluded from the realm of adult men, where major economic and political decisions are presumed to take place. Yet a central finding of this research has to do with how much women are involved in decision making and in maintaining and preserving the values and principles of this patrilineal system.

Chapter 8 looks at gender and marriage and the importance of marriage in creating a viable domestic unit. Chapter 9 investigates the significant internal relationships that ensue after a domestic unit is established, and chapter 10 examines women's relationships with individuals beyond the domestic unit. I show how certain customs and practices are seen by women as vital to their interests while at the same time they function to support the patrilineal ideology.

The system of male relationships described in earlier chapters could not exist or flourish without the support of women. Women not only initially instill the ideological values of patrilyny in their children, both male and female, but they also monitor, guide, and set limits on the behavior of men using appeals to traditional values and customs. While much of their influence is subtle and unobtrusive, what became obvious to me on a number of occasions was how much women were involved in ritual, economic, and political matters, affecting the decisions of the men who held the dominant political and economic positions.

In chapter 11, I conclude that many of the institutions and customs associated with this patrilineal system may well have been inspired, created, or instituted by women in furtherance of their and their children's interests as they perceived them. The custom that I have called "Njem" (chapter 10) is a clear example. This study provides the first and only in-depth description and analysis thus far of a custom identified in the literature as "cicisbeism." During the second year of research, I collected numerous data about this practice that allows women to legally take lovers after marriage. I was intrigued by its ramifications and especially the revelation that it was primarily women (and children) who benefited from the custom and who continue to support it.

This study thus raises questions about the nature of patrilineal systems and how they have been perceived and interpreted in the past. The analysis suggests that one reason for the dominance of patrilyny as an organizing principle in human societies is that perhaps many of its critical features were invented by women. Certainly women have protected and promoted the values of patrilyny in many other societies, but ethnologists have not always understood the reasons for this. It has long been accepted in some anthropological circles that women are naturally conservative and distrustful of change, as Edward Evans-Pritchard (1965) once suggested. This presumed quality appears to explain the wide prevalence of patrilyny as a product of women's passivity or conservative nature. However, my study of the Birom contradicts the vision of women as passive agents in the construction of social realities. It suggests a different perspective on the nature of patrilineal systems and women's roles within them. Part of that different perspective, I argue, is to recognize that ideas of patriarchy and patrilyny should not be perceived as covarying phenomena. Patrilyny is not a single uniform phenomenon but varies from one society to another just as the exercise of male power varies independently of forms of descent.

Since the roles and activities of men and women are so different in Birom society, this study presents and summarizes the analysis, in the final chapter, by posing a different model for the roles of women. This provides the best insight into the functioning of Birom society. Although it has its detractors, the use of theoretical models has long been recognized as a valuable technique for examining, understanding, and explaining human social systems. Given the extraordinary complexity of the Birom social system, the value of the models is that they translate large amounts of data on structures, institutions, customs, and processes into a series of clearly understandable principles. Not every ethnographic fact can be or need be encompassed by the models, but the reader can judge the effectiveness of explanatory paradigms by how much they contribute to the overall comprehension of this social system.

Most of this study was prepared within a few years after I left the field. The rest was completed during a period of two years while I was in residence as a fellow of the Radcliffe Institute in the early 1970s. When I first offered a version of this study for publication, it was during a period of the rising feminist movement in the United States. Several publishers' representatives informed me that a work of this type would probably not "go over well" in the atmosphere of enhanced feminist consciousness, as it did not reflect the dominant feminist philosophy of the times. As one editor informed me, the current rage was for documenting the pervasive oppression of women worldwide, not rationalizing male dominance. This was a great shock. I did not believe that anyone familiar with the social sciences, particularly the anthropological need for objectivity, could draw this conclusion from this manuscript.

Times have changed. Several women anthropologists have criticized the ways in which Western feminist philosophy, beliefs, and issues have been applied to indigenous African peoples (Amadiume 1987; Obbo 1980; Okonjo 1976; Oppong 1981), and new studies of African women have documented realities about their lives that often contradict Western assumptions (see Hodgson 2000; Mikell 1997; Oboler 1985). My hope is that this study will contribute something more to our understanding of how successfully some peoples have adapted to extreme ecological circumstances and especially to our understanding of women in Africa and around the world and the adaptive roles that they play. It should raise questions about the assumptions we have associated with "patrilyny" and "patriarchy." More nuanced understandings of social interaction among women and men in different societies are clearly necessary.

Since most of this book was originally written shortly after I came out of the field, it describes a contemporary reality of that time. Except for when I am referring to experiences, customs, and traditions of the remote past, I have left the descriptions in the ethnographic present, even though it should be clear that many circumstances have changed. It describes a people as I knew them and retains the freshness of that description. It presents a way of life that may well be no longer extant. The peoples and cultures of the plateau no doubt have undergone dramatic changes since independence (there has been a university in the town of Jos for over three decades). However, there is great value in preserving descriptions of indigenous cultures before they become totally engulfed by globalization processes and the transformations that they bring in their wake. This ethnography provides a baseline for understanding more recent changes that have occurred. More important, however, is the theoretical perspective that invokes a different approach to gender relationships in a traditional society and enables us to break through the limitations and possible misinterpretations of older views of patriliny.

Many anthropologists have criticized the use of certain terms like "traditional" and "modern" to refer to social systems of the Third World prior to and after contact with the Western world. And I agree that these are often inaccurate terms for designating cultural phenomena. They sometimes suggest an erroneous and illusory abruptness in dynamic processes of change and dramatic transformations that are deceptive. We should recognize that most real changes take place rather slowly. Moreover, there are precontact features of many cultures that persist into present times and circumstances, and sometimes these can be so adapted to contemporary realities that they indeed may become "modern." At the time of this research, most Birom villages were still intact, and most people still carried on a way of life that was clearly indigenous to the plateau. Fortunately, there were individuals still alive of both European and native backgrounds who were present when the first contacts were made as early as 1918. (In some parts of the plateau, the first European was not seen until the 1930s.) They were able to help confirm the existence and persistence of traditional cultural features as well as observed changes. Given the wealth of information that I was able to obtain, it is possible and necessary to make important distinctions between folkways and institutions that clearly pre-date the colonial presence and postcontact transformations in indigenous lifestyles.

Finally, the Birom sociocultural system is extremely complex. I have tried not to generalize or oversimplify, but this is always a danger where space is limited. My only expectation is that the reader will understand how I reached an important conclusion. The data from this study suggest that many of the institutions and practices associated with this patrilineal system and ideology were generated in the past and perpetuated in the modern context by women in furtherance of their own individual and collective interests.

Notes

1. Some of the earliest works include the papers in Reiter (1975) and Rosaldo and Lamphere (1974) and books by Friedl (1975) and Schlegel (1972), among many others. The list of publications on women has grown enormously, and theoretical perspectives have likewise been transformed, some confirming, some contradicting older positions. See an overview in Mascia-Lees and Black (2000).

2. For examples, see Ardener (1975), Boserup (1970), Friedl (1975), Lerner (1986), Ortner and Whitehead (1981), Rosaldo and Lamphere (1974), and Sanday (1981).

3. For brief accounts of these and other theories, see di Leonardo (1991) and Mascia-Lees and Black (2000). For a broader exploration of theories of patriarchy, see Lerner (1986).

4. Women appeared as leaders in many African societies. They have "founded cities, led migrations, conquered kingdoms" (Lebeuf 1960, 94.) See other articles in Hafkin and Bay (1976), Hay and Stichter (1995), and Paulme (1960). These are just a few of the well-known works on African women. Because of space limitations, I have limited the references and bibliographic citations in this study.

The Birom People and Their History I

T HE BIROM-SPEAKING PEOPLES are the largest distinguishable cultural group among the so-called pagan tribes of the Jos plateau. The plateau itself is part of a much larger geocultural region of formerly non-Muslim, non-Christian peoples known as the Middle Belt of northern Nigeria.[1] This is an area of great cultural and linguistic diversity, with an estimated forty or fifty different ethnic groups and as many different languages. There has long been a great paucity of anthropological knowledge about the multiplicity of indigenous peoples who are scattered over the region (see Greenberg 1956; Gunn 1953, 1956; Isichei 1982; Murdock 1959).

The Birom are a conglomerate of peoples speaking dialects of mutual similarities who had no centralized form of political coherence prior to the imposition of British colonial rule early in the twentieth century. Until the middle of the twentieth century, even the name Birom was not consistently applied to a territorially delimited society whose component members bore some semblance of common organization and culture that made them distinct from others. At varying times in the past, different names have been applied to different sections of the present-day Birom peoples (Gunn [1953] records Burum, Burumawa, Borrom, Kibo, and Kibyen, among others). The Birom have been intermingled with many other peoples, some of whom have also been classified as Birom largely because of cultural similarities and patterns of immigration and settlement.

At the end of the colonial period, many Birom see themselves and are seen by their neighbors (the Jerawa, Anaguta, and Afusare to the north; Rukuba and Irigwe to the northwest; Ganawuri and the Katab-speaking people to the west; and other groups, such as the Sura and Angas to the south) as an ethnically distinct people. Yet there is a fair degree of similarities in material culture, economic features, and the physical settings of village life throughout the plateau. The major criterion for the division of people is language, but recognized similarities of languages or dialects are not sufficient to evoke sentiments of common feelings. Greenberg (1963) places Birom along with some forty-four other plateau languages in a separate subdivision of the Benue-Congo subfamily in the large Niger-

Congo family of languages. In the peopling of the plateau area, all these peoples have interpenetrated extensively, and ethnic identities are often very fluid (Isichei 1982). To my knowledge, Birom is the only plateau language to have been extensively studied by a trained linguist (Bouquiaux 1970, 2001).

In addition to language, dress and personal decorations differ from one group to another, in some cases from one village to another. Within the Birom region itself, there are local cultural variations with regard to food habits and taboos, major and minor rituals, dress and adornment, as well as dialectal differences that increase with distance. Significant also are differences in political organization at any one point in time, from a few communities having hereditary chiefs to loosely organized acephalous communities whose members are traditionally bound together by ties of common origin, kinship, and ritual affiliation.

With the coming of British colonialism early in the twentieth century, several attempts were made to unite the Birom-speaking groups under a single Native Administration. By the end of the colonial period (1960), all the Birom villages had been organized by the British under a hierarchy of officials ranging from village chiefs to district chiefs to the "paramount chief" of Jos. In 1960, the chief of Jos was head of the Native Authority in Jos Division, which included seven non-Birom districts. Even so, he was commonly referred to by most Birom as well as by non-Birom as the chief of the Birom.

At the time of first European contact, all the plateau peoples inhabited scattered settlements, primarily within the hill masses. These settlements were described as villages, village areas, or hamlets in the early literature of missionaries and colonial administrators. Each village was apparently politically autonomous, while at the same time each had special types of ties with other villages or village clusters. Relationships among villages were extremely complex, being based on trade, intermarriage, and an intricate system of ritual and ceremonial ties. These functioned in a quasi-political manner to structure the interconnections of villages throughout the plateau to one another among both Birom and other ethnic groups.

The census of 1963 gave the total Birom population in all of northern Nigeria as 118,685 persons. The vast majority (over 95 percent) was concentrated in the rural areas in thirteen of the twenty districts of Jos Division in Plateau Province. An estimated 1,788 were settled in areas of the province outside Jos Division. Most of these inhabited small settlements or mining camps in Pankshin Division, a neighboring region contiguous to the southern Birom territory. Of the total provincial population of 114,292, only 3 percent were designated as living in urban centers, and most of these were in Jos and Bukuru towns. Birom people were not highly motivated to migrate to non-Birom areas. A few young men have been able to acquire education and have found careers primarily in government service and as clerks, laboratory assistants, military personnel, and workers in textile industries.

The Birom constituted some 25 percent of the total population in Jos Division, living primarily in the northernmost districts. Theoretically, they occupied some 1,020 of 1,435 square miles in Jos Division and of 12,426 square miles in the province. But such statistics are misleading in that most of the province has been under mining leases for several decades or are barren, denuded areas of little value for human occupation.

For centuries, this has been a region of apparently frequent turbulence. Beginning in the twelfth century, the leaders of surrounding Hausa states increasingly turned to Islam and began to wage holy wars (jihad) against their neighbors. They also fought among themselves from time to time for control of the southern entrepôts of the trans-Sahara trade and for commercial dominance. Among the goods traded across the Sahara were slaves, albeit in nowhere near the numbers that were later to be transported across the Atlantic. Hausa middlemen also received slaves from the plateau communities when the latter periodically raided one another. Historians and geographers who have attempted to reconstruct the history of the Middle Belt area agree that most of the peoples now on the plateau are descendants of refugees who arrived here in the wake of the disturbances caused by warfare and slave raiding. According to Gleave and Prothero (1971), "A further response to slave raiding was to seek refuge in hill areas, and this was widespread in the Middle Belt of Nigeria as elsewhere in West Africa" (321).

The Encroaching Modern World

The first European on the plateau was Henry William Laws, an Australian mining engineer who was hired by the Royal Niger Co., a British overseas trading company, to investigate rumors of tin deposits near Bauchi in the north. Just before Christmas of 1903, he, his assistant Tom Lowry, and an entourage of African servants, soldiers, and carriers arrived in the area. They made camp near a village called Bukuru and proceeded to attempt to establish relationships with the surrounding peoples. His party was received with suspicion on the part of even the friendlier villages and with open hostility from others. While he described the people of Vwang (Vom) as very friendly, his outfit had a three-day "skirmish" with the Gyel forces.[2] With military assistance from the colonial government, Gyel was defeated; later, other hostile groups were subdued, and Laws was able to make a tenuous peace.

Laws brought in 600 carriers to outfit his first camp. These men (and a few women) were predominantly from the southern regions of Nigeria and included both Yoruba and Igbo people. Within a decade, Laws had established the first tin-mining company on the plateau, Naraguta Tin Mines, Ltd. Increasing numbers of Hausa people from the north were also hired on in varying capacities; Hausa became the lingua franca of the area. A little marketplace called "Guash" (pronounced "Jos") by the Hausa retainers became the center of commercial activities for the mines and eventually the administrative center for the entire plateau. From that time on, there were to be large numbers of foreign peoples migrating onto the plateau, nearly all of whom were associated with the rapidly developing mining industry and those ancillary industries that serviced it. In 1912, the first Native Administration was introduced in Jos Division to deal with the nonindigenous peoples. This was a significant political event as the railroad reached Jos in 1914, and the plateau was permanently connected with the south and its peoples.

In the early 1960s, Jos was a bustling and sprawling town of about 50,000 inhabitants. It was second only to Kano as a leading commercial and transportation metropolis in the northern region. Because of its location in the Middle Belt area, it is the main gateway to the north. The African population is predominantly foreign to the area and includes representatives of up to thirty different ethnic groups from other areas of Nigeria as well as from Ghana, Sierra Leone, Cameroon, and other neighboring states. The non-African population, numbering 54,122 in the entire province, included a smattering of British, French, Scandinavians, Lebanese, Indians, Italians, Americans, and a few other nationalities. Most were men working by contract on special projects and rarely had any interactions with the indigenous peoples.

Ten miles south of Jos is the new town of Bukuru, which almost exclusively services the mining industry. At any one time, there are perhaps 12,000 to 15,000 inhabitants of Bukuru, and it shares with Jos a similar heterogeneity of people. The oldest section of Bukuru, known as Clerks Quarters, was laid out in 1929 to provide housing sites for mining employees. Further plots were opened in 1931 and especially during the 1940s, when an acceleration in the production of tin and columbite was demanded by the Allies for their World War II operations.

To accommodate all this growth, some of the indigenous peoples who had settled in the area had to be displaced. There are no records of how many homesites or people were removed or what happened to these peoples. Nearly half the present-day inhabitants of Bukuru are from southern Nigeria, and they make their living in the mining industry as white-collar workers, artisans, skilled workers, contractors, engineers, truck drivers, and heavy-machinery operators. Others are storekeepers, barbers, bar owners, hotel workers, and street vendors. The remainder are Hausa and other people from the north, the majority of whom made up most of the unskilled workers, hiring themselves on as casual laborers and tributers who contract labor on their own. Very few of the original inhabitants of the plateau live and work in the towns. In 1961, for example, there were only 671 persons from all the "pagan" groups listed as residents of Jos and many fewer in Bukuru. Virtually all of them have become assimilated to a Hausa way of life as converts to Islam or have converted to Christianity, with their home lives, dress, and behavior reflecting missionary influences.

After World War II, public primary schools were established in several of the larger districts of the plateau, although mission schools had been in operation irregularly since 1909. By 1960, there was at least one junior primary school in all districts, and there were several senior primary schools, with others in the planning stage. There is also a secondary school for boys in Kuru District, and both boys and girls may be educated at the secondary school level at Gindiri, founded by the Sudan United Mission (a British-based Protestant missionary organization), about fifty miles south of Jos. The gradual process by which schools were established means that until 1960, relatively small numbers of young people had some formal education. Some of the large mining companies have training schools in Bukuru and in several other areas where mechanical and driver education is available.

The peoples who still live in the indigenous villages are on the whole visibly distinct from townspeople. Isolated in the hill masses or on the lower slopes, they live on the borders of chronic poverty. Few can afford the Western- or Hausa-style clothing worn by townspeople. The severity of their lives on the plateau in the precontact period has been transmuted into impoverishment at the lowest level in a now stratified industrializing society. It is no exaggeration to observe that individuals in most other ethnic groups, Europeans and other Africans included, look down on the "pagans" as dirty, primitive, and illiterate. For Europeans, they embody all their stereotyped prejudices about African peoples. To some Nigerians, they are a nuisance, for most others a source of embarrassment. Their way of life as well as their religious beliefs are viewed with contempt by many Muslims and Christians alike.

At the time of this study, the towns, the mining and labor camps, and the ubiquitous foreigners were a potent, omnipresent part of the larger Birom ecological setting. The few urban centers especially represent a field of strong countervailing forces, both attracting and repelling. On the one hand, the Birom must deal with these centers out of mounting dependence on the market products they provide. On the other hand, there are features of Bukuru and Jos that attract men and women away from the obligations and responsibilities to which they were conditioned in the indigenous culture. Traditional values become easily subverted by the expediency of immediate gains in an economic realm wherein different sets of rules and expectations operate. New lifestyles, new ideologies, and new concepts of work/pleasure/leisure threaten the foundations of the Birom sense of rightness in personal and social relationships. It is an alien world that is becoming more and more familiar, so that in some instances it is becoming difficult to separate the old and traditional from the new.

Problems of the Colonial Era

The encroachment by outsiders into an already occupied habitat did not proceed without the production of inordinately difficult and virtually unsolvable problems for the indigenous peoples. Problems originated in the first decades of European hegemony, and these were connected with the growth of the mining industry along with its associated proliferation of foreign immigrants. At the end of 1903, there were only Mr. Laws, several aides, and their retinue of servants, carriers, laborers, and interpreters to launch the mining industry. In June and July 1910, there came a rush of prospectors, and the following year saw an estimated 400 Europeans in Central (Bauchi) Province and over 9,000 foreign laborers, constituting a floating mining population.

So rapid was the development of the mining industry that little thought was given to the strain on food and forestry resources for the burgeoning population or the impending shortage of farmlands as more and more acreage was alienated to mining. In 1914, there was a serious famine throughout the Bauchi territories (as they were then known) with the result that native production, which had hitherto been the main source of food supply to the laborers, was found to be wholly inadequate to meet the needs of both the indigenous and the immigrant peoples. Subsequently, several abortive efforts were made to establish cash crops, such as Irish potatoes. For a variety of reasons, the potatoes would not grow, so the project was soon abandoned.

Meanwhile, other foodstuffs began to be imported onto the plateau by truck from more productive surrounding areas, such as the lowlands and from Bauchi Province off the plateau. By 1930, most of the foods for the foreign population were imported, with large amounts being shipped from overseas for the growing European population. The colonial government anticipated that the indigenous peoples were able to supply themselves with foods indefinitely. But some observers were already suggesting that food was becoming in short supply even in large villages.

The demand of the foreign settlers for firewood led to rapid deforestation of the plateau without any form of private or public program for the restoration of wooded areas. It was noted as early as 1912 (Annual Report) that the deterioration of sylvan products in some areas was occurring at a great pace. In 1924, an estimated 250,000 head-loads were being sold annually in the markets of Jos Division alone. A brief note in the Provincial Annual Report of 1923 observed that "firewood has become quite a problem." Despite a few efforts at reforestation, the rate of denudation and soil erosion accelerated, creating vast tracts of treeless land.

With more than two million cubic feet of wood fuel being consumed each year, the government by 1959 had established 162 square miles of forest reserves to ameliorate some of the problem (Birom Tribal Notebook 1959).

Land Alienation and Compensation

No problem of either the administration or the control of native and stranger populations has been so persistent, so complex, and so vexing as that of the irreconcilable claims to and demands for land by the two groups most interested in the land. The requirements of the developing mining industry for large areas to be exploited principally by opencast mining techniques became greater during each successive decade, becoming more acute during the decade 1945–1955. At the same time, the indigenous farmers were being hard-pressed to find enough farmlands to provide for a population that began to expand gradually with the introduction of modern medicine.[3]

Conflict between these two groups was generally avoided during the early exploitative period because hunting lands and reserve bush regions were not habitually farmed. Mining activities in these areas initially did not much disturb the native peoples. However, some of the lands were sacred areas, containing the sites of ritual shrines and associated activities. Others, such as certain tracts of rich land along the streams and streambeds, were the village preserves for wild vegetable products, such as bamboo thickets, wild greens, and sisal grass. Additionally, large amounts of seemingly uninhabited bushlands were actually farms under long-term fallow. Alluvial mining[4] began in the aged river valleys out on the plains and from there expanded into other areas as a result of more widespread prospecting. It was when miners began to penetrate into these areas that the Birom began to complain and occasionally physically obstruct the mining activities. Following initial hostilities with the British-led troops that resulted in the deaths of a few men and the burning of selected villages, the plateau peoples were understandably reluctant to further resist the encroachment of the miners on these lands.

The subsequent history of conflict over land between the indigenous peoples and mining companies persisted into the postcolonial era. Throughout World War II, efforts had been made by the government to formulate a clear policy regarding mining interests and the need for compensation for farmlands. Eventually, a special formula was introduced and applied to the most congested areas, first demarcated and documented in 1947, accompanied by much resistance from the mining companies. The general acceptance of the idea that farmers should be compensated for the loss of their land was only reluctantly achieved after massive demonstrations and protests by the native peoples in the late 1940s and early 1950s.

The long-range significance of these developments for the plateau peoples perhaps cannot be fully estimated at this point. Virtually all lives have been touched by the phenomenon of land alienated to mining and the bitter atmosphere surrounding disputes over compensation. The decade from 1945 to 1955 and subsequent years saw what was for the farmers large amounts of cash coming into their hands, particularly in villages centrally located in the congested area (for example, Gyel, Zawang, and Du). Compensation for total disturbance rose from two pounds per acre in early 1940s to a peak in 1955 of over fifty-three pounds per acre. In some cases, realization of compensation was an event that occurred only once, being a sudden windfall, the unique nature of which was completely lost to the farmers. Some of these men tragically yielded much of their farmlands for the boon. In many if not most cases, however, cash income from compensation extended over a number of years as older mining leases were gradually worked and exhausted. Some families have had recurrent payments as these areas are gradually being worked. Thus, each year, relatively large amounts of money in lump sums were and still are paid out by mining companies, and there is no question that many farmers look forward to, expect, and even depend on some form of compensation.

Nevertheless, land compensation is a self-limiting source of income. It is sporadic and unpredictable at best. With the congested areas now completely closed to further mining leases, once the present areas are exhausted, compensation will certainly cease. There is already a decline in the amount of tin produced from this region as mining companies seek new unexplored veins in less populous regions, and most of the accessible alluvial tin has already been removed from the congested areas. This poses a dilemma of undeniably great magnitude in the future: What happens when compensation is no longer forthcoming on the high plateau and new farmlands are not available for the next generations?

The plateau peoples were ill-prepared for the dislocations that accompanied both the loss of their land and the sudden bewildering shower of compensatory moneys. Until this time, very little cash had actually been used by the Birom, although many persons had become accustomed to the few pennies or shillings earned daily in the mines (more often the payment was in grain). But as we will see later, this kind of employment was limited to a few days, a few weeks, or perhaps a month at the most during the year. The small amounts of cash changed hands quickly in purchases of foods and clothing from the markets or beer from women vendors.

With the coming of land compensation, some men individually received five, ten, twenty-five, and upward of fifty pounds in one payout. Members of the mining community and government officials claim that since these large sums represent up to ten years' value of the crops lost, the farmers are adequately compensated and ought to be able to subsist by finding new lands to cultivate. Many assumed that the farmers would relocate and purchase better lands in the lowlands.

In reality, very little of these moneys was utilized in long-term ways, such as investment in new lands outside the villages or in property in the towns. Some few men who had sufficient experience in the wider culture did purchase training for themselves or their sons in certain trades such as tailoring, boot making, or mechanical skills. But most of the money was soon dissipated in unwise purchases of material goods in the market or was taken from the farmers in various swindling schemes by outsiders. In the sometimes fatuous arguments used by Europeans to show the ineptitude of the "pagans," nearly everyone forgets that the plateau farmer had no traditions or precedents to guide him in the use of these relatively large sums of cash. There was no impartial agency to offer any form of counseling on the management of these funds for long-term purposes. More important, the reality of the situation on the high plateau went against the possible investment in farmlands. There literally is no farmland available for purchase, as all cultivable lands are already held under native rights of occupancy. Traditionally, native rights in lands are heritable but not purchasable. And it had been demonstrated on several occasions (such as the aborted Sabon Zawang Resettlement Scheme) that the native farmers of the villages on the high plateau did not want to move down to what they believed were unhealthy areas in the lowlands, where some land was available under government aegis. Thus, even with the payment of land compensation, the disadvantages accrued to the farmers. They were members of a preindustrial society forced to take actions and make decisions as if they were familiar with the uses of money in an industrialized capitalist economy.

The consequences of these circumstances have penetrated into all areas of Birom life, invading even the ritual relationships of those who still cling strongly to traditional beliefs. It would be impossible in this book to analyze all the ramifications of the effects of land compensation as it becomes substituted for the land. Its far-reaching effects have still to be seen in terms of the displacement and reorganization of people. In later chapters, I deal further with the effect that the money/market economy is having on the structure and functioning of the domestic unit. Suffice it to say here that money and the manner in which it came to the

Birom have altered the relationship of men to land and as a consequence have added a new dimension to the relationships of men and women to one another.

Native Labor and the Minefields

From the beginning of contact with the plateau peoples, attempts were made to enlist them as laborers in the mines. Such efforts were found mainly to be futile in the early years, so mining companies turned to outsiders. With the establishment of government offices in Bukuru, the demands for labor for building roads, transport, and construction increased, and a few farmers were enlisted by force. Headmen or chiefs of villages were required to produce a stated number of men for work, particularly during the dry season. But the Birom offered great resistance for a very simple reason: They thought this to be a method by which the government planned to exterminate them. Among the first forced laborers were men who, when they returned to the village, were exhausted by the heavy labor to which they were unaccustomed as well as having been exposed to new diseases. Perhaps coincidentally, some of them died shortly thereafter, and thus the belief became established among the village peoples that death was the consequence of working for the Europeans. The latter soon found that impressed laborers simply disappeared overnight into the nearby villages. Such resistance persisted for more than a generation, for it was not until the late 1920s that significant numbers of people, both men and women, came into the labor force, all but a few as casual labor. By then the Birom were beginning to feel the pressures of their own declining economics and the need for the use of cash to pay taxes.

The influx of strangers connected with mining operations presented a three-pronged problem to the colonial administration. First, there was the necessity to control and to keep separate the mining camps from residents of villages situated near the mining camps and to establish colonial authority over all hostile regions. Second, there was the problem of "unruly" mine laborers. Hausa men from the north as well as southerners, who constituted the bulk of the miners, sometimes pilfered the crops of the native farmers and tried to entice their women. Third, there was the need for settling and controlling the large numbers of southern workers, a predominantly male population of semitransients whose juxtaposition to both Muslim Hausa and the plateau peoples caused a constant turbulence. Special courts had to be set up in the mining areas to deal with these discordant groups, and special policeman were recruited whose main duty was to keep these groups apart.

The mining camps have been the vehicle through which the Birom have received the greatest influences from the outside world. The heterogeneous African populations in these camps introduced to the plateau new lifestyles, customs, values, and knowledge. The European miner or political officer was much too remote to have had much direct contact and influence with the villagers, and even when he did so, it was always through an intermediary, usually a Hausa man. But the African inhabitants of mining camps often had contact with the nearby village people. Soon there were many relationships based on comaraderie, indebtedness, trade, and work between residents of mining camps and peoples of the nearby villages. Despite sometimes quite friendly intentions, there were also numerous occasions of active hostility among the indigenous plateau peoples and foreigners, especially those who came from the south. Such enmity continued on through the civil wars that have plagued Nigeria since independence.

At the time of this research, most of the mining camps were owned by large commercial companies or by individual miners. Some of the more stable permanent camps, such as at Rayfield and Barakin Ladi, became substantial suburban settlements, comparable to small towns. They house workers and their families who have lived for a generation or more on the plateau and provide numerous services, including schools, churches, markets, and places of entertainment. But the majority of camps are much smaller, maintaining for the most part a relatively transient population. In addition, the smaller camps tend to house workers of more homogeneous ethnic backgrounds; many camps are composed entirely of northerners, with Hausas predominating. The large camps are very cosmopolitan and may contain members of a dozen or more ethnic backgrounds. Not only are they more ethnically diversified, but they include men with a greater variety of skills, incomes, and social statuses, from the Ibo white-collar worker who may be a store manager, typist, or clerical worker to the unskilled daily laborer who generally subsists at the bottom of the income scale.

The camps are dispersed throughout the plateau so as to give the workers easy access to the paddocks and the areas in which mining operations take place. What makes them particularly relevant to the kinds of images perceived by the indigenous people is that virtually all of them are within walking distance of villages. Each large camp has, by statutory obligation, a market within the campground, and it is this feature that attracted the villagers early on. Every mining company provides housing and stall space for vendors, the vast majority of whom are Hausa and Ibo. These entrepreneurs sell almost every commodity, both edible and otherwise, that may be found in the larger markets at Jos and Bukuru but on a somewhat smaller scale. Many of the native Birom, especially the women who would not or could not go to the large markets in the towns, will utilize these local and rather informal mining camp markets. When they have money, they purchase small items, such as salt, tobacco, oils, and prepared foods, particularly fish and meats. The amounts are very small. Some Birom women go to these markets to try to sell what extra goods they themselves may have. A few women regularly prepare food to sell to the mineworkers.

Perhaps of equal attraction and significance to the village people is the fact that every large mining camp also has "pubs" and/or quarters for women to sell native beer. Large mining companies have provided the pubs, each camp being allocated drinking spots roughly according to its population. The ratio was about one pub for every fifty or sixty men. Most of the mining companies also sponsor the women who sell beer in the camps, although the latter are responsible for obtaining their own liquor licenses. The pubs are inspected by the Medical Department, which imposes minimal requirements for such establishments. Although the pubs are primarily for the men living in the camp, no one refuses to sell to outsiders as long as they behave themselves. Most of the women who run these establishments are northerners, including Hausa, and a few non-Muslim women. They are known as excellent businesswomen, astute, and skillful. Many have well-run businesses and will tolerate no nonsense since a good reputation is important for maintaining the support of the mining company. On the other hand, such drinking spots are frequently the scenes of local fights and much quarreling over money, women, gambling, and drink. Much of the hostility is commonly between northerner and southerner and between plateau men and foreigners.

Until recently, houses of prostitution were also supported by the mining companies in the camps. Many were established in the 1920s to attract laborers. All these establishments were run by women (called *magajiya* in Hausa) who lived in houses provided by the company. Each *magajiya* made all the arrangements for the girls and established prices that depended on the customer's social standing and income. The *magajiya* invariably owned one or more of the pubs, and with all these enterprises, she frequently obtained substantial wealth in a short period of time. It was and still is in this capacity that the *magajiya* took on another activity that soon became widespread throughout the mining region: She became known as the moneylender. Easy loans, with high interest, were available to most of the men, including the plateau villagers who did not live in the camps. Gossip and custom have it that the average northerner is "an addict on borrowing money or getting things on credit," and the *magajiya* found a ready market among both the Hausa and the plateau customers.

Within the past six or seven years prior to this study, the companies ceased to support brothels in the larger camps because of the spread of venereal disease. As soon as the companies were compelled to provide medical care and hospital services, the support of prostitution became too expensive. However, the *magajiya* still functions primarily in her role as moneylender and petty trader. Illegal prostitution also persists in some camps, often attracting Birom girls.

The Birom view the mining camps with a great deal of ambivalence. To the Christians and most older people, the camps are dens of iniquity because of the drinking, gambling, and prostitution. On the other hand, many Christians almost always have contacts or acquaintances among the Ibo and other southerners in the camps who are useful to them from time to time. Young Christian men have also been known to borrow money from either friends or the *magajiya* of some of the camps, and many of them know the prostitutes of neighboring camps, particularly since perhaps half of them are Birom girls or from other plateau groups. Village men frequently make purchases in the camp markets, as do some of the women, although the men try to prevent their women from doing so. The non-Christian Birom object to the camps because they introduce the young men to ideas and beliefs that contradict Birom traditional values. It is from contact with southerners, especially in the larger, more sophisticated camps, that young Birom men become influenced by such alien values as the notion that farming is dirty work and beneath their dignity. They prefer to go and have "fun" rather than work, a concept that is new to Biromland. They learn gambling and confidence tricks from the more worldly Africans, get involved in illegal tin mining, spend their money on the town women instead of sharing with their Birom kinsmen, lose respect for their elders, and disobey their fathers.

The Influence of Missionaries

Soon after the first Europeans arrived on the plateau, various mission groups, many of which were already in other parts of Nigeria, began to show some interest in the area. The first mission to enter the territory and proselytize the Christian gospel among the pagan peoples was the Sudan United Mission (SUM), an evangelical group composed of British Protestant sects. In 1904, the head of its first expedition, Dr. Karl Kumm, was given permission by Captain Frederick (later Lord) Lugard, the high commissioner, to send an investigatory mission onto the plateau. Dr. Kumm spent almost a year in the area establishing contact with different plateau peoples.

In 1907, the first SUM station near Bukuru was opened, and by 1913 there were four missionaries in the Birom districts, including one medical missionary. The first mission school was opened at Gyel in 1908 and was later (1910) moved to Du village, where the Gwom (chief) gave the mission a piece of land that is the present-day site of the SUM school and church in Du. For many villagers, this was their first sight of a European. Some of the older people informed me that they believed that white men were men with no skin.

From the beginning, preaching and attempts at teaching were in Hausa, which was the lingua franca of the plateau area. In a few years, however, Birom (as spoken by peoples of Du and Forum villages) was reduced to writing, and the mission published some simple biblical texts in the transliterated language. Outside these texts, the language has never been used in a written form, as Hausa and English are the basic languages in the school system for written and verbal communications of all sorts. Few Birom have actually seen these small texts in the Birom language, and fewer still are able to read them; they have thus far had virtually no effect on the spread of Christianity.

There appeared to be little overt or violent objections to the existence of missionaries and their peculiar behavior among the Birom. But the reactions of village leaders were highly varied. Baker reports that the chief of Bachit expressed very strong objections to missionary activity. On the other hand, while the chief Chunung Nyap (deceased around 1935), who first allowed them to settle in Du village, never became a Christian himself, he was unusually accommodating to their presence, partly because of self-interest and curiosity and partly because of personal pressure from touring district officers. He was required to provide laborers to build and maintain the mission houses, and some of his own grandsons were sent to work as houseboys and other servants to the mission. It was to these latter individuals that the missionaries made their initial appeal. Years later, these young men were among the first converts to Christianity.

The most striking development in the first few decades of SUM activity was the complete lack of evangelical success among the Birom. All attempts to reach the pagans were met with a passive but tolerant resistance that caused much frustration among the missionaries. Even after the appointed chief of Du recognized the Christian Sabbath, thus freeing people to attend the outdoor ceremonies, the services were still only lightly attended by the curious few.

In 1913 and again in 1918, missionaries reported that they had not made much progress among the Birom. Not only were there problems of lack of funds and inadequate personnel, but it soon became apparent that there were other competitors and other attractions. Islam is frequently mentioned as a force spreading its influence into the pagan areas. In 1913, the Reverend Charles Barton at Forum spoke of "definite Islamic activity in all the important centers of the Birom tribe." He added, "Between me and the town lies the Hausa market, which always proves an attraction to the pagan. Hence very few pass it to come on to me" (Sudan United Mission 1914, 189–90). Another missionary wrote:

> The counter-attraction from the tin mines in this district are increasing year after year. . . . Our most promising hands are leaving their homes allured by the love of money to go to these mines to do some menial work. The probable result will be corruption and love of thieving, besides love for big money as wages. (Sudan United Mission 1918, 163)

The first convert among the Birom was baptized in 1921, and from then on small numbers of Birom have become at least nominal Christians. Roman Catholic missionaries arrived on the plateau later (1949), and this faith has been discernibly more successful than the evangelical and puritanical Protestant groups. Overall, Christian beliefs and dogma have had limited influence within the villages. Young people who became Christians often did so in order to get a job, to get educated, and to leave the village and settle in towns. And it is true that many young people say that they are Christians because they feel it gives them better standing with outsiders when in fact they have not become members of a church congregation and do not attend services. It is common, however, for young people to "hang around" the local church in order to meet members of the opposite sex. There is little observable difference in actual behavior between those who are sufficiently influenced by Christianity to attend church regularly and those who may be described as peripheral Christians. In most villages where there are churches, church attendance consists primarily of several dozen women and older girls, along with young children.

Even with such difficulties, the missionaries have been the main channel through which formal education has been introduced into the plateau, and they have provided important models for the personal behavior associated with Europeans and subsequently emulated by some of the village leaders and young people. How profound the influences from missionaries may be is difficult to assess. Of the five young men who first converted in the late 1920s, only one remained a Christian. He worked as a dispenser at a nearby infirmary. Young people have become aware that some of the more fundamentalist mission groups (such as the American-based Sudan Interior Mission [SIM]) are in fact exotics in their own culture. They perceive quickly that other Europeans do not dress and behave like the missionaries and generally have little contact with them. From a pragmatic point of view, it is the other Europeans, government officials, commercial representatives, bankers, mining engineers, and so forth (the purveyors of worldly success) who represent the kinds of goals for which these young people strive.

At the same time, they accept many of the moral tenets taught by the missionaries, as these are generally consistent with, or at least not opposed to, basic Birom beliefs. Young people voice the opinion that they can learn a lot about the European way of life from the missionaries who are often more visible than are the commercial or government people. In their contacts with missionaries, they are ready to accept whatever they can learn and to use their friendship for personal advancement. But they are also very much aware of the areas of inconsistency and hypocrisy observed in the missionaries' behavior, especially their racial attitudes. The American SIM, comprised at that time of white Americans, particularly from the southern United States, imported racial and segregationist ideology; they established separate schools, churches, and hospitals for whites and blacks regardless of ethnic identities, education, background, or social standing. Representatives of the SIM complain bitterly about their lack of success and the overwhelming attraction that some of the Irish Roman Catholic groups have experienced. The Catholic missions have had far less funding than the American fundamentalist groups. Yet in one village area to the south of Jos where the Americans have established both elementary and high schools along with churches, one Catholic priest was able to gain more adherents than the entire American establishment with its considerable wealth. At the time of this research, no students had been enrolled in the American schools.

Notes

1. At the time of this study, regional boundaries for what is known as the "Middle Belt" were not precise. Generally, it is the area north of the confluence of the Niger and Benue Rivers and includes savanna lands on either side of both rivers.

2. Initial resistance to European penetration came from Bukuru, Jal (Ganawurri), Rukuba, Forom, and Hoss. The names of other villages are not known or were not recorded. See Laws (1954).

3. From 1907 on, there were missionaries in the area, and until they made their first converts in the late 1920s, they served principally as dispensers of medicine. Vom (Vwang) Hospital, the first to be constructed in the plateau, was established in 1922, and shortly thereafter the government began to provide local dispensaries.

Ecological Features of the Precolonial Past 2

THE HIGH PLATEAU APPEARS as largely a barren area today with areas that stretch for miles with little sign of tree or bush. This topography is relieved only by great variformed rock outcroppings dispersed here and there, forming low, hilly extrusions that give the appearance of rolling downs in parts. Dry shrub grasses cover some of the surface, in a few areas rising several feet high. Other surfaces are barren rock worn to a waxy smoothness by the agents of erosion—wind, water, and sand. It is among the sprawling hills and the great rock masses with their sculptured profiles that most of the villages were and to a certain extent still are clustered. Since the "pacification" of the area, however, the population has been spreading out over the open plains at varying rates. Dotted around among older, traditional settlements are numerous trees—eucalyptus, the African elemi, cassia cottonwood (kapok), and the rare mahogany—some of which grow remarkably large. Outside of and beyond the settlement areas, the absence of trees highlights one of the more serious problems of the plateau, which once contained far more extensive woodlands, fertile swamps, and thickets than it does at present (Grove 1952, 37).

The lands of the plateau rise about 3,000 feet above sea level, and some of the larger hills may be several hundred feet higher. The plateau is hedged by rugged escarpments that drop several thousand feet to the surrounding plains on the east and west and as much as 3,000 feet on the southern borders. With this elevation, the plateau enjoys a comparatively cool and pleasant climate. There are two definite seasons with wide variations of temperature in each. The rainy season lasts about six months, from the end of March to the beginning of October, with the greatest concentration of rains in July and August. Especially toward the end of the rainy season, heavy thunderstorms are frequent and often disastrous to crops. Rainfall may reach between fifty and sixty inches per year, but the rainfall pattern is erratic and unpredictable, varying greatly from area to area and from year to year. The distribution of rainfall is so uneven that while one area may get four inches in one downpour, an area only a few miles away may get none. At the height of the rainy season, there is abundant water in natural streams and wells.

Except for the dams built by the mining companies, most of these sources dry up for a time in the dry season. Temperatures during the rainy season can get quite low, varying from the mid-forties (Fahrenheit) to above seventy degrees.

From late October to March is the normal dry season, which is characteristically sunny and pleasant with temperatures rarely reaching above eighty-five degrees and averages in the mid-seventies. Scattered showers may come on rare occasions. Between December and February, the harmattan, a cool north wind from the Sahara, desiccates the area and leaves in its wake a silty covering of fine sand. Wind-borne disease agents accompany the harmattan, and the indigenous people especially are much troubled in this season by respiratory infections, eye diseases, and skin ulcers. In some areas, the scarcity of water becomes acute by January and February.

Farming, Trade, and Material Culture

The Birom were and still are hoe cultivators, typical of the West African savanna or grasslands zone. The description of economic activities that follows applies mainly to the northern part of Birom territory. Where major changes have occurred, such as the virtual cessation of hunting as a source of food, or where alterations in traditional customs have taken place, I have indicated this. The greatest change with respect to farming activities has been primarily in the amounts produced but also in the types of crops grown, not in the manner of farming.

The Birom exploited the environment with a relatively simple technology. Digging sticks of varied sorts were universally used, particularly to unearth tuberous plants when needed throughout the year. But a simple hoe made of iron, smelted and shaped by local smiths, was the basic agricultural implement. Perhaps the one major technique that gave the plateau peoples superior adaptive advantage in such a harsh environment was the knowledge and use of iron. Hoes, spear tips and arrowheads, swords, a wide variety of knives, and some decorative items, such as greaves and bracelets, were made of this metal, which was smelted in crude but efficient earth ovens. Because of the hardness of the granite-derived soils of the plateau, especially following the dry season, it is likely that had these people not had iron, they could not have occupied the plateau as successfully as they did.

Small amounts of brass and copper were traded in by barter, but these were used solely for decorative items of dress for men and horses, smoking pipes, and the handles of swords. Bamboo, a scarce and valuable resource on the high plateau, was utilized for containers and for small cutting implements, especially those of women, and more important for the frames for the grass-thatched roofs. Among the other grasses and plants that are native to the plateau, fibrous ones are or were moderately abundant, and woven mats, door covers, storage containers, winnowing and other types of pans, rain capes, parts of horses' harnesses, penis sheaths, straps, bags, rope, and string were made. Clay, which is also available in limited supply in certain known areas, was used by the women in some villages to fashion simple utilitarian pots for cooking, storage, and transport. Although some women are still known for their quality workmanship, these items now are not greatly in demand, as they have been replaced to a large extent by the less bulky and lighter-weight metal and enamel pans available in the markets.

Goat skins and horse hides were formerly used to create various types of containers, such as the men's tobacco pouches and bags for holding small implements, knives, awls, pipes, and so forth. The manufacture of these items, however, has long declined, as inexpensive bags of cloth, plastics, and hopsacking can be bought in the market. Moreover, younger men no longer smoke the ancient bamboo, clay, and wooden pipes with their brass fittings but prefer the modern cigarette. More and more cooking implements, containers of various sorts, cutlery, and other items are purchased from local markets. As would be expected, those settlements closest to the centers of industry and commerce or within easy contact of markets and mining camps are most affected by these material changes. More remote villages still utilize items of traditional culture, although even here it is usual to find many market items that have been brought into the "bush" areas. Most remarkable of these newly introduced implements and perhaps the most widely diffused is the modified native "hoe." To end native smelting and its presumed consumption of large quantities of firewood and to prevent the stealing of iron railings from the railroad, the colonial government flooded the plateau with cheap metal shovels that the Birom hafted to a wooden or bamboo shaft. This innovation began in the 1920s and was soon widespread over the upper plateau.

On the high plateau, the native peoples depend almost entirely on rainfall for the growth of crops. Unlike the southern, or lowlands, peoples, some of whom have terraced farms fed by irrigation systems, Birom farming has never been based on intensive irrigation, nor is their habitat suitable for terracing (compare Netting 1968). The Birom made use of furrows and ditches, mound building, and euphorbia plants for the temporary retention of running water, and where possible they sometimes divert running water from natural streams for irrigation purposes. In more recent times, the use of wells and shadoof mechanisms has been a source of irrigation for garden farms in some areas, but few villagers have wells that are deep enough to provide water year-round.

Farms are worked for a period of time, today usually three to four years, until the soil is exhausted, at which point they are then left to lie fallow for a period ideally double to triple (eight to twelve years) that of the cultivating period. In the past, the length of fallowing depended on the nature of the field and the crops grown or to be grown therein. The fallowing period is shorter now, usually about three and rarely exceeding five years, and the total yields have decreased. Land shortage is such that few families can afford for land to be idle for an adequate fallowing period.

Fields are prepared by burning the wild growth, stubble, dried grasses, weeds, and bush at the height of the dry season or shortly thereafter (late February to March). The First Fires ritual, which precedes the burning, serves as a notice to commence the preparation of the soil and is the beginning of the ceremonial year, so that March is roughly the first month of the Birom year. There are thirteen months, most of which derive their names from some planting or harvesting activity.

Most of the grain and vegetable crops are planted during April through June, and there is deliberate staggering of certain crops to tide villagers over during the preharvest hunger period. The Birom have developed an estimated twenty varieties of *acha* (Hausa, *fonio*), or *Digitaria exilis*, a staple crop of the western Sudan that has different growing periods and maturation rates. Three varieties—*were*, *ndat*, and *akan*—are the fastest growing with harvests ready in September. Unfortunately, these do not give the biggest yields, though *ndat* and *akan* can give moderately good yields under optimum conditions. *Were* is fairly popular because of its taste, which the Birom prefer. Of the ten or eleven other varieties of *acha* identified in the area where I lived, the most popular, *ndei*, is also the longest growing. It gives a good yield but requires about seven months of growth to reach its peak of ripeness. Along with *peng*, another slow-growing variety, it is harvested in late November and early December.

In addition to *acha*, the major indigenous cereal crops are bulrush millet, finger millet, guinea corn, sorghum, beniseed, and small amounts of maize. All are stored in granaries in the compound. Both guinea corn and maize (two varieties are grown, brown and black) were known and grown in most parts of the plateau prior to European contact but have generally been of minor importance because of the difficulties attendant to their growth and storage. They require fertilizer, weeding, and protection from birds and are more subject to attack by insect pests and fungi than any of the other cereals.

Yams are planted from late November through early January. A few are planted as late as April, although the mounds in which the cuts are embedded are prepared at the end of the rainy season, when the soil is still soft. Yams, legumes and pulses, cucurbits, squash, melon, and other vegetable plants, some of which are unknown in the Western world, are either consumed or harvested, left stored in the ground and used as needed (the case of most yams), or harvested and prepared by being dried or smoked and stored in the rafters of storerooms and cooking huts.

Crops are rotated, normally according to standard patterns, and intercropping is practiced with all except the millets and *acha*, and even here some people will intercrop these cereals with Indian roselle. Fertilizer, in the form of animal manure, was known before European contact and is used very modestly only in the garden farms for finger millet, the seedlings of bulrush millet, and a few other vegetables. *Acha* is not normally manured because the Birom are aware that higher yields would not be produced and that manuring frequently leads to weak vegetation growth in the open areas, increased erosion, and lodging. However, today, because of the decreased fertility of the lands and the annual migrations of large herds of Fulani cattle (an estimated 140,000 head in Jos Division), Birom farmers often make use of the droppings that cover some of their fields at the end of the rainy season for garden farms.

All edible wild plants and animals were apparently utilized in the Birom diet, with minor taboos affecting only a portion of the population at any one time. Only the older people, particularly women who were barred from eating certain portions of animals from the hunt, still observe these taboos. It would appear that the traditional Birom diet was not rigidly circumscribed by prohibitions and restrictions. New food items have been and still are accepted with facility, though people may say they prefer the indigenous foods because they are better for one's health. Food dishes from the southern parts of Nigeria and traditional Hausa foods have found their way into nearby Birom villages, and European vegetables, potatoes, carrots, cabbage, string beans, cauliflower, cucumbers, onions, and so forth are readily consumed when available. A few farmers grow small amounts of these vegetables, hampered only by the poor soils and inadequate water supply.

There were no full-time specialists in traditional economic production; the smelters and smiths were also farmers who engaged in their nonfarming activities during the quiet period of the dry season, as was the case with all other nonfarming productive activities. All men were able and expected to build their own houses, thatch roofs, and weave bags, rain capes, doorways, and so forth. Those with the greatest skills were sought after by relatives and neighbors who could obtain their services in return for grain. Today, it is not uncommon for these men to hire out their skills for cash. More of a part-time specialist was the blacksmith (*vosun*). While these men did not constitute a distinct class of people, their trade was passed on in family lines. They enjoyed heightened individual prestige reinforced by their abilities to conduct certain rituals and thus control certain unknown forces not amenable to other men. They also received payment in kind.

All able-bodied men participated in the hunt in traditional times, when hunting was much more important than it is now. Some wild game were available up until the late 1940s, but the rapid expansion of human population into the "bush" hunting areas quickly adversely affected the supply of game. Fishing was apparently of secondary importance in precontact times while at the same time fish was favored in the diet of many people. There was not an abundance of fishing areas since many of the small streams accessible to the villagers became dry in the dry season. Today, most streams on the high plateau have been destroyed by mining activities.

The Birom never kept significant amounts of livestock. In the memories of older men, dwarf cattle were apparently common in some districts, but it is claimed that on the high plateau, only important men in the villages were able to have cattle. Perennial grazing was insufficient for maintaining large herds, and herding itself is not considered a traditional Birom activity. Moreover, the conditions of hostility and threat of slave raiding on the open plains where herds could be grazed precluded their use. In the past, some groups occasionally raided Fulani herds for meat. In contemporary times, some Birom have purchased cattle from local Fulani; I know of one family that kept a milch cow, but this was most unusual. The keeping of goats and sheep is a tradition of virtually all plateau groups, in addition to chicken and dogs, which are part of the diet of the northern peoples. Rabbits and pigs were also found in the village where I worked. Goats and sheep were killed not for their meat but primarily for funerals, as the skins were used for shrouds. Subsequently, the meat was consumed in the funerary rituals. Villagers always claimed that there were many domestic animals in past times.

The most important animal was the horse, a small, pony-sized animal adapted to the sparse and hilly terrain of the plateau. As the most versatile form of wealth, the horse was highly valued by the Birom in that its ownership conferred a degree of prestige. The horse functioned primarily as bridewealth without which no marriage could be legitimized. But it was also the basis for the superior mobility of plateau warriors engaged in strategic warfare. It provided one of the major forms of recreation in the villages, some of which were famed for horse racing. Finally, a horse's skin was used as a shroud for an important man, especially if he were headman of a kin group.

In the 1960s, with a few exceptions in some western villages, there were virtually no horses on the high plateau. The decline is the result of a number of factors that reflect on Birom relationships with the outside world and the internal changes that have occurred in Birom culture. During the first decades of colonial administration, many horses were commandeered by colonial administrators, sometimes in lieu of tax payments from the village at large. On some occasions, horses were deliberately shot on orders of British officials as punishment for some alleged misbehavior or as object lessons to rebellious villagers. In addition, several extreme hunger periods, such as during the droughts of 1914 and in the 1920s, led to the selling of horses by peoples of the high plateau to lowlands areas for food.

While the number of horses were dwindling, the social, economic, and symbolic functions of the horse were undergoing drastic changes. Bridewealth began to be transformed into cash beginning in the 1920s and was later standardized by a legal ruling of the colonial administration. Internecine warfare had been outlawed over a decade before that. The one function that remained (albeit diluted by 1960) was the use of a horse's skin in funeral rites. A son who wished to honor his father at the time of his death would go far and wide and to great expense to provide a horse for the latter's shroud. Even many years after a burial, if the body were not properly provided with a skin, some sons would claim that it was their unceasing ambition to provide a skin in a reburial ceremony for their fathers before the end of their own lives.

The Birom had no traditional marketplaces. Most goods were distributed by reciprocal gift exchange and by bartering. However, because of the slave trade, the localized production of certain materials such as metals and clay for pots, and the need for salt on the plateau, some amount of trading among the villages of the plateau and between the plateau peoples and Hausa specialists occurred at certain times through the year. These were mostly times at which plateauwide ceremonies were held. It was on these occasions that hostilities among villages ceased by common agreement. Under such truces, visiting traders, many from off the plateau, arrived and plied their trade. There was apparently widespread upholding of the "peace of the market." Birom traders (*bi-jiik*) were part-time specialists, often the same individuals who engaged in metalworking, and they bartered their wares with neighboring villagers. They also acted as channels of contact with Hausa traders, with some of the *bi-jiik* maintaining a sort of client–patron relationship with their Hausa compatriots. The Birom claimed that even in the time of organized warfare (*chomo*, or fighting with spears), native traders were known to everyone and would not be killed.

Clay pots, animals, decorative items such as shell beads, red ocher, brass anklets and bracelets, bamboo, wooden implements, and certain foodstuffs were thus spread about the plateau to remote villages by indigenous traders. The non-Birom, particularly Hausa and Kanuri men who traded with villages at the periphery of the plateau, were full-time commercial specialists who bought slaves, iron pieces, and tin rods from the plateau in exchange for salt, foodstuffs, shell jewelry, brass disks, and sometimes goats and horses. It was through them that European traders first learned about the tin deposits of the plateau.

A type of special-purpose money (Bohannan 1963, 348) existed in the form of flat plates of iron metal (*yere*) about four inches square. After making hoes and weapons sufficient for the needs of the villagers, native smiths fashioned these plates from whatever was left of the metal and used them for trading purposes. They came to have a function as a means of exchange of other goods. The Birom had a multicentric economy that disintegrated with the introduction of British money. Although the ethnographic data are sketchy and somewhat unclear, there seem to have been three fairly exclusive spheres of exchange. In the most exclusive sphere (Bohannan's "supreme" sphere), the items involved were horses and people, particularly women. A wife could be obtained only through the payment of a horse, an exchange that legitimized the union and the children produced from it. No other item of equivalent value could be substituted. In addition, it was possible for a man, should none of his sons live to maturity, to obtain a son from a kinsman or from a fellow Birom through the exchange of a horse. Other people could be purchased with salt (ten bags), bracelets and anklets, or twenty-four bags of *acha*. Some of the persons so purchased were slaves, but slavery was not feasible in Birom society, and most soon became incorporated into patrilineal kin groups as kinsmen. Many were further sold to neighboring peoples or to traders. In some cases, they served as ransom for kinsmen captured in war.

A second sphere of exchange (the "prestige" sphere) involved goods of high value, and it was in this context that the iron disks, or *yere*, were used widely in exchanges. Salt, bracelets and anklets, goats, bags of *acha*, finger and bulrush millet, beans, and (rarely) small farm plots were interchangeable in this sphere, with the *yere* setting the standard of exchange. One goat, for example, was the equivalent to three *yere*, and one bag of *acha* (sixty pounds) equaled one *yere*; and a horse could be obtained with twelve (or if it were an especially fine racing horse twenty-four) *yere*. Horses could not be exchanged for any other edible goods with the exception of a storeroom of *acha*. The third sphere of exchange (the "subsistence" sphere) contained foodstuffs, including all vegetables and grains, meat, fish, frogs, birds, and so forth, as well as some small utilitarian items. There were no standards of value used here and no methods by which payment not in kind could be received since all exchanges were by simple barter and/or gift giving.

Warfare and Slave Raiding

Much of the literature on the Middle Belt characterizes it as having had extensive internecine warfare prior to the colonial period. The Birom themselves speak of hostilities among some villages and village areas before the coming of the white men. Missionaries and travel officers were prone to portray the plateau peoples as wild, bloodthirsty savages. But the image of constant warfare, coupled with head-hunting and/or slave raiding (compare Archbold 1942; Tremearne 1912), is a product of Western fears and ignorance and is misleading. It is contradicted by information from elders in the villages who clearly remembered the precolonial period. But more important, it is not compatible with our knowledge of the harsh conditions of the plateau, which required much energy and time devoted to economic pursuits necessary for mere survival. The portrayal of unceasing violence and brutality seems to have stemmed in part from the felt need on the part of the colonial officers, early miners, and missionaries to overdramatize the dangers of residence in an unknown area and the savagery of its indigenous peoples (compare Curtin 1964, chap. 13; Hammond and Jablow 1970).

Armed physical conflict among human societies is a complex, many-faceted phenomenon, a fact that has generated much debate on the meaning, definitions, and functions of war (see, for example, Vayda [1961] and Wright [1965] and the various papers in Bohannan [1967] and Fried, Harris, and Murphy [1967]). The Birom data substantiate the position that it is erroneous to treat warfare as a single entity separable conceptually from other ecological features. They also suggest some additional correlates of warfare that may broaden our understanding of the ecological significance of such organized hostilities.

The Birom discriminate clearly among different types of hostilities, ranging from skirmishes between small groups of men (some of which may have been motivated by purely personal considerations) to warfare. Armed combat, what we might readily identify as warfare, involved the mobilization of militia, planned strategies of action, use of military leaders who were semispecialists, and coordination of movement and support tactics. It is known in the Birom language as *chomo* (fighting with spears) and involved the use of both mounted warriors and foot soldiers. Evidence for this kind of warfare is clear from early reports.[1] It shows not only that there were some villages able to recruit considerable numbers of men for defensive purposes but also that there existed a political mechanism for uniting the forces of two or more villages. That there was a wide variation in the military capacities of different villages is also fairly clear. Major John Vitoria, in personal reminiscences of his earliest tour, claimed that the fighting forces of some of the smaller villages were a mere handful. According to oral history, several of the largest villages engaged in full-scale warfare much more frequently than the smaller ones. Gyel village (which may have had a population of 5,000 or more) appeared to have had the reputation of being the most bellicose village prior to European penetration. Baker suggests, and my information concurs, that Gyel was in the process of expanding and that her conflicts with Kuru, Vwang (Vom), Du, and other villages were over acquisitions of lands. Elders of Zawang, a village in Du District, claimed that they gave the Gyel people the land on which they are now settled. But there were subsequent quarrels over Gyel's greed for more land, and the latter waged war with Zawang people both before and shortly after the British arrived. In the past, villages have been known to have migrated en masse from a former site (Baker 1954, 51), although such large-scale movements were apparently rare. In any case, conflict with neighboring peoples often ensued. Thus, we can see that competition for land must have been one of the motivations for organized aggressive warfare. Other reasons given by informants were revenge for slave raiding or horse-raiding attacks.

Localized skirmishes were more variable in form, motivation, and content. What they had in common were the small sizes of the groups involved and the use of swords, sticks, and knives rather than spears. The objectives of some limited-scale attacks on small groups were primarily to obtain slaves or horses. But other reasons given had to do with revenging a wrong, continuing a feud, or personal enmity arising out of quarrels over women, destruction of crops, stealing of livestock, and other slights or arguments. Occasionally, such personal grudges might escalate into villagewide hostilities.

While some foresight and planning might occur as a prelude to secret attacks and ambushes, no military strategy or tactics were involved. Sometimes the fights were ad hoc affairs or accidental encounters between groups of men who had reason to bear malice against one another. These attacks occurred in areas distant from the villages and thus were never considered a threat to an entire village. Normally, the skirmishes did not result in deaths. Fighting was terminated voluntarily when the men wearied of it or someone was seriously wounded. If the attacking group was superior in number, the victims would more often than not be bound and sold as slaves. It was for this reason that such attacks on the open plains were greatly feared.

Clearly there were variations in the frequency of occurrences of these different types of physical hostilities. Older informants were in agreement that local skirmishes and slave raiding were far more prevalent than all-out warfare and the most constant source of external danger, especially to women and children. Large-scale armed combat required the suspension of farming and the disruption of the day-to-day activities of making a living. The infrequency of full-scale warfare is attested to also by the evidence of old men (from eight kin groups) who were teenagers or young adults at the time of European contact. None of these men actually experienced warfare, although some had been involved in skirmishes. The accounts of wars related to me were based on tales told to them by men of their fathers' and grandfathers' generations. Often they described battles among other villages about which they had been told. Battles that had occurred in the far more distant past may very well have been telescoped in time because of their importance or their dramatic impact on demographic patterns. Du village and its satellites had apparently not engaged in warfare for many generations despite accepted institutionalized patterns of enmity between Du and other villages (see the discussion under "Intervillage Relationships in the Precolonial Era").

Not all villages were involved in hostilities with one another, nor were the existing hostilities without periods of cessation. What is important about all the hostilities, whether full-scale wars or local skirmishes, is their effect on villagers who saw in them a constant threat of danger. It affected their patterns of farming and hunting, their conceptions of sex roles, the customs regarding land tenure, the social value attributed to particular crops, and especially the arrangement and locations of villages. It is my hypothesis that some of the most important elements of the Birom social system and many other cultural habits, including their characteristic ways of relating to strangers, must be seen in terms of protective responses to the perception of imminent danger. The potent ecological factor was not the reality of warfare but rather the villagers' *fear* of warfare and slave raiding. It is quite likely that the actual incidence of armed conflict among villages was very minimal, but (and this became clear in interviews) the *belief* in the probability of warfare and slave raiding was great.

Intervillage Relationships in the Precolonial Era

In the circumstances described so far, the perceived necessity for defense was a primary determinant of the pattern of distribution of villages on the plateau and a major influence in the relationships among villages. What is clear is that such relationships were highly variable, ranging from what I call "institutionalized enmity" on the one hand to friendly and sometimes strongly binding alliances on the other.

In Plateau Province, there were over eighty villages designated as Birom. Some were quite ancient in age; others were of more recent founding, but all antedate British contact. Villages ranged is size from quite small settlements numbering little more than 100 persons to large villages like Gyel, Von, Riyom, and Du, which in the 1960s had populations of 3,000 or 4,000 people. While the population sizes of all villages have varied considerably from the precontact period, oral histories clearly portray some large villages as dominant ones in their regions, with smaller villages having subordinate status to the larger ones. In some cases where it appears that several smaller villages were closely allied to a senior or dominant village, Baker (1954, 56) has designated these as minor federations, or village areas, and suggests that they shared a common foreign policy. This would be based on several factors: the protective role of the larger village, its ability to recruit militia from the smaller villages, plus in some cases its status as the senior village from which the smaller ones were founded (see the section "Pseudokinship").

Legends and myths of common origin tell us very little about the nature of the actual relationships among villages as they vacillated over time. The existence of such legends did not preclude hostilities, although at the same time they were advanced as explanations or rationalizations for ties of friendships and cooperation among some villages. Baker (1954) points out that despite the large number of villages alleged to have been founded from Riyom, some "might yet have hostile relations with Riyom and with each other; some villages founded from elsewhere had relations of peaceful friendship with Riyom" (61). One concession made out of deference or respect to Riyom was that villages that shared a common origin did not take heads from one another when hostilities occurred between them.

Of the many different ways of relating villages to one another, one can identify five types of interconnections that pre-date European contact and that characterized all villages at one time or another. I have given names to these linkages that reflect the central theme of the relationship.

Pseudokinship

Where contiguous villages were ranked as senior and junior to one another and where there was no recent history of hostilities between them, kinship terms were often employed to symbolize and reiterate the closeness of the ties (compare Cunnison 1956). This was most often the case when a settlement that was once an offshoot of a larger village matured as a full-fledged village of its own sometimes with a chief (*gwom*) and a separate body of elders and ward heads (see chapter 7) who functioned as a village council. Thus, Sop was founded by immigrants from Bachit village (Baker 1954, 69), and the people of Sop are "sons" or "children" of Bachit. Shen village in Du District was founded by immigrants from Du, and Shen is considered a "child" to Du. (It is of interest to note that some elders contradicted the relationships as stated and said that Shen is a "brother" to Du.) Heipang and Forum are called "brothers" to Du because it is said that they were founded by members of the same migrating family that first settled in Du. Where such kinship terms are used, it is claimed that these villages never fought one another. Like true kinsmen, they also had obligations to support one another in cases of conflict with "outsiders."

Friendship Pacts

Less constant and enduring than pseudokinship, pacts of friendship between villages were apparently determined in large part by regionwide influences that affected large numbers of villages. Most of the alliances of this sort were formed for purposes of collective defense against a common enemy. The best examples of this would be some of Baker's minor federations mentioned previously. No postulates of kinship are ever expressed. Thus, the people of Hwoss (who are Birom) and the people of Jal (Ganawuri-Birom) were known in ancient times to have had strong ties of friendship. "They affirm that they (Hwoss) had a closer relationship with the Jal than they ever had with the people of Riyom" (Baker 1954, 52). Later these two villages quarreled, and the alliance was terminated. In another example, Baker points out that "Vyang (Vwana), which was not founded from Riyom, had a tradition of friendship with the people of Riyom which was never broken, and the two villages never fought" (57). Vyang also joined with the other people of Kwon (Irigwe) against the Gyel villagers, although these latter had once been a part of Vyang, according to oral history. Even villages that were traditional enemies to one another might join together against invasion from some external source when the perception of a major threat demanded such unity.

Ritual Alliances

The most ubiquitous, complex, and significant of all connections between villages were those based on ritual alliances. Each village contained two or three major collectivities of corporate kin groups whose distinctiveness is that they hold or own certain rituals or ceremonies that others in the same village do not hold. These "ritual groups," as I have called them (chapter 6), have corresponding members in a number of other villages, usually in the same locale. The intravillage ritual groups have the right and the obligation to perform certain major rituals for the good of the whole society and are allied with corresponding groups in other villages. Such linked groups cannot engage in any form of violence among themselves for fear of angering powerful supernatural forces. The pan-village rituals, which I have called the "Great Ceremonies," have names, definite identifying dates during the year, and formal techniques and procedures. When two villages, some of whose members are thus ritually allied, enter a period of enmity, regardless of the cause, individual members of the ritual groups cannot engage in the battles for fear of harming a "brother" member from the opposing village. More important, however, during the time of the Great Ceremonies, known in most areas by common names such as "Mandyang," "Pei," "Tyi," and "Ngasang," all warfare must cease among all villages involved. For some rituals that are performed in a definite sequence, the truce periods may last as long as a month or more. Thus, Mandyang begins at Riyom sometime in late March as part of the ceremonies commencing the new farming year. After three to five days, Vwang follows Riyom (although the Vwang elders claim that Riyom cannot start before a messenger procures a special sacred staff held at Vwang); then, groups at Kuru, Gyel, Du, Forum, and Fan follow in approximately that order.

Intervillage Marriage

Nineteen percent of all marriages of girls in the village where I lived were with men of neighboring villages (Gunn 1953, 33). Most of the marriages were arranged between men in villages already conjoined by one or more of the previously mentioned types of connections. Such marriages need not involve only members of common ritual alliances but often also groups that did not participate in or recognize such rituals themselves. There were also some marriages that occurred among members of villages that had long traditions of enmity. In the knowledge and memories of informants, there were no villages that had isolationist customs of strict endogamy. That many of these marriages served specific political functions is recognized by the Birom themselves, who pointed out that those individuals taking most of the wives from outside villages were men who held powerful positions of leadership.

One well-known custom of institutionalized intervillage marriage arrangements was that between the people of Du (and also possibly Gyel) and the Anaguta-Jerawa (non-Birom) villages to the north of Birom territory. In modern times, it has been disputed that these were marriages since they involved exchanging a very young girl for foodstuffs and not a proper bridewealth. The girls were later married in the receiving villages. The Birom themselves commonly referred to these exchanges as marriages but distinguish them as Pyomo marriages. And it is true that the consequences were the establishment of ties between a Birom and non-Birom group that were often much like kinship ties, especially in some of the economic aspects (see chapter 10).

Gunn notes that perhaps 20 to 30 percent of all marriages of Buji men were with Birom girls.[2] My own data confirm a heavy investment in such ties since they show that nearly three of every four agnatic groups in Du have had at least one girl transferred and married in Pyomo lands. I estimate that such marriages constitute 6 to 10 percent of all marriages of girls in Du village over three generations. These arrangements were established primarily for economic reasons, but some exchanges also resulted in new political alliances.

Institutionalized Enmity

Hostilities among certain villages have already been mentioned, particularly in their association historically with slave raiding and/or abduction and the subsequent retaliation measures. Some villages were described as being traditional enemies to one another, but the original cause of the enmity is either unknown and/ or lost in the haze of a history long forgotten. I was even told about some villages that were enemies to one another, but no one ever recalled their warring together. The fact that villages in close proximity to one another appeared to be on relatively friendly terms and that "enemies" were more often than not at a great distance from one another (except on occasions of migration) suggests the possibility that such enmity was not arbitrary but that there was some pattern to it. How did these groups get to be "enemies" to one another, and what was the point of retaining the notion of perpetual antagonism among certain villages? Such institutionalized enmity may well represent an ecologically significant mode of spacing the human population, particularly in an area of meager resources. But there is another possibility for which the Western world's experience with the Cold War might provide a parallel. If two or more societies have sufficient fear of one another and find the posture of threat a useful device, this may well prevent them from actually fighting one another.

It is clear from the available evidence that relationships among villages were neither haphazard, sporadic, nor, as some early visitors would have us believe, based on constant hostility, savage warfare, and proclivities for head-hunting. Although presently there is insufficient evidence to be able to identify the total patterns of specific relationships or interactions between known villages, the clues suggest the need for careful and detailed investigation here and in similar areas.[3] Of particular significance is the fact that every village has a certain percentage of its women married outside the village, a mechanism well known in the histories of human societies for establishing alliances between distinct communities.

Hunger as a Dominant Cultural Theme

During the years of this study, the Birom described themselves as a hungry people.[4] Hunger is indeed a pronounced fact of life among most if not all of the villagers at some time or another. At the beginning of the twentieth century, the staple crop of *acha*, along with other grains (such as millets and guinea corn), a variety of yams and cultivated vegetables, a range of wild plants, nuts, berries, insects, eggs, and occasionally meat brought home by hunters, constituted the entire diet. Today the population is greater, as is the variety and availability of foodstuffs. Every year an abundance of food is imported onto the plateau, but this has been directed largely to the alien population. Since the 1920s, there has been a decline in the production of native crops and products of the hunt. With an expanding population, native production was clearly not sufficient to support the indigenous peoples. By the end of the colonial period, the Birom were rapidly becoming an impoverished peasantry, dependent to an unexpectedly high degree on the market economy.

Much of what Birom farmers experience and accept about their condition today is a feeling of hopelessness as they compare their own poverty with the proliferation of material affluence in the foreign settlements. In many cases, land, the major resource and form of wealth, was devoured by the mining companies, and farmers found that recourse to the law and government was ineffectual. Thus, many Birom farmers are poor in spirit as well as in foods and material goods.

Yet evidence indicates that hunger may have been an even greater problem earlier over the past century. The theme of hunger became part and parcel of historical traditions that persist into modern times. Innumerable folktales and anecdotes have developed around this fact of life as well as many special ceremonies of major significance to Birom life. Hunger was an element in the themes of every ritual that came to my attention. Both "Christian" and "pagan" Birom pray to their deities for surcease from hunger. When you ask a man to relate the history of his family, he will invariably begin with the statement that the first man came here (or settled at some other place) because he was hungry. In precolonial history, desperate men sold their sons and daughters into slavery because of hunger or raided neighboring villages for food.

The intensity of hunger varied with seasonal cycles, with the most acute periods occurring just prior to the first harvesting of early crops from July to September. Early missionary reports from 1914 to 1919 reveal that the preharvest period was one of dire hunger and frequent starvation. Daily mourning rituals and "wailings on the air" signaled deaths of the young and very old (Sudan United Mission 1919). Such preharvest hunger is a common phenomenon in the savanna regions of northern territories of coastal states and indeed throughout the Sudan (Johnston 1958).

The anticipation and fear of hunger has become part of the worldview of the Birom that feeds back into social practices. The Birom actively perceive their changing world in terms of categories, values, attitudes, and beliefs derived from the imprint of previous experiences. The expectation and fear of hunger is part of the "mind-set," an intellectual coping mechanism, and the strategies for coping developed in times past are applied and utilized as well in changing circumstances. Because the theme of hunger pervades nearly every aspect of life among the plateau peoples, I speculate that it must have figured as an important causative factor in the origin and/or elaboration of indigenous social institutions, customs, and practices. The proliferation of many and varied ties among small, easily fragmented kin units through their women (detailed in later chapters) is a direct response to ecological conditions described here and in other chapters. The experience of extreme hunger, as during periods of drought, or of heightened warfare or fear of slave raiding must have restricted farming activities to the safest areas. As will be seen in the next two chapters, this would mean expanding the need to focus on women's farms and their activities in providing foods to replace foods supplied by men. An erratic and generally inadequate food supply and the relatively uneven distribution of food crops in the absence of an indigenous centralized mechanism for the control and redistribution of available food resources require strategies for survival that focus on the interlinkage of domestic units via women. Any analysis from an ecological perspective must recognize the adaptive significance of processes taking place at the level of the domestic unit (see chapter 8) where food is prepared, distributed, and consumed. It is in this domain that we find important mechanisms of short-term adjustment.

There were qualities of resilience and flexibility in the Birom culture that made it possible for them to develop new strategies for coping with and adjusting to changes brought about by colonialism without losing their fundamental cultural integrity. Today the sporadic nature of income-producing activities, especially the patterns of casual labor among adults, may be, from an economic point of view, one of their most important adaptive strategies. It is an energy-efficient way of acquiring some income for people who have to subsist on a low-calorie diet, and it permits them to continue farming and other activities that are part of the traditional economy. Opportunity to recuperate from the stress of extremely enervating and demanding work is also more easily afforded by such work patterns. In appendix A, I delineate the many sources and patterns of income that Du Birom have and argue that, although cash income prompts interest in the outside world, the Birom do not see this income as fundamentally transforming their way of life.

Notes

1. The Tildy expedition under a Captain Gallagher made the first government-sponsored trek across the high plateau in the fall of 1904. Among their hostile encounters was a battle with the Ganawuri that left "over a hundred killed and wounded" out of an estimated force of "seven or eight hundred pagans" (Bauchi Province Reports 1904). This same expedition later encountered a defending army from Kuru and Gyel. According to the report, "The combined tribes of Kunkuru and N'giel must be able to put several thousands into the field; they possess a great number or horses and are courageous fighters" (Bauchi Province Reports 1904). In addition, R. A. Archbold (1942), describing his contact with the pagan armies around 1910, wrote, "The besieging army was no more rabble, but was disposed in an orderly and systematic manner. In the forefront was a double line of bowmen set in echelon, each protected by a large shield held by a man kneeling. Behind these were mounted spearman." See also Laws (1954) and Provincial Annual Reports (1903, 1905, 1906).

2. Gunn (1953, 33). The British considered such exchanges to be the selling of children and outlawed them under the antislavery laws. All women are "girls" until married.

3. An interesting attempt to explicate alliances of a similar type in East Africa in terms of game theory is Hallpike (1970).

4. Audrey Richards's (1948) pioneering thesis gave full appreciation to the significance of hunger in tribal societies (27, 202 ff.). See also her classic work (1939) on the Bemba.

Du Village: Organization of Space and People   3

THE RESEARCH FOR THIS STUDY was undertaken in a traditional, long-settled community called Du, or Udu, the land of the Du people. Du is a large village of about 3,500 people, some of whose members are fairly well scattered now. For the first three or four decades of the twentieth century, Du was a fortified hill village typical of most of the plateau settlements before European contact. Access to the village was made difficult because of the rows of twenty-foot-high prickly pear cacti that lined the pathways. Today Du is the senior village in the Du District, and because of its location in the midst of the demarcated "congested areas," it is well representative of the impact that mining has had on the plateau lands and people.

Du is one of three large villages that lie in the southernmost extension of Du District, rising from Bukuru town east to the edge of the plateau. Following traditions under which a zone of "no-man's land" separated the territories of neighboring villages, there are no precise boundaries between Du village and the villages of Zawang to the west and Shen to the northeast. Over most of the area today, some farms of the people of Du and Zawang and of Du and Shen are becoming intermingled in a confusing array. Indeed, in some locations the ownership of farms is constantly in dispute, and attempts to settle these disputes form the bulk of the work of the Grade D Native Court established by the colonial regime. The idea of permanent physical boundaries is alien to the native peoples. The Birom see their territorial space in terms of human occupancy or some other human association, not in terms of definitive spatial limits.

The hub of Du village is the courthouse located in a traditional gathering place of the elders, an area called Nlo, which is dominated by a huge baobob tree. It is about four miles southeast of Bukuru town. Six miles north of Du is Rayfield, a European mining settlement dating back to 1911 and the headquarters of the Amalgamated Tin Mines of Nigeria, Ltd, the largest mining company in Nigeria. Du is also just under four miles north of the main camp and offices of the third most important company, Bisichi Tin Co., Ltd. Thus, the village is sandwiched between two of the largest mining centers in Nigeria. Within a radius of ten miles of Du there are sixty-four labor and mining camps owned and operated either by private miners or mining companies or by the Northern Region government. Most of the land in Du District is under contract to mining companies and their affiliates through mining leases, exclusive prospecting licenses, certificates of occupancy, or grants of specific water rights. One European miner of almost thirty years' residence in the area has estimated that nearly 75 percent of the land in the congested areas (which includes Du, Gyel, and Gabong Districts) is subject to commercial or government titles.

Throughout this area, there are fairly good dirt roads, most of which were built by mining companies to connect their extensive paddocks. One such road runs through the western edge of Du village area, and on it taxis and trucks run during early morning and evening hours from Bukuru to Sabon Gida camp at Bisichi and back again. It is, however, mainly a dry-season road. On the main roads there are buses and trucks from Bukuru to Jos and from Jos to Bukuru to other areas of the plateau and of Nigeria. Many Du people consequently have some contact with the people and markets of Jos, and many more attend the Bukuru market.

Du village is the administrative center of the Native Authority of Du District. The Grade D Native Court provides judicial services for the district and is also the main vehicle for the administration of local government regulations. The seven members of the court who are legitimately recognized by the government and the public come from Du, Zawang, Shen, and Gabong. But all Birom men who are considered elders are permitted to sit in on cases and participate in the decision making, albeit informally. There is a district chief (Da Gwom Du) who is head of the court, an office that was invented by British administrators during a period of reorganization of native territories and the establishment of administrative districts. There is no native term or concept for either the district or the district chief, the latter of whose responsibilities are the collecting of taxes in the entire district and presiding over the weekly native court, which has jurisdiction over minor civil and criminal cases and cases involving native domestic issues. Although the prestige of the district chief is therefore high in the contemporary context, his influence in matters of native customs and law is in practice not greater than that of other men and is subordinate to that of the elders.

The village is composed physically of compounds that vary in size from several rooms to one that has over forty. Until the early 1940s, all the compounds in the village were located tightly clustered together high in the interstices of the hill mass, called Lo Ku Lo Du, which sprawls more than two miles long and rises several hundred feet above the flat plains. The largest compound in the village was still located at the northern apex of the hill mass and had approximately forty-one rooms. Most of the larger compounds are traditional in their architectural form, consisting of a series of grass-thatched round rooms arranged around a larger entry room of the headman of the compound and sometimes connected by mortar and daub walls. The smaller compounds tend to be "modern" (square houses with corrugated zinc roofs) and are almost always the offshoots of larger compounds. The smaller compounds are also generally the newer ones, built out on the open flat plains away from the rocky hills and separated from other dwellings. This difference in the pattern and size of compounds represents differences in their social composition, with the larger, more traditional ones still housing multigenerational patrilineally based kin units and the smallest ones generally containing nuclear families or a single polygynous family. The newer housing does reflect better economic conditions for some as well as population pressure on land that has induced young married couples to move from the paternal compound to areas where more land is available.

Compounds consist of an entrance room, sleeping rooms, storage rooms or granaries, huts for animals if there are any, cooking huts for the rainy season (and sometimes special sleeping rooms), rooms for newly married women, and a variety of other rooms with special functions, such as the sleeping rooms for young unmarried men and a special room for the ancestors. In compounds established within the last generation or so, fewer rooms are the rule, and often there is one large rectangular dwelling with several rooms under one roof. Compounds are usually surrounded on most sides by fences constructed of the long-stemmed euphorbia plant, which resembles a tall cactus with poisonous needles and can grow nearly twenty-five feet tall. Neighboring compounds and the small farms interspersed among them are connected by networks of footpaths.

Wards

From the administrative point of view, every compound in the village is located in a particular ward, which is a colonial unit for assessing and collecting taxes. To the colonialists, the ward was a territorially discrete division of a village with determinable geographic limits. In time, the administrative idea of wards became adapted to and confused with an indigenous term, the *manjei*, which represents social divisions within the native villages. There are no precise territorial boundaries expressed in the traditional Birom concept of *manjei*, and colonial ward divisions appear to have no relationship to the traditional *manjei* except in the use of their names. The farms of individual kin groups are usually scattered over several *manjei* without regard to the ward membership of the owners. This has prevented the government from establishing and maintaining rigid physical boundaries and assessing precisely the farmlands owned. Tax records show that some "houses," although remaining in the same location undisturbed, have been placed in different wards from one year to the next.

There were originally only five *bajei* (plural) in Du, with the names Janda, Madu, Rugut, She, and Le chom. However, with the cessation of hostilities among villages beginning in the 1930s and the expansion of the population, newer areas have been settled, extending out onto the plains, that came to be identified as separate *bajei*. Ropwang, Moh, and Beg were created contiguous to the older *bajei* as offshoot settlements of Du people.

The eight sections, perceived as true *bajei* of the village, are clustered in and around the hill mass, called Lo Ku Lo Du, whose peaks rise several hundred feet above the main plateau level. The entire mass stretches two miles north and south and is nearly one mile at its widest section. All the Du people lived within this area until the third decade of the twentieth century. One can still see the ruins of many houses in the hills, and hundreds of small garden plots are still used. The majority of people continue to inhabit the *bajei* surrounding the hills, with nearly all the compounds located within a mile of its lower slopes.

Population Size

The research for this study was confined largely to the eight inner wards (Janda, Rugut, Lechom, She, Moh, Madu, Ropwang, and Beq) primarily because they are areas of longest settlement and more traditional in outlook and because, taken together, they are territorially distinct from the more distant settlements. In addition, these inner wards are the only areas that are fully Birom. Most people do not consider the outlying areas as part of Du village. Two separate censuses were taken in the eight wards, one in 1960 and the other in the spring of 1961, with the results shown in table 3.1.[1]

There were several reasons for the discrepancy in numbers that are of interest for the understanding of social interaction in the village. First, there is within certain families a high rate of individual mobility of residence. A few individuals frequently move, today not so much from one large native village to another but

Table 3.1   Du Village Census of 1960–1961

Year	Adults		Children		Total
	Male %	Female %	Male %	Female %	
1960	735 (22.8)	845 (26.2)	900 (27.9)	747 (23.1)	3,227
1961	652 (22.2)	777 (26.4)	835 (28.4)	677 (23.0)	2,941

rather into nearby towns, outlying wards, or mining or labor camps to stay with relatives or to work as laborers for periods varying from several weeks to several years. In addition, during the rainy season, many people move onto bush farms; some stay for the season, others for only a few weeks. Second, there are a small number of young people who remain away for long periods of time. The question is whether they are still to be considered Du people. Virtually all these young people return each year during the farming months to participate in the farming activities and to share in the produce. Moreover, where kinship ties are close, they will visit frequently at other times during the year.

Finally, there is a question as to the limits of ward membership. Ropwang and Beq are wards at the southern edge of the hill mass, and according to the tax records, each contained about 140 persons. As we conducted our census survey, some people in this latter area were still claiming that they were of the Beg or Ropwang *manjei*. The same is true of areas three miles north of Lo Ku Lo Du, where undoubtedly a few people included themselves in Madu or Janda during my census taking. This emphasizes that the traditional *manjei* was a unit based on consciousness of social propinquity, without precise geographic boundaries.

Social Organization: The Political–Jural–Ritual Domain

There is an arena of social interaction that is comprised exclusively of structural relationships among males. These are membership units formed by principles of agnation, descent, alliances based on propinquity, and the common ownership of important rituals. The peoples of the plateau developed very complex and elaborate ways of relating men to one another that helped make possible the high levels of mobility that characterized the area.

Structured Kinship: Lo, Yere, and Chang

The basic unit of Birom society is an agnatic kin group, called *lo*, composed ideally of patrilineal descendants of a known founding ancestor from whom the group receives its name. This ancestor appears in genealogies recounted at a point some four to seven (rarely more) generations from the youngest generation living. Although birth and legal paternity, established by the payment of brideprice, determine membership in the group, affiliation may also occur by adoption or other fictional means. The *lo* is a discrete unit with corporate identity and functions, the most important of which is its embodiment of all rights and privileges and all obligations, priorities, and responsibilities with respect to the holding and use of land and other strategic resources. The very concept of patrilyny as an ideology of group formation means that the critical structural relationships are among men only. This is the "bony framework" of the social system (Barth 1966).

There is no other unit, superior to the *lo*, that reckons its membership through unilineal descent from a higher level of genealogical segmentation. Thus, the *lo* is not a minimal or minor segment within a hierarchically structured lineage system.[2] Patrilineal descent as an ideology of social placement is a minimal element in the rationale that aligns persons and groups to one another, while agnation, the notion of men and groups having relationships based on their settling together as "brothers," in the past has had greater political significance, as later discussions will show. The point regarding descent ideology should not be misconstrued. Descent is still the primary mechanism by which members are recruited into the kin group, and its influence is symbolized in the still relatively undiluted concern and interest in things pertaining to the ancestors along agnatic lines. The collective ancestors (*bivu-vwel*; lit., "dogs of the earth") are thought to have considerable mystical powers over their descendants. They function to legitimize claims to landholding. They provide sanctions for the behavior of living men and women and are often held to blame for the illnesses of children. Moreover, who they were and where they came from determines the kinds of rituals and associated beliefs and values held by living descendants. A Birom man greatly desires sons whose existence can elevate his status, enhance his reputation and influence, and confer on him the kind of immortality that comes only when they found a kin group in their father's (pater's) name. Descent then is important and relevant in different ways, but it does not provide the sole charter for the structuring of Birom society.

Birom conceptualizations of kinship classify all patrilineally related groups and persons into three orders, expressed by the terms *lo*, *yere*, and *chang*. *Lo* kinship refers to the close agnatic ties of men, women, and children who belong to the corporate kin group. These persons are "the people of the house" (*bimad lo*) and as such are distinguished from all other types of kinsmen, cognatic and affinal. The term necessarily only includes patrilateral kinspersons and not the descendants of female agnates. *Yere* refers to the relationships, in a structural sense, of close agnatic groups to one another. Two separate *lo* groups that stemmed from a single *lo* as a result of fissioning and segmentation several generations past will call themselves *yere* of one another. This term also has the connotation of descendants but is rarely used to refer to individual relationships. When a man does use the term, as, for example, "Ma sei yere lo Rwang Shom" ("I am *yere* of Lo Rwang Shom"), he is referring not to personal relationships but to the structural position and to the continuity of himself and his sons within the agnatic system. The concept of *yere* is not personal kinship, nor does it apply to women, although women will use the term in reference to agnatic kin groups that presume a close relationship among themselves. Because of its function as the property-holding, -managing, and -producing unit and its autonomy in quasi-political matters, the *lo* is the critical unit of adaptation over a range of time that encompasses many generations. Its viability, and therefore one might say its adaptive success, depended on its ability to adjust to environmental changes, to the unpredictability and instability of food resources, to demographic fluctuations, and to the requisites of peaceable interaction with its neighborhoods. In the next chapter, I give a detailed account of the sociocultural features and processes that give identification to the *lo* and an analysis of the salient ecological correlates that have been the primary determinants of its forms and structural arrangements. The term *chang* is much less specific; it refers to a generalized notion of kinship and includes many categories of kinsmen.[3] It is loosely and widely applied to all nonspecific kinspeople of bilateral or bilineal connections, known and unknown. Thus, all cognates, exclusive of the *lo* members and its predecessors and derivatives, are included, as, for example, father's mother's people and mother's cognates. It also includes affines of both primary and secondary links, such as the families of the wives of men in whose *lo* group one's daughter is married and any other peoples considered related but with whom one has no structured, formal behavior or expectations of such. *Chang* also applies to ties between *lo* groups that share a common ritual, a common tradition of origin in a distant place, and a common shrine where no agnation is postulated between them. To say of a family, "Yin a man chang zong" ("They are only *chang*") is to place them outside of what I call structured kinship, involving the institutionalized operation of rights and obligations. At the same time, this statement identifies these people as having certain kinds of minimal ties with one's own group. Beyond the *chang* are other Birom of the village (*kafiring*) with whom one has no kinship other than the community of custom and language, residence, and mystical beliefs. Non-Birom peoples are identified by ethnic group or place of origin, and all others are "strangers."

Traditional Political Structure

The Birom, prior to the imposition of colonial rule, would have been identified as an acephalous society. With few exceptions, each village or village area was an autonomous community. A common understanding in anthropology is that such societies display several characteristics that are related to their low level of economic specialization and absence of government structures of a centralized nature—administrative agents, legislative bodies, and judicial machinery.[4] Power was not concentrated in the hands of one person or party, but decisions about all community matters were made by the elders in concert or as ritual leaders. Among such societies also is the absence of class distinctions and rigid stratification of permanently unequal social elements. Such societies are described as "egalitarian" wherein adult individuals of the same sex have relatively equal access to wealth and power and to positions of prestige sanctioned by custom and law (Fried 1967, chaps. 2 and 3). This is not meant to imply homogeneity or sameness among individuals, for personal prestige, positions of influence, reputation, and social standing are all sorted differently in society even where there are no formally ranked statuses. The range and scope of differentiation runs along numerous axes, reflecting or emphasizing qualities that may be primarily achieved or categorically ascribed or a combination of both.

In this sense, inequality of individual social standing and prestige is an important characteristic of the Birom community, although the society is not a stratified one, and the ranking of individuals is more informal than formal. The measurement of a man's position, relegated by virtue of his sex to the public arena, is determined by a number of factors. These include the traditions of origin of his kin group, the number of wives and mistresses (in the cicisbeian relationship; see chapter 11) that he has, the amount of land held by his kin group, its efficiency in the production of the critical food resources (especially *acha*), the nature of the rituals that he and his kinsmen command, his role(s) in the performance of certain public rituals, and so forth. Added to this are certain qualities of personality that are considered essential ingredients in the status adhering to a big and important man. These are wisdom, knowledge, health, maturity, diplomacy, tact, and (most important) generosity.

Most important distinctions are those that emanate from questions of origin. We have already seen that Birom villages are composed of individuals and family aggregates of diverse ethnic and geographical origins. The cognitive recognition of this diversity of origins has formed the basis for the establishment of social categories and social groupings that, in addition to the agnatic kin groups, comprise the social divisions in the village.

Many persons in Du village claim to be descendants of immigrants from northern territories; others claim ancestors originating from the western and southern lands. Many if not most village peoples are generally classed and known by their "land" of origin, a distinction that appears to be of only superficial significance in the conduct of daily affairs. Thus, the Bi-Jal ("bi" = plural) are any of the settlers from Jal, the Bi-Kuru from Kuru, Bi-Vwang from Vwang (Vom), and so forth. There is no regularity or consistency in the number of such *lo* groups that originated from these separate areas. Of particular significance to the sociopolitical cohesion of the plateau villages in former times is the fact that the majority of the various kin groups, in villages where I collected data (Du, Shen, Forum, Vom, Kuru, Riyom, and Gyel), also claim to have ties of remote kinship (*chang*) with peoples in these other villages.

Folktales, myths, and oral history depict fairly frequent but unpredictable movements of peoples throughout the plateau. Each migrating unit carried cultural features peculiar to its own background, such as a special mode of decorative dress or body jewelry, a unique type of minor household ritual, certain food taboos and notions of malevolent spirits, or ritual alliances with other like groups centering on a specific shrine or sacred area. For example, the people called the Bi-Jal (Ganawurri) have meat taboos such as the prohibition against eating a certain type of small snake. There are also some minor linguistic distinctions. Although the Bi-Jal in Du are considered Birom and speak the language of the Birom, there are slight differences in vocabulary, such as words denoting a special type of yam, or there are differences in the pronunciation of some words common to all the Birom. Differences according to alleged place of origin of immigrating groups have not resulted in the formation of distinct classes or ethnic subdivisions. However, the divisions vary greatly in population size, and sheer numbers alone enhance the importance and prestige of kin groups in certain categories.

Most of the kin groups of the village (sixty-three of eighty-five *lo* groups) belong to one of four large divisions: the Bi-Lei, Bi-Kabong, Bi-Bwata, and Bi-Pyomo. The Bi-Lei are said to be descendants of peoples from the far north, through Buji lands. The Bi-Gabong are also from the north, via Gabong. The Bi-Bwata are a heterogeneous mixture of peoples from the west, from the village areas of Kuru, Kwi, Rim, Jal, Vwang, Wering, and Riyom. The Bi-Pyomo, who of the four are the fewest in number, are said to be of Jerawa origin, representing more recent immigrants from the north and east. The remaining kin groups (twenty-two *lo* groups) claim to have their origins from a variety of regions, some nearby villages of Zawang or Shen and others from non-Birom areas. Ten of these twenty-two groups claim to have no relationship to one another or to other peoples in other nearby villages.

Each of the four major divisions contains smaller clusters of kin groups that claim close ties inter alia. In such clusters, when a relationship between two or more kin groups is said to be *yere*, genealogical evidence generally shows that they are junior units formed as a result of segmentation of a former *lo* in the remembered past (see chapter 5). Additionally, there are groups of five, six, or seven or more kin groups who feel themselves united for particular purposes. The relationship among them is expressed in the general term for kinship, *chang*; it is neither agnatic nor based on descent but rather a recognition of a common bond by virtue of origin: "Our ancestors once dwelt together in the same place and therefore we are brothers." Thus, the agnatic kin groups—Lo Pam Dyet, Lo Gyang Pam, Lo Man, Lo Gyes, Lo Mak, Lo Ja, Lo Godus, and Lo Bwei—consider themselves as closely related groups within the category of Bi-Bwata. The same is true of the groups called Lo Matta, Lo Gan, Lo Ko Dusu, Lo Da Jang, Lo Chun Tok, Lo Da Reng, and Lo Bot Tok, who form a distinct unit of *chang* and whose background is also Bi-Bwata. There is no native term for these groupings so formed, but they are distinguished by the fact that they are the exclusive owners of certain shrines and have specific rights to the performance of particular rituals. For the sake of clarification and simplicity, I will call these groupings "sodalities," by which is meant a nonresidential (nonlocalized) "association that has some corporate functions or purposes" (Service 1971, 13). I will discuss the nature of these ritual functions later.

If prevailing interpretations are correct, the peoples of all the villages of the plateau represent a mosaic of remnant immigrants, some of whom came from the larger, more politically unified states to the south, east, and north. These "strangers" to one another were held in tenuous but orderly relationships by ties of fictive kinship, of ritual alliances (sodalities), and sometimes of hostility. As the movements of these groups continued through space and time, the patterning within each village was, like a giant kaleidoscope, reformed over the generations into many different arrangements. The coming of Europeans added momentum to the already existing dynamics of various groups aligning and realigning themselves vis-à-vis one another. The description presented here of the relationships among these groups in Du village shows the pattern as it developed in the early twentieth century as well as subsequent modifications brought about by the emergence of some groups to positions of power and eminence and the decline of others in recent decades.

The Core Groups

The people who call themselves Bi-Lei and Bi-Kabong differ from all other groups and categories in the village in that they consider themselves and are so considered by others as "true Du" peoples, descendants of the original founders of the village. Member *lo* groups in each sodality maintain an oral history demonstrating and thus proving their descent from the first man, Du Bute. A few elders in these groups can volunteer genealogies ranging to eight generations in depth, tracing the ancestry of their various component *lo* groups to Du Bute, his "brothers," and followers. However, within these genealogies, connections beyond the five- or six-generation depth of the corporate kin groups are uncertain, or unknown, and usually subject to much dispute. I have obtained as many as five different versions of the ancestral links by which one *lo* traces its genealogy to Du Bute.

Legend has it that Du was a man of Gabong, and the narrative accounts of how he came to settle in Du differ somewhat in their details, the various places at which he is supposed to have stopped, his motivations, his companions, the rituals they founded, and so forth. At the same time, the basic skeleton of the story is the same in all accounts. Du Bute stopped at Buji and erected a special stone that was to become the site of some of the more important rituals. He stopped at Gabong, and some of his followers remained there. After arriving at Du, some of his followers, including relatives and companions, continued on to Forom; this explains the special links to that village. As we will see later, certain member *lo* groups within the Bi-Lei and Bi-Kabong are today rival claimants to supremacy in the villages. Their different versions of the founding of the village are employed to validate their claims. Each group denies that the other people actually descend from Du and hold that it was from one of his companions that they stemmed.

Member groups of the Bi-Lei and Bi-Kabong are fairly well scattered throughout the village lands. However, the rule of virilocal residence and the values that maintain close propinquity of fathers, sons, and brothers have resulted in a greater concentration of members of these divisions in certain parts of the village. Generally, the Bi-Lei *lo* groups are scattered over the northern and eastern slopes of Lo Ku Lo Du, while the Bi-Kabong tend to inhabit the southwestern wards of the village. The original homesites of both groups were in the valleys and slopes of the mass of hills. While none of the Bi-Kabong live in the hills today, they maintain a homesite and a shrine in a place called Kabang on the southernmost tip of Lo Ku Lo Du. It is here that some of the old men still perform some of their major ceremonies. The Bi-Lei have two "original" homesites and shrines, one on the northern hill top and the other on an eastern and more southern peak.

These sites and shrines correspond to what the Birom view as irreconcilable differences among three factions struggling for power. All the member groups who call themselves Bi-Kabong constitute a single sodality or ritual group. The Bi-Lei, on the other hand, are divided into two subgroups, Lo Gwom and Lo Du, each having separate sets of rituals and political interests. Like the larger units, the Bi-Lei and Bi-Kabong, the people of Lo Du and Lo Gwom are antagonists; they are counterposed in perpetual opposition as rivals over claims for precedence in the village.

These sodalities today have lost some of their internal adhesion. The ancient symbols of their unities, the Great Ceremonies, have largely been expunged by British-imposed law or eroded by the lack of faith of the young and present-day conflicts of power. Appeals to common descent have little real meaning among some of the younger people, except as just one of the strategies to be utilized in struggles for power or strategic resources. The identity and functions of such sodalities in precolonial times had greater significance, but even so, the significance was limited to very specific spheres of village public life. Sodalities are not, for example, exogamous groups, nor do they have control over marriage arrangements or the collection and distribution of bridewealth. Their primary functions around the time that Europeans came up onto the plateau had to do with performing the Great Ceremonies that spanned most of the plateau populations.

Each kin group of the Bi-Kabong (Lo Kwei, Lo Bogom, Lo Pam Teng, Lo Bwa, Lo Kwon, Lo Go Zang, and Lo Bwengei) is a completely separate agnatic kin group, with its own lands and headman. If there were ever any genealogical ties among them, these are unknown, and it is considered unnecessary to trace them. Members of these kin groups can and do marry one another and speak of themselves as *chang* to one another. On the other hand, certain of the groups are regarded as being more closely related than others. Thus, Lo Go Zang, Lo Bwa, and Lo Kwon people do not intermarry, and in some situations Lo Bwa and Lo Kwon people will state, "We are all Lo Go Zang" as well as people of Kabong. At the time of my research, these groups were in the later stages of the process of segmentation. There are still some known genealogical links among older individuals within these groups, indicating that their social identities as separate, mature, corporate *lo* groups have only recently fully emerged. A similar situation obtains among some of the groups within the Lo Du and Lo Gwom sodalities.

Neither the Bi-Bwata, the Bi-Pyomo, Bi-Jal, nor any other peoples in the village make claims to early settlement or relationship to the founder, Du Bute. Although many of these people have held land for generations in the village, none give genealogies of more than five or six generations. They all distinguish themselves from the Bi-Lei and Bi-Gabong by the term *Bimad pweng*. The word *pweng* has been translated in modern times to mean "poor." In the traditional context, however, it appears to have meant only those who were not of the "first or founding families." Some of the Bi-Bwata are comparatively large and wealthy kin groups.

Unlike the "first families," related groups that form sodalities among the Bi-Bwata and Bi-Pyomo categories do not claim descent from a common ancestor. As noted previously, the most frequent reason given for their common membership in the sodality is origin in a common place or "living together as brothers."

The Bi-Lei and Bi-Kabong are different from the other peoples of the village in that they emphasize descent from the founding ancestor and preserve genealogical knowledge or myths to corroborate this. Each cluster of kin groups is subsumed under a name—Lo Kwei (Bi-Kabong), Lo Du, or Lo Gwon—that gives them a distinct identity. These differences are not predicated on class or wealth.

In each division, there are some members who are extremely poor and a few who are relatively well off. In any case, the differences between those who are better off and those who are poor is not very great when viewed in terms of the wider context of plateau society.

Despite the differences that separate the Bi-Lei and Bi-Kabong from other peoples in the village, those clusters of kin groups formed into sodalities have a number of characteristics in common. One of these is that there appears to be at the center of each sodality at least one large influential kin group around which the sodality is organized and which becomes the focus of the activities of the total unit. Among the Bi-Kabong, it is a kin group known as Lo Kwei. Other kin groups, such as Lo Go Zang, Lo Pam Teng, and Lo Boggom (out of the thirteen groups that make up this sodality), are larger in size. And Lo Boggom today has greater prestige because it was from this *lo* that the present chief of Jos was appointed. But it is the Lo Kwei men who hold the traditional positions of ritual leadership in the sodality, and it is quite likely, as some claim, that the Lo Kwei were at one time the dominant kin group in terms of both numbers and status. Even today, old men of related kin groups in this sodality will often say, "We are men of Lo Kwei" to underscore their evaluation of the high status of Lo Kwei.

Among the peoples who belong to the Lo Du sodality (Lo Dong, Lo Gorot, Lo Hwelling, Lo Wet, Lo Vogon, Lo Yang, Lo Dung Zong, Lo Chun Tok, and Lo Pam Shom), it is the kin group Lo Dung Zong that occupies this central position. The Da Lo, or headman of Lo Dung Zong, is also called the Da Lo of all the Lo Du peoples by virtue of his leadership in the performance of major rituals owned by this sodality. It is also the largest kin group numerically, and its older men use the name of Lo Du interchangeably with Lo Dung Zong. Likewise, the Lo Gwom sodality has its focus in the kin group that calls itself Lo Gwom Rosso. For reasons that have to do with modern political circumstances, this sodality is less unified than the others. While I cannot explore here the full nature of the contemporary political conflicts, I will have more to say about factionalism among the Lo Gwom group and the role of women later.

A most important characteristic of all sodalities and essentially what they all have in common is a particular type of traditional function, the performance of certain important ceremonies, some of which are exclusive and specific for each sodality. The dominant kin group or groups in each sodality can be envisioned as the focal point of distinct ritual spheres. Around them other kin groups have sorted themselves, some being considered genealogically related, others not. Some of the evidence suggests that the ritual alliances that bind these *lo* groups to one another may be loose and ambiguous, yielding a condition similar to internal agnatic kinship where connections are manipulable. There were a number of situations in which one kin group claimed to have Lo Gwom or Lo Du status, but others would deny it. The people of Lo Go Det, for example, sent their elders to me to demonstrate via the recitation of history and genealogical data that they are also Lo Du. Elders from some of the other Lo Du kin groups had not included them in an earlier historical reconstruction and had denied that Lo Go Det were also Lo Du. Two old men argued that Lo Go Det people were really Lo Gwom. Others were uncertain. Ritual connections or membership within either sodality confers status and prestige, but the contentions could not be resolved by agreement among any of the elders. Yet late in 1960, one old man of Lo Go Det did appear and participated in the Pe ceremony that was held by the Lo Du men and was not turned away.

These and other examples evince a special characteristic of all indigenous communities on the plateau. While membership in various alliances was seemingly stable over long periods, it was not rigidly fixed or indefinitely secured. Groups at different structural levels, from the agnatic kin group to the sodalities and even to village levels, moved into and out of alliances within the lifetime of a man so that the kinship and alliance patterns with which he might have been familiar as a young boy will have changed drastically by the time he became an elder.

Such complex and dynamic patterns of group interaction, especially of agnatic groups moving into and out of numerous alliances over time, may well have deep historical significance as I suggested in the introductory chapter. This mode of interaction may have been the catalyst for the growth of larger states, such as Old Ghana, Mali, Songhai, and Kanem Bornu, and the mechanism by which unification of autonomous communities was secured. Ritual linkages such as the Great Ceremonies may have been strategies of organization capable of unifying increasingly larger numbers of disparate kin groups and village communities. What were autonomous villages could have been bound together and brought to high levels of cooperation and defense, including the unexpected and sophisticated military organization described by the first Europeans. In the evolution of plateau society, kin groups developed certain features that could allow them to readily respond to the requisites of changing political, economic, and demographic circumstances. For this reason, among others, I identify the kin group as the major unit of adaptation.

All the groupings specified here are conceived as male membership groups. Women are not critical for such membership groups except as wives and mothers of the men. What I found of interest through all the research into this elaborate sociopolitical structuring of male relationships is how many men were uncertain about the identities of other men in these groups. Wherever I went in the village, after older men would speculate on who was a member of which groups, there would be disagreements. Nearly always toward the end of my visit, several older women would then intervene and venture to relate the "correct" information. Women do not spend much of their own time speculating on relationships at these different levels, but they tended to agree among themselves that they alone knew the most accurate information. Why were women so circumspect about the relationships of men to one another? We will begin to see some answers to this question beginning in chapter 5.

Notes

1. The discrepancy in numbers between males and females in the categories of "adults" and "children" appears to be due to the differences, both on the part of the Birom and myself, in the perception of the ages of males and females. Most girls are married shortly after the onset of menstruation, and, though some may not as yet have attained the age of fifteen, they are classified as adults because of their status as wives. My calculations as to the ages of young unmarried men aimed at precise dating on the basis of certain events that occurred in the year of their birth or weaning. The Birom insist that a young unmarried man, even in his early twenties, is still just a "boy."

2. This lack of higher-level structuring on genealogical grounds is in contrast to the Tiv, in a neighboring area of northern Nigeria, and others peoples, such as the Tallensi or the Nuer of the eastern Sudan, who have hierarchically arranged segmentary lineage systems or clans that form umbrellas over clusters of smaller lineage segments.

3. C. K. Meek was, I believe, the first to mention, although briefly, a kind of "kinship," not expressed in the genealogical idiom, among "pagan" peoples of northern Nigeria. He speaks, for example, of two types of relationships between kindreds among the Chamba. In one, kindreds are related to one another in the male line and are "brothers." In the second, kindreds are "comrades" to one another. Furthermore, "It is stated that the founder of the Kwasa kindred married the sister of Longa, and that it is for this reason that the Kwasa are "comrades of the Sama and Janga kindreds" (Meek 1950, vol. 1, 339).

4. The Birom were not lacking in forms of governance, as will be seen later in this volume. This included both "agents" and strategies for resolving conflicts, issuing and interpreting regulations, and maintaining social order. For general and comparative discussions of such "acephalous" societies, see Colson (1974), Fortes and Evans-Pritchard (1949), Mair (1962), Middleton and Tait (1958), and Schapera (1967). In this book, I am concerned primarily with the nature of the distribution and operation of socially recognized authority and the forms in which it is expressed.

The Ecological Basis of the Kin Group 4

THE IDENTIFICATION OF THE agnatic group (*lo*) as the property-holding unit in Birom society through which all resources are channeled and their production and use controlled requires consideration of the ecological circumstances under which the unit functions and which have in the past helped give it its definition and form. In this chapter, I delineate the specific historical and ecological factors that were most relevant to the structure, size, and functioning of kin groups. I especially note how decisions about the gender division of labor were effected in the interactive process and the conditions that influenced the construction of gender roles. In the last section, I examine the implications of changes brought about by the coming of tin mining and colonialism to the formation of kin groups and women's positions.

In this analysis, my first concern was to distinguish what we might call the cognitive arena of interaction: the Birom peoples' perception of environmental features that can be specified as significant to their lives. The crucial element in the Birom ecosystem is, of course, their land, both as an exploitable milieu and as territorial space. Traditionally, as I have shown, Birom conceptions of mobility and distance were circumscribed by fears of warfare and predation, especially slave raiding, from other human groups. I have already described the age-old patterns of settlement in better-protected hill areas that were one response to this perceived hazard.

The Birom divide the whole of their territorial space into five different zones that appear to be based chiefly on considerations of propinquity and distance. But there is a great deal more to these areas than the factor of space. Each zone also has different cultural-economic meanings associated with it. The zones correspond objectively to geographic distance (but also to some degree to natural elements), topographical features (such as land elevation), and differences in the natural fertility of the soil, vegetation patterns, and wild animal habitations. These five zones constituted the known territorial world of the Birom villagers from remote times.

Three of the zones are of major importance because they contain the farmlands from which villages traditionally derived their sustenance. In the following sections, I identify each of the zones and describe their particular characteristics, in their natural form and with respect to human use, with which they are associated. The boundaries of these zones are not set but are elastic and subject to change over time.

Zone I: Garden Farms

The first of the farmland areas is called *bwi* in the Birom language and is today probably the most important in terms of economic value to the Birom. I have translated the term as "gardens" or "garden farms." Every compound has some *bwi* around it, sometimes on all sides, and most are surrounded by tall cactuslike euphorbia plants. The purpose of the euphorbia fence, the Birom say, is to protect the crops from goats and other animals. The crops are also protected from malevolent spirits by special medicine sticks whose movement incidentally frightens away birds and other predators. These gardens are more fertile than all other types of farmlands, receiving human and animal waste, and some of them are deliberately manured for particular kinds of crops. Located in the hill areas by virtue of their attachment to compounds, they are better watered and have the further benefit of decayed vegetable matter from small clusters of trees, brush, and tall grasses that dot the hillsides. Unlike farms on the open plains, garden farms are protected also from water and wind leaching by the surrounding brush, trees, housing, and huge rock boulders of the hill mass. With a greater humus content, the topsoil is subsequently deeper and more permeable. Partly because of their location, *bwi* are small in size, averaging less than one-third of an acre. A few garden farms in the foothills tend to be somewhat larger.

Because of their greater fertility and proximity to the compounds, the crops that require more nutrients from the soil, manuring, or more care and protection are grown in these *bwi* lands. So also are crops that the Birom do not or cannot produce in large quantities or that do not require an extensive area for a desired return. Thus, staples, including three types of yams, guinea corn, sweet corn (maize), cassava, and some finger millet, can be grown here. Vegetables such as cowpeas, beans, onions, peppers, tomatoes, Indian Rosselle, beniseed, and many other native plants that have not been given English names are intercropped with the grains and tubers. Although *acha* (*Digitaria*) is the staple grain of the western Sudan and Du villagers recognize more than a dozen different species of *acha*, only one of these is grown traditionally in garden farms. It is one of the fastest growing and is planted in May and harvested in September. As it does not give a high yield, the majority of farmers say they prefer not to plant it, especially if the *bwi* are still giving good yields of other crops. In other words, this variety is grown only in gardens when the soil is too exhausted to take any other crop.

In addition to the ordinary *bwi*, there is another area, consisting of strips of land nearest to the compound called *lo bwi*, in which a type of native spinach, some squash, some types of yams, runner beans, marigold plants, and Indian Rosselle are grown. These plants are normally relishes that are not regarded as providing a main dish and are not grown in abundance.

Garden farms are divided annually or periodically among the men of the kin group who are the "owners," but women and children do the planting, weeding, and caring for these crops. This reality puts women and children in a spatially distant region during the cultivation period, out of contact with men, and this no doubt has allowed them to develop practices and habits that may not be shared with men. The implications of distance for the enhancement of distinct gender identities are considerable. I will return to this topic later. The only time men are seen in garden farms occurs at the beginning of the farm cycle. Men prepare the ground by slash-and-burn techniques, hoeing after the burning and forming mounds or ridges of varying sizes, depending on what is to be planted. Today, some women prepare the ground by hoeing it themselves if they cannot find male kinsman or affines to do so. Women never prepare yam beds and, according to informants, did not do any of the hoeing for *acha* until recent times. Garden farms are intensively farmed and today are rarely left to fallow. With the exception of the one variety of *acha*, crops grown in garden farms are considered women's crops and are perceived to be inferior to the more prestigious *acha*.

Zone 2: Intermediate Farms

For convenience, I call the farms lying in a zone immediately beyond the fenced *bwi* "intermediate farms," which suggests their spatial position in relation to garden farms and the larger "bush" farms. The Birom term for these farms is *chuel*. Such farms also occupy an intermediate position with respect to the kinds of crops grown, the general fertility of the land, and their water and labor requirements. As these farms are farther away from the compound, they are not surrounded by a cactus fence, although sometimes *chuel* boundaries may be marked off by the use of a special piece of wood from a tree of the ficus family. Occasionally, one sees a *bwi* garden scattered in among the intermediate farms on a spot that is unusually fertile. *Gakap chop*, the small strips of land farmed only by women, may also sometimes be found in this zone. The average size of intermediate farms is less than one acre, but the variations in sizes are much greater than that of the garden or bush farms. *Chuel* farms may be on sloping areas of the foothills or on flatter, more even areas of the plains. They are rarely manured but are left to lie fallow for rejuvenation. Today, for certain crops, the droppings of Fulani cows may be spread over a small portion of an intermediate farm.

The crops grown in *chuel* are varied, but not as many different vegetables types are grown here as in the *bwi* zone. Sweet potatoes, several types of native plants (intercropped), beniseed, and three types of *acha* (*were*, *san*, and *peng*) are the normal crops found here. Three kinds of yam, those that are not the "water" yams, are also grown in *chuel* lands. None of the people grow all the crops that are considered fit for the different zones. Their choices are contingent on numerous factors, including soil fertility, desire for certain foodstuffs, availability of workers, location of the farms, and many other personal decisions.

Both men and women work the intermediate farms, as the sexual division of labor depends largely on the kind of crops grown. All vegetable plants are the province of women and children no matter where they are grown. All grains, especially *acha*, continue to be grown by men, although in these *chuel* farms, women today may do the planting of *acha* (it is sown broadcast). Men still do the majority of tasks, such as preparing the ground, sowing, and cutting, tying, and threshing associated with the harvesting of *acha*.

Zone 3: Bush Farms

This third area of farmlands, called *hei* in Birom, is located at the outermost rim of the village's cultivable area and thus is the most remote of the farmland areas. Bush farms are located on flat, relatively level grasslands, and their average size at the time of this study was about an acre, but the range in sizes is considerable. They are the least fertile of all different types of farms, have never been traditionally manured, and, on account of their position in open plains, are highly subject to wind and rain erosion.

All the varieties of *acha* recognized by the Birom may be grown in bush farms, although the more usual ones found here are those that are slow growing (planted in April–May and harvested in November–December). Bulrush millet, also a late crop, is sometimes transplanted to bush farms as seedlings. Like *acha*, millet does not require much water, and the plants will grow strongly under a wide variety of moisture conditions. Some types of yams may also be planted in these farms, especially in areas closest to the village, but only if the soil is rich enough and there is a source of water from a stream or rivulet to maintain the plants. By far, the dominant crops of the bush farms are the many varieties of *acha*.

Bush farms are not fenced as are the garden farms; the Birom say that they are too far away for the goats to bother. But perhaps the feature of greatest import is the fact that the crops grown in these lands need not be watched or weeded. Sowing is preceded by burning over the stubble (wild grasses and brush), a process that kills the weeds and provides nutrients for the soil from the resulting ash and the chemical changes in the soil caused by the heat. And because *acha* and millet are relatively immune to fluctuations of temperature and have few insect pests, the main work of the villagers occurs generally at two periods of the farming season: sowing and harvesting time. Because of the fear of slave raiding and warfare in the past, it is obvious that there was an ecological advantage to growing crops that did not require constant human attention on lands that were most remote from the village. Moreover, work on bush farms was formerly done only by men. Traditionally, at the beginning of the rainy season, a work group of a dozen or more men, usually from neighboring kin groups, would move out onto the flat plains and cooperate in preparing all the farms and sowing the *acha*. They would move into these farms fully armed in case of an attack by slave raiders or another village and spend several weeks together preparing the farms of all their kin groups. Harvesting, likewise, is done by men in cooperating groups.

Today, a few women may work together with their men, especially if the farms are not too far away or if there are few men and boys available to do the farming. Older women who live alone do not grow *acha* for themselves, but all women have ties with some men who are able to cultivate *acha* for them or provide it as gifts. *Acha* has long been seen as the staple crop of the plateau area. It is also identified as a man's crop—the supreme prestige crop of the Birom—and there are many elements in the value system that symbolically or metaphorically associate it with a man's strength, virility, and reputation. I will return to this point in later chapters.

Zone 4: Hunting Lands

These are special areas beyond the cultivating zones of the village where hunting rights of different villages were recognized in the precontact period. There were nine major areas belonging to Du village, all of which were located generally beyond four miles from the village center. Most of the areas are north, northwest, and northeast of the village, and some as far as twelve to fourteen miles distant, where also are some of the sacred lands. All were forested areas or hilly, rocky places at the time of European contact. This zone has been one in which some of the most significant changes have occurred. There was no farming, nor were houses built in these hunting lands prior to contact, but in the last two generations some of the hunting areas have become regions absorbing the expansion of population and forming the sites of newer wards. Birom informants agreed unanimously that it was dangerous in precolonial times to venture into these remote regions, and no one ever did so alone. Young men formerly went hunting two or three times a year in groups of ten or twelve or more. Most of the men of the village participated in a major hunting ritual once a year, usually after the harvests. Expansion onto and settlement of these areas became possible and desirable after the establishment of the colonial government.

Prior to the colonial period, some portion of the hunting lands appear to have served as reserve lands for the cutting of bush farms (see discussion later in this chapter). Birom informants agreed that a man could cut farms in this zone, as there was no prohibition against it. But he would be foolish to do so unless he had easy access to some protected area or hiding place. While making a survey of some of these areas with me, some of the older men could point out the farms of men who had expanded their cultivating onto these lands before the Europeans arrived. All agreed that the frontiers of village farming could be pushed only so far before one risked the danger of going beyond what villagers considered to be a safe or protected region.

Zone 5: Sacred Lands

These are small areas or specific locations, some of which are situated beyond the village cultivating boundaries, where the special Great Ceremonies are performed and where the major spirit force(s), the various *chit*, reside or manifest themselves. No hunting, house building, or farming was traditionally permitted in these areas, and in those particular sites in sacred lands that I have designated as "ritual areas," no cutting of wood or brush was permitted. Ritual areas (*tsafi*) are specific locations, marked often by some unusual natural feature, that are found in sacred lands. These special places are avoided by the Birom, and there are several taboos that still strongly operate over these areas, such as the taboo against touching these grounds with metal in any form. The sacred lands harbor many spirits, some of which can be malevolent, so one is always careful when traveling through this zone. Some of the ritual groups of the village have their shrines in these areas; those that are most important belong to the core groups who perform certain ceremonies at shrines that are thought to be beneficial to the entire village.

Sacred lands, like hunting territory, collectively belong to the village as a whole, and each village has separate areas that are sacred to its people as well as some ritual areas it shares with the people of a "brother" village. Recognition of each village's sacred areas was an important rule of the customary intervillage law that prevailed in the precontact period. Such recognition still operates today. People of different villages do not violate one another's sacred lands.

From the earliest contact with miners, mining has generally not been allowed in those areas considered most sacred (that is, where there are shrines). Opposition to the mining brought many disputes between miners and native peoples over the boundaries of these areas. Throughout the 1940s and 1950s, miners were accused repeatedly of defiling these areas. District and court records reveal that there were widespread conflicts on numerous occasions. Such conflicts often tied up the courts with extensive litigation. At the same time, some of the government records indicate a shifting of boundaries from time to time by the Birom ceremonial leaders—the older men in the various ritual groups who have the special medicines and must perform the ceremonies. In some cases where sacred lands have been mined, land compensation has been paid to the ceremonial leaders as "owners" of the land in an attempt to diminish opposition.

In precolonial times, it appears that the hunting and sacred lands were largely nonproductive areas (except for hunting) and served rather as barriers or limits to expansion or farming. This was so because of their positions as buffer zones between potential warring villages. On the other hand, the existence in some of the sacred lands of the shrines to which related ritual groups from two or more villages made annual pilgrimages produced an orderly method of maintaining intervillage communication and exchange.

The three farming zones have quite a different kind of significance, and I will emphasize the detailed variations in their individual importance. In order to take advantage of the differences in nutrients and growth capacities of different types of soil, especially important in a habitat that is generally low in fertility, each kin group as a producing unit ideally should have holdings of land in all three farmlands zones. The three-zone system is felt to be basic to their economic well-being. This means that holdings in farmlands of necessity are discontinuous and dispersed. None of the kin groups in the village had compact areas in which all their farmlands were located. Each of the three types of farms (except for *bwi* farms, which are more localized) for any one kin group are irregularly scattered throughout the village areas, and even within a single category, such as garden farms, the plots need not be completely contiguous. A man may have two or three gardens around his compound but others located half a mile away in different directions. One of the chief reasons for this type of fragmentation is the present-day custom, quite widespread, of alienating these farms through gifts, loaning, and pawning. The scattering of farms was also brought about in part by some of the social mechanisms by which emerging new *lo* groups could obtain farmland from older groups in the village that were declining or had died out.

There were precedents for this pattern of cultivating in three zones that pre-date the colonial experience. The dispersal of farms permitted farmers to take advantage of recognized differences in the fertility of the soil. Fine-tuned recognition of soil variations allowed the development and maintenance of a wide repertoire of food crops—an astonishing variety of native plants with differing requirements that the Birom were able to adapt to plateau soils. The *acha* itself is a wild grasslike plant native to the plateau. Birom ingenuity allowed them to ennoble this crop and to ultimately develop some twenty varieties, most of which are extremely hardy. *Acha* (also known as *fonio* in the Futa Djallon and sometimes called "wild rice") emerged as the staple crop on both the Futa Djallon and the Jos-Bauchi plateau; it was the mainstay of the survival of all the plateau peoples. The open flat bush farms were suitable to its cultivation, as is the case with most grains.

One effect of this situation is that no concentration of large landholdings is possible. There is indeed no advantage to holding large numbers of farms in any one area or in any one zone. In fact, there is a distinct disadvantage in that such concentration might limit the diversification of crops that is considered so essential to the Birom diet. Moreover, farmers are aware that widely dispersed farms are good insurance against the possibility of natural disasters (extreme eroding, wind- and rainstorms, locust invasions, occasional flooding, and animal predators), depriving them of all or most of their crops. Thus, the scattering of landholdings in farms in different zones must be considered as an ecologically adaptive characteristic.

A system that depends on a variety of crops grown in different areas has a further consequence. Among subsistence-level horticulturalists, one must accept as a basic ecological principle that the amount of and the productivity of the land (that is, the total available food resources over time) will determine or affect to a high degree the size of the group that feeds from it. Granted that there is some leeway because of sharing, ultimately some kind of balance between the total amount of food available and the size of the consuming units most probably is established, but the relationship is a dynamic one and by its very nature not capable of sustained equilibrium. The Birom are well aware that more mouths to be fed means that more land must be cultivated. Their ideal is that as the landholding unit expands, so also ideally must all three types of farms. In the absence of further room for expansion within the three zones, the only alternative is that the landholding unit itself, when it reaches optimum size for the available resources, must be able to respond to the selective force of this limiting aspect of the ecology.

The situation becomes more immediately perceptible and acute when we consider the most direct connection between the sociocultural system and the land—that is, the system of land tenure. Native laws and regulations under which farmlands are held and cultivated differ considerably from one zone to another. By tradition, bush farms are held solely on the basis of priority of occupation and cultivating rights. The first man who cuts a bush farm holds exclusive rights for his kin group as long as he or any other member of his *lo* cultivates the farm. But the holding of rights to the use of the farm becomes immaterial once the farm has become exhausted. It is then returned to fallow, and the rights of the previous occupant and his kinsmen cease. The fallowing period ideally is two to three times the period of cultivation, and during this long hiatus no one person or kin group has "ownership" of the farm. It reverts to village tenure or to "no-man's land" and may not have any economic use at all. When the land is again capable of bearing crops, any man of the village has the right to open it, and he need not confine his farming to the boundaries of the previous farm.

Informants who had been young men and were farming in the early decades of the twentieth century claimed that their particular kin groups customarily cut bush farms each year in the same general area (that is, north, south, and west of the village), but this appears to have been because of convenience and habit rather than because jural rights were recognized in these areas. All informants agreed that any man of the village could legally cut a farm anywhere in virgin bush areas. In late October, November, and the early days of December, men can frequently be seen with their hoes over their shoulders, wandering over *chuel* and bush areas seeking good land, usually small fertile strips, on which to build yam ridges. They will build these ridges in any suitable bush area and will often have no idea who previously worked the land. But there are several conditions that must be observed. A man must not disturb areas where another man's crop is growing, and he must recognize prior possession signified by recently burned, freshly hoed lands, or the presence of the special demarcating posts. Yam ridges are large, measuring two to three feet across and about eighteen inches deep; they are the result of much hard labor, and, with one exception, it is virtually a mortal sin for someone else to disturb them. The erection of yam ridges signifies a man's right to cultivate this area for his kin group.

The tenure with respect to *acha* differs from that which obtains for yam beds. This is understandable because yams were not traditionally grown on bush farms until fairly recently. One may notice that several kin groups that customarily use the same bush farm area are considered to have some degree of priority in the use of these farms. The rotations of grain crops enable a man to continue cultivating the same farm for five or six years before allowing it to revert to fallow. This is not the case with yams, for which normal usage of a plot of land (usually a small section of a farm) is only one year. Today, with the shortage of farmlands, the increased value of all lands for mining, and movements of residents onto what were once bush areas, permanent rights to the holding and use of certain bush farms are gradually being established. This has occurred in several areas but not without much heated quarreling. Both government files and my field notes include many records of disputes over bush farms where the lands officers are attempting to establish "ownership" based on the previous users or those who customarily farmed in the area. A great many people now press the argument that they were the "original," "previous," or "last" users of the farms as competition for such land increases.

Chuel lands, the intermediate farms, are subject to the laws pertaining to the corporate rights of the members of the *lo*. These farms are normally acquired on marriage from the holdings within the kin group, the "ownership" of such farms being exclusive to the kin group. Intermediate farms may be increased by cutting them from nearby bush farms with claims to new *chuel* farms signified by the placement of a special wood post on the area. The only limit to the cutting of new *chuel* farms is the condition of the soil, which might prevent its use for certain crops. Generally, a kin group holds fewer intermediate farms than either garden farms or bush farms, and during some period of their adult lives some men never cultivate *chuel* farms. They are more flexible and can be dispensed with more easily than the other types of farms.

Garden farms (*bwi*) are the richest farms; they are in limited supply and therefore of great value, and they are acquired only through the inheritance rights defined by membership in the *lo*. Virtually every foot of available land within this zone is today allocated to some landholding group that maintains perpetual rights to these gardens. Older informants revealed that at the turn of the twentieth century (and perhaps for generations before) all areas within the *bwi* zone were cultivated and that there was small room for expansion. In the contemporary situation, garden lands are very tight; even those small gardens scattered in the *chuel* zone are only technically *bwi* farms, and they are recognized to be poor areas for gardens. There were several occasions when I discovered that a former garden farm was being allowed to revert to an intermediate farm because garden farming was too exhausting for it. The cutting of *bwi* farms has long embraced all the best land. The extent of the zone for garden farms is fundamentally limited by the fertility of the soil. The availability of garden farms to any man, under the traditional system and today, is based on the holdings of the *lo* group into which he was born or to which he is affiliated. This is true even though from time to time some vacant farms occasioned by death or emigration would be available to other villagers. The present-day scarcity of such farms is great; very few men stated that they had enough garden farms for their families.

The relationship then between the land as the basic resource and the sociocultural system becomes quite specific and direct with respect to the holdings of garden farms.[1] Occupying the most limited zone of farmlands, they provided the crops most crucial for the survival of the group. This would seem to have been especially critical during those periodic occasions when, according to oral history, heightened fear of warfare forced the villagers to retract their cultivating activities to the better-protected farmlands closer to the village. The only really indispensable cultivation areas were the garden lands, a much constricted zone but capable of supplying sustenance for a limited amount of time. I suggest that the garden farms can be seen as the barometer of the extremes of conditions to which the generations of Birom had to adjust and are thus most crucial for understanding the structure of the *lo* and the processes that occur within it.

The salient features of the *lo*, the landholding unit, in its relationship to the land are 1) its relative smallness of size, 2) its exclusiveness of membership and the narrow limits of genealogical connections of its members, 3) its fragility, or tendency to segment at low genealogical levels. It is my hypothesis that these features, especially the friable nature of the *lo*, are directly related to the fragmentary nature of the land, to the limitations for expanding on the land, and to the differential fertility and crop potentials of critical cultivable lands under a horticultural technology.

When exploring the area of interdependence between the kin group and its lands, it should be noted that there are three means by which the landholding units can be adjusted to the productivity and availability of the lands. One of these is via the system of land tenure. Different rules about holding and exploiting land in different zones afford some flexibility for adapting the different *lo* groups as they vary in size through the generations to the available bush and *chuel* farms. With respect to this, the short-term and temporary tenure on bushlands is important. No kin group can control or utilize under this type of tenure more land than it needs. It used to be the case that additional bush farms could be acquired in response to increased need, but mining has interrupted this reality.

Garden farms are held, as we saw, under more strict and formal tenure, but the ease with which these farms can be transferred from one *lo* group to another also provided a means for adjusting the property-holding units to the overall supply of farmland. Yet these factors would be effective only if the population remained fairly stable, with the number of deaths and emigrations canceling out increases by birth and immigration.

No society ever maintains this kind of equilibrium for long. Normal population growth constantly puts pressures on resources. A period of unusual abundance may stimulate a disproportionate increase in the population, and such a period may well be followed by a decade of drought and greatly diminished production. Furthermore, the high mobility of the peoples of the plateau and the sporadic unpredictable disasters to which these people were subjected undoubtedly complicated the maintenance of equilibrium in the relationship of people to resources.[2] One would expect, then, that other social mechanisms must operate that have the effect of regulating the relationship of men to one another and their adjustment to available land.

One such mechanism is the custom by which a kin group can slough off some of its members individually when short-term and immediate reductions, without splitting the group, are necessary. In nearly every genealogy recorded, there were a few individual men in most generations who were described as "wanderers." They were men who never married in the village but left the area on attaining adulthood and usually never returned. When one investigates the cause or reason for "wandering," it becomes clear that these men were usually one of many sons for whom there was not enough land and no brideprice. The most common way of explaining why these men became wanderers is the simple statement *vide be* ("no garden farms"). Reduction in the size of the *lo* group by wanderers is a mechanism of immediate reaction to a situation already characterized by maximal holding and use of garden farms and the unfeasibility of further fragmentation of the *lo* group's lands. Were these wandering sons to marry and remain in the village, the chance of increasing the number of mouths to be fed would be magnified out of proportion to the crop capacity of the kin group's lands.

There is clearly another device that limits, decreases, and transforms the number of people who can claim hereditary rights to hold and cultivate the limited lands of a kin group. Birom customs provide small kin groups with institutionalized methods of breaking kinship, such as segmenting at genealogical levels of four to six or seven generations, a process often remaining within the memories of the oldest living men. Such segmentation is an adaptive response to the increase in the size of the kin group and the limitations of cultivable lands. It is a built-in device for maintaining or restoring some type of equilibrium between the land available and the number of mouths to be fed. It is normally accompanied by dividing some of the garden farms and intermediate farms that already are held in the segmenting *lo* group, but it also requires the attachment of new farms to the developing new *lo*. Much of the newly claimed land comes from areas of vacant farms whose previous holders have died or moved on to another village. Occasionally, new garden farms are obtained as gifts from a man's maternal *lo* group or, in a few cases, from another *lo* within a ritual group. Today, gardens are frequently borrowed, rented, or pawned, and in some cases a few have actually been purchased—that is, permanently alienated—although this is not part of Birom traditions. In the very few areas where I discovered new garden lands cut from zones that had not previously been used for garden lands, the owners were individual men who farmed the European way using modern fertilizing and irrigation techniques.

Not only do *lo* groups segment and change the form of their kinship or eliminate agnatic kinship altogether, but the cultural recognition of modes of segmentation signifies an attribute of maneuverability of kinship ties that can work in two directions. Kin groups not only can be divided into separate segments but may also be joined together. Because of the subordination of genealogical ties beyond the fourth or fifth generation, a new ideology or myth of connectedness can be generated. This feature is the basis for the many linkages of kin groups to one another where men with their families are known to have settled together as "brothers" and no genealogical connections are known or actually present. It is also fundamental to the new types of connections, now being developed among some kin groups, that have derived from the sharing of land compensation.

Let me stress here that I do not argue that the multifaceted nature of landholding and use is a unitary single cause of the anatomical structure and fissile nature of the *lo*. Also significant is the fact that the labor requirements of the different crops grown are limited, and increased numbers in the labor force of any producing unit would not increase the yield of the farms.[3] I have already noted that the small size of farms, especially the garden farms, is in part a consequence of the irregular and uneven surface of the land. The only time during the cultivating period when larger numbers of hands are needed—that is, the hoeing of *acha* farms and harvesting—can be well provided for by use of ad hoc and informal work groups, including friends and neighbors who are not fed from the land. Moreover, if we accept the implication of oral history with regard to the mobility of people on the plateau in the precontact period, we must assume that the groups migrating over the plateau were small, independent units that were able to maintain some autonomy because of such flexibility in structural kinship relations engaged with known historical and ecological conditions.

The segmenting process produced distinct units, some of which had to separate and sometimes physically move away to other villages. The histories of many recent groups in Du village attest to this fact. People fleeing from warfare and slave raiding and wanderers seeking places to settle also were part of the immigrant force that continuously peopled the plateau. These various fragments of peoples, men alone, or several brothers with their nuclear or polygynous families of procreation must have formed a considerable portion of the population of any one village. The empirical heterogeneity of Du village and other villages substantiates this point. The conglomeration of many unrelated peoples at any time was probably not conducive to the formation of large inclusive kin groups such as are found among more stable and more homogeneous societies (such as Nuer and Tallensi). An additional suggestion is that without pack animals and little surplus of food (most people moved because there was not enough food), a large group could not be as mobile as smaller groups of people. Thus, mobility and the heterogeneity of the population also promoted small-scale property-holding groups. All the crucial ecological factors in combination, it seems, mitigated against the establishment of large exclusive landholding units.

Later Ecological Changes and Their Effects on the Kin Group

I have already indicated some of the changes that were occurring in the relations of men and their kin groups to the land during the colonial period. The most basic changes have followed on the expansion of farming and of people onto once uninhabited and uncultivated areas. Outside the sacred lands—the mining areas and hunting lands that are generally hilly and unsuitable for farming anyway—all the land is now under some form of cultivation. Even those bush areas considered most infertile will bear a crop or two of *acha*.

One major effect of this expansion has been the dispersal of individual *lo* members to bush farm areas and the subsequent establishment there of permanent residences. This permanency has modified the tenure of areas that were formerly bush farms and caused a reduction in the amount of lands that remain under traditional bush farms tenure. For a few kin groups, having *lo* members permanently residing in bush areas has increased the production of stable grains and encouraged a kind of specialization and mutual exchange and sharing of farm products that is not traditional to the Birom. But this applies to only a minority of groups that have such an arrangement.

The dispersal of *lo* members may have had the effect of facilitating the process of definitive segmentation in some cases. A study of the many complaints to district officers and local lands officers shows that the Birom are quite conscious of this social effect, the increasing ease with which especially young men separate themselves from the group. The complaints included statements about the failure of kinsmen living in the bush to carry out the corporate functions of the *lo*, performing the various rituals, sharing food and labor, participating in marriage arrangements, and so forth. In a majority of cases, those members of the *lo* living in the bush are a set of brothers or a father and his adult son(s). The idiom of *lo* membership is still maintained by the splitting group, so the tendency is overtly toward the establishment of independent households (*lalla*). Many kin groups in the village have some members living in bush areas on lands where all members may customarily do their *acha* farming, that is, on lands that are considered to be held by the group. An acknowledged threat to the cohesion of the *lo* exists when some members in the bush areas begin claiming prior rights to the land, after a generation or so, and eventually opting for exclusive rights to hold or use it. Conflicts always surface when land compensation is to be paid for some of these farms. Many disputes arise over how the payments should be divided and who should receive some portions of the money. Older men in the village deplore the neolocal residence of their sons in bushlands. They say it divides the kin group. At the same time, these same men admit that there are not enough farms for their sons in the village area.

The introduction of money compensation for land has had another effect realized only since the 1940s. That has been the increase in the number of men who claim rights to farm the land but who are not necessarily dependent on it for a living. In some cases, the anticipation of land compensation has apparently delayed the process of segmentation and of the transformation from *yere* kinship to that of *chang*. In a large number of cases, the trend has been to define rights to land compensation so that only those who are still *yere* to one another may share in the monies. The relationship of *chang* terminates the right to a share of the compensation. The result has been the maintenance of kinship ties and their extension at the level of *yere*, producing larger entities with clanlike connections. Where ties would have been severed before and become transformed to *chang* level, now some *lo* groups simply realign themselves as *yere* vis-à-vis one another.

An interesting example of this sort of manipulation is the case of Lo Go Zang, Lo Kwon, and Lo Bwa. These groups, who identify themselves as *yere* to one another, have long been independent and autonomous with respect to the corporate functions and symbols of *lo* group status. And, although they hold and cultivate separate lands, cash compensation for land has been shared in all three units. The pattern of sharing within less than a decade reveals the ways in which kinship among the groups has been manipulated. In 1955, a large sum was paid for some bush farms that had been customarily held and worked by some old men of Lo Go Zang. The first division of money was in two lots, half to Lo Go Zang men and the other half to Lo Kwon and Lo Bwa together, as these two groups were thought to have closer genealogical ties. Subsequent divisions were made along generational lines within these kin groups, five such divisions all together, until every man had a portion, varying from three pounds to some men who got twelve or fifteen pounds. This is a typical Birom method of sharing land compensation money. In 1959, another lump sum was paid and divided, but this time Lo Bwa had been shifted from Lo Kwon and received its money together with Lo Go Zang. The older men of these three groups had decided that Lo Bwa was really closer genealogically to Lo Go Zang—within the space of four years!

Another example, of a slightly different sort, is that of Lo Pam Teng, which is a very large agnatic group, numbering 116 members who have successfully delayed the process of segmentation and remained a single corporate entity, even though genealogical ties among all the members are either not known or at best are vague. This kin group is one of the few units whose members gave genealogical information dating back eight generations. The people of Lo Pam Teng are comparatively wealthy, primarily because they were among some of the first kin groups to receive compensation in the late 1930s. Subsequently, they have received large sums of money and have used it to educate some of their young men or train them in new skills so that they function economically independent of the land. The members appear to be quite conscious of the normal pressures that would tend to divide the kin group. One of the most interesting experiences of fieldwork occurred when, as I was collecting data about the kin group, some of my questions prompted angry reactions. To my first queries about who owned or held which farms, who performed what rituals, and so forth, I was summarily silenced by the exclamation, "Kai! are you trying to divide the house?" What was most fascinating about this reaction and that of older people in other kin groups was the fact that those individuals who reacted with the greatest vehemence were older women, wives of the men who had borne children for the *lo*.

There were many examples of various kin groups attempting to claim *yere* kinship with one another for the purpose of sharing in the land compensation. In one case where one *lo* was contesting the claims of another over a bush farm for which forty pounds were being paid, men of the two kin groups agreed that the ancestors of both groups had farmed the land at some time in the past. The quarrel over which kin group had prior rights went on for several weeks and was finally resolved when some of the older men agreed that two of their ancestors were "brothers." They subsequently concocted a genealogy that placed both groups together six generations in the past.

It is clear from these examples that the introduction of land compensation has effectively transformed the relationship of men to the land and to one another. This is reflected in increasing attention to genealogical connections and much disputation about how kin groups were connected or not connected in the past. The creation of genealogies at more remote levels than four or five generations in some groups, it can be argued, is a recent development. It is contradictory to the more usual experience, as suggested by many anthropological studies, of kinship units undergoing segmentation and their members losing all knowledge of higher-level genealogical ties as they disperse into smaller lineage units and eventually reconstitute themselves as full, independent kin groups. In the next chapter, I take a close look at the processes among the Birom by which agnatic kinship groups are generated, reach full maturation (and population limits), eventually split, regenerate, and continue the cycle. Anthropologists familiar with kinship-based societies will recognize this pattern as reflecting the life cycle of kinship groups. This study adds greater detail to our knowledge of the life cycle processes and identifies the material symbols, in this society, that denote specific stages in that process.

Notes

1. Worsley (1956) has emphasized the importance of garden farms (what Fortes [1949] called "compound farms") for the Tallensi, whose social systems show interesting parallels to those of the Birom). As among the Birom, there is "great population pressure on the land" (Worsley 1956, 48), and it is the compound land, "with its high fertility" (59), that binds a man to his nuclear lineage. Worsley noted that there is a "high degree of regularity in the relation between the food unit and family units" (40).

2. Goodenough (1955) has observed that unilineal groups "fluctuate considerably in size" (80) and that a problem must arise where land rights are held strictly within the group and land is not abundant. See also Peters (1960) on the mobility of client groups among the Bedouin of Cyrenaica that "facilitates a more efficient adjustment to the ecological situation from year to year" (43).

3. This point is supported by discussion with Lawrence Fom of Riyom Government Farm, himself a Birom man with knowledge both of Birom techniques and values as well as vast knowledge of European practices and methods of scientific analysis.

The Life Cycle of the Kin Group **5**

I N THIS CHAPTER, I outline in greater detail the structural forms and processes that are basic to Birom social organization at the level of the agnatic kin group. I do so without exploring the content of the interpersonal relationships of which these forms and processes are composed, a subject that is covered in later chapters. The presentation here not only provides important ethnographic information that has been lacking about the plateau peoples but also gives a meaningful outline and background for later discussions of the complex personal relationships that exist within and between kinship groups.

The Agnatic Kin Group: Composition and Principles of Organization

The most important social unit for any individual in Birom society is the agnatic kin group, or *lo*. The Birom term has been translated into English as "family" or "house," but these words do not convey the full complement of Birom meanings associated with the term. There are both physical and social meanings that are usually determined only within the context in which the reference is made. From the point of view of its physical meaning, the term can be translated as "compound" or "homestead," referring to a physically discrete cluster of huts generally set apart from other such structures and often surrounded by euphorbia plants. Every compound has a name by which the social unit that owns and (theoretically) occupies it is known, and this brings us to the second meaning of the term *lo*, its social meaning, with which this work is most concerned. There are two aspects of its definition as a social unit—the first referring to the residents of the physical compound as just stated and the second referring to all the (male) members of a given agnatic kin group who may or may not have residence within the physical compound. The first social definition encompasses all the people who reside in the households of a compound, including unmarried girls, women married into the kin group, and any others attached to the kin group. The second reference denotes the specific social structural unit derived from the principles of patriliny and agnation, the relationship of male members of the kin group who usually are or are considered to be descendants of a common ancestor. In normal everyday usage, it is this second meaning, the structural unit of male kinsmen, to which the term *lo* always refers. This distinction is significant for understanding the social organization of the village and the structural rules that govern the way groups of patrilineally related kinsmen interact with one another. Unless stated otherwise, then, I use the term to refer to the male membership group that I call the "agnatic kin group" or simply "kin group."

Agnatic kin groups are not coterminous with territorial units; the households and compounds that belong to a single *lo* may be scattered throughout the village area. However, common residence within a single compound or in compounds that are close together is in the Birom system of values highly preferable and ritually sanctioned. Thus, in the majority of cases, men who are fathers, brothers, and sons to one another still living in the inner wards of Du will occupy a single compound or a compound area where several homesteads may nestle quite close together. On the other hand, of the eighty-five identified *lo* groups in this study, all but sixteen had one or two members of the group living away in towns or temporarily in distant bush wards. The increasing dispersal of *lo* members today is a major change in the traditional pattern of residence. Historical data on the processes by which *lo* groups segment and divide confirm that it was the norm for agnates within the *lo* to live contiguously most of the time.

The *lo* is a unit of people who are normally related to one another by descent within four to seven generations from a common ancestor, as noted in the previous chapter. Thus, the *lo* often has the *form* of a patrilineage or lineage segment. In many cases, however, there are often a few individual men whose genealogical connections are obscure. Sometimes the common ancestor postulated is not known by name, or the name is not agreed on by all the men of the group when interviewed. I noted while collecting genealogies that there were frequent disputes among the older men of a group concerning the identification of ancestors and about how to place them in genealogies. It seemed to follow from this that actual genealogical connections and descent from a particular ancestor were of secondary importance. The factor that seemed most significant for the cohesion of the group comes out in the statements frequently made by older men that two or more ancestors "lived together as brothers" or "were brothers and lived together." Some of the genealogical charts that I collected demonstrate graphically that collateral links of "brotherhood," regardless of whether they were putative or real, were uppermost in the minds of informants.

In the conduct of ordinary affairs within the *lo* group (which rarely involved more than three generations of living males), emphasis is often placed on collaterality rather than lineality. The parting of brothers, for example, is considered an even greater tragedy than the parting of father and son. Some conflict between fathers and sons is indeed expected in Birom society and is assumed to be part of the normal state of relationships. Cooperation is the province of brothers. Further evidence of this tendency is the significance of the male sibling (real sibling and patrilateral parallel cousin) relationship in nearly all of Birom oral history, mythology, and folklore. Origins of villages are historically seen in terms of brothers settling together, and they are portrayed never as the founders of separate lineal segments in the stories themselves but rather as the "first man" of a single unit. Explanations of present-day relationships among kin units that have no known kinship links are always in terms of a kind of social "brotherhoodship." In the past, slaves captured in raiding and warfare were attached to *lo* units as "brothers" or "sons" and given land and wives, and even in the folktales and myths involving animals that are personalized, they enter into temporary or permanent relationships with other animals as "brothers" (compare Colson 1958, 45).

These data suggest that two basic principles for the formation of kin groups were and are operative in Birom society: *patrilineality*, which poses the model of membership as legal descent in the male line (that is, a principle of *descent affiliation* or its fictional counterpart), and *agnatic collaterality*, which has to do with the norms and mode of cohesion of the kin group (compare Radcliffe-Brown and Forde 1950). These two principles, certainly part of the normal institutions of patrilyny found everywhere, operate in most spheres of Birom life but produce different kinds of social consequences.

Within the eight wards of Du where the most intensive census work was done, groups varied in size from a unit containing one living man with three small sons to the largest with sixteen adult men. The total membership range was from four members to fifty-seven living persons. In some cases the smaller groups, containing from two to five or six people, were only branches of a larger *lo* unit, most of whose members had moved away from the village or were residents of other villages, mining camps, towns, and so forth. The average size of the residential *lo* (pl., *nlo*) groups was twenty-three individuals, with approximately four adult men, just under six adult women, and the rest children under approximately fifteen years of age. Thus, the agnatic kin group, whether seen in terms of the male members only (average number of male members, men and boys together, was eleven) or in terms of the total membership, is comparatively small for a West African people.[1] Still, the Birom attach great social value to large kin groups. The ideal mode of increase is through many male births and the survival of young male children to manhood. However, as noted previously, in the precolonial period men could acquire sons through an institutionalized exchange system, and they sometimes attracted other landless men, both strangers and distant kinsmen who may have remote uterine or agnatic connections, to settle with them as "brothers." Wealthy men found it relatively easy to attract "clients" who might eventually be grafted onto their groups as kinsmen through fictive ties. On occasion, men and boys captured as slaves were commonly adopted and affixed onto the genealogy in kinship positions.

The larger the kin group, the higher its status in the village and surrounding village communities and the more secure its status. A group's size is indicative of wealth in land (of all types); of a membership of hard-working, ambitious, and successful farmers; and of the health and fertility of the women it has married. It is also seen as proof of a high level of cooperation among male agnates and, most important, the presence of a successful headman renowned for his administrative abilities, sagacity and good judgment, and other qualities of leadership. Men who are headmen of such groups have personal powers broader than the confines of their own kin groups; they are indeed "Big Men," and their reputations may be known in distant villages. Certain of these men had such great reputations in the past that their names and exploits have been handed down as legends through the generations. It is no coincidence that many of these men were also those who held traditional positions as leaders of certain Great Ceremonies or military leaders.

According to Birom custom, compounds and *lo* groups are normally named after the person who built the homestead originally and who is seen as the founder of the *lo*. This was true in most cases, especially where the head and founder died, leaving an adult son or several sons and their families occupying the same premises. Thus, Lo Matta is named after the person who four generations from the youngest today settled in this particular homesite. Out of respect for their father, the sons, now elderly men and grandfathers, continue to call the original compound and their kin group by the name Lo Matta. In a very small number of cases, the compound may bear the name of a living older man, be he an elder brother, a father, an uncle, or a grandfather to all the other men and boys. The headman of a compound may even use his own name as the *lo* name when the group is small and in the process of separating itself from another unit by segmentation and if there are no other males within the kin group living elsewhere. A son may use his father's name as the homestead name under the same circumstances, particularly if there is a need to distinguish his group from another bearing the same name. But there is the possibility that an old father may interpret this use as an unstated wish for him to die, so it is not common practice.

In most cases, a single compound of long standing still bears the name of a person who died many years ago but from whom the compound inhabitants stem regardless of who erected the compound. For example, Gyang Pwara lived six generations ago, according to his descendants. His elder brother Kwon founded and built their first compound (Lo Kwon) in Du when as young men they migrated from the southeast. Kwon had one son who died, while Gyang had many sons, two of whom lived to create families. Their descendants in the homestead call themselves the people of Lo Gyang Pwara although admitting that Kwon was the founder of their homesite. In several other cases, the founders' names are used as the *lo* names even though they left no descendants. Thus, the rule for naming a compound is not totally invariable. What ultimately determines the name is always a combination of facts peculiar to that kin group's situation.[2]

The Life Cycle of the *Lo*

The *lo* as a unit of structured kinship is composed of subdivisions called *lalla*. Like the term *lo*, the term *lalla* functions in different contexts with different meanings, a fact that is not confusing to the Birom but poses some problems for an outsider. A *lalla* is a physical setting, a social unit, and an economic unit concerned with the preparation and consumption of food and is comprised of a married woman (or widow) and all those whom she feeds. In this essentially economic context, I call the *lalla* the "domestic unit" and analyze its major characteristics in later chapters. In this section, I discuss only the attributes of the term *lalla* as a structural subdivision of the *lo*. From this point of view, the *lalla* may be defined as a unit within the agnatic kin group consisting of a married man, who is the head of the group, and his legal offspring. The Birom speak of the *lalla* in this context as a branch (*nlang*) of the *lo*. When asked to list the names of persons belonging to this *nlang*, they invariably give only the names of males: men and their sons (or in some cases men and their brother's sons). Wives are members of the *lalla* when it is viewed as a residential unit, and they are certainly necessary for the perpetuation of the *lalla* as a social and economic unit. But no women occupy positions in the structure of the *lo* or *lalla* or function in these units, as do male members.

A *lalla* originates some time after the marriage of a young man, when he has set up his own household within his father's compound. It becomes a clearly distinguishable unit within the *lo* when he has a wife and sons of his own. For example, there are six *lalla* in the kin group called Lo Chuang Dong (figure 5.1). Dung Chuang, the eldest living male member of the *lo* (and headman), occupies a *lalla* with his wives and his son Pwol, who is also married but has no children. Pwol remains in the *lalla* of his father sharing in the farming of this father's lands and storing the produce with his father. Thus, the physical *lalla*, the economic unit, and the *nlang*, the agnatic branch, coincide. The other sons of Dung Chuang, Bot and Ryang, have separate living quarters in the compound with their families.

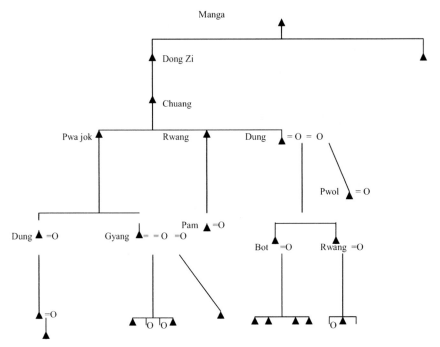

Figure 5.1   Lo Chuang Dong agnatic kin group

Although they are known as Lalla Bot and Lalla Rwang, out of respect for their father they also continue to use the identity of "Lalla Dung Chuang," which terminologically also distinguishes them from lines (*nlang*) founded by their father's brothers, Pwajok and Rwang. When their father dies, "Lalla Dung" will no longer exist. Although Pwol and his mother may continue to use his name for a while, during a kind of mourning period, in time it will become known as Lalla Pwol.

The physical and social separation of bi-*lalla* (pl.) within the same agnatic kin group provides the point of cleavage for the process by which a *lo* group eventually becomes divided and two or more distinct new *lo* are formed, a process that social anthropologists call "definitive segmentation." Two generations ago, Pwajok Chuang, Dung Chuang, and their brother Rwang were members of a common *lalla* (that of their father) at which time the unit was called Lalla Chuang of Lo Manga (not illustrated). After the splitting of Lo Manga, a process that takes at least three to four generations for completion, two new *lo* emerged, one of which was Lo Chuang Dong. As time has passed and new generations have been born, the separate bi-*lalla* of Pwajok and Dung may become the points at which further segmentation will take place, especially since Dung and Gyang Pwajok have large families, as have the sons of Dung Chuang. Pam Rwang will undoubtedly choose to remain with one or the other sets, as he is not strong enough (he has no sons or brothers of the same womb) to establish a *lo* of his own. The social separation and the physical separation of *nlang* within a *lo* always coincide during this phase of the process of segmentation. After they had both married and started raising families, Dung and Gyang Pwajok built a compound close to but separate from that of Dung Chuang and his sons. Thus, the division lines were already starting with two brothers under the principle of "agnatic collaterality," erecting a compound together. As they have become men of substance and increased their families, they have started on occasion calling themselves "bimad Lo Pwajok" (men of Lo Pwajok). Eventually, not only will Bot Dung's four sons and potential grandsons establish separate bi-*lallas* of their own, but, together with Ryang and Pwol Dung and their sons, their particular descent unit may also for a time call themselves Lo Dung Chuang or Lo Bot Dung. Not all men become the named founders of *lo* groups; much depends on strength of numbers, especially sons, personal character, the ability to command the loyalty of collateral agnates, and the unpredictable hand of fortune.

In about four generations, then, the name of Lo Chuang Dong, that of the earlier agnatic unit, will be discontinued; it will be replaced by the names of the succeeding *lo* and will in time be forgotten. This is a cyclical change, a basic characteristic of the social process that unquestionably pre-dates the colonial period and accounts for the shallow depth of genealogies of living groups. Many genealogies give ample evidence of this kind of repetitive segmentation, and many old men remember the names of *lo* groups that preceded those in existence today. The processes and cycles of segmentation and their critical diagnostic points will be discussed further in connection with an analysis of the functions of the *lo* in the next sections.[3]

The Corporate Character of the *Lo*: Functions and Symbols

The traditional *lo* was an autonomous segment of the wider Birom society. It had control over the welfare and behavior of its members and was traditionally subjected to no higher political authority. In certain spheres involving the welfare of the larger society, the village, the kinship groups were subordinate to the authority of ritual leaders. They also yielded, at least temporarily, to the wisdom of accepted military leaders whose powers were also partly sanctioned by ritual in matters relating to the defense of the village. One might view the village as a very loose organization or confederation of kin groups. The alliances among them evolved for specific occasions under certain kinds of external pressure and did not result in the consolidation of political power in a central office or the rise of a permanent government structure.

Within the kin group itself, social control was maintained by the etiquette of kinship, particularly by norms demanding deference, respect, and obedience on the part of younger to older persons. The sanctions against improper behavior were institutionalized, such as fear of the wrath of ancestors, but they were also very pragmatic, as many of them centered on access to economic resources. Under colonialism, the political autonomy of the *lo* has been replaced legally by the power of the state. But from the point of view of the Birom, more immediate factors, such as changes in economic relations among members of the *lo*, have had a greater impact on the exercise of control within the kin group. Except for taxes, most of the villagers have yet to feel the political and persuasive power of the state.

The impact of external influences on these kin groups has varied considerably. A few groups are quite obviously becoming more rapidly modified than others under colonial conditions. These are usually the groups that have some educated or semiliterate members in which movements of its individual members have largely divided the kin group into separate nuclear families and in which members have many contacts with non-Birom elements in the wider plateau society. But for the great majority of people, the traditional features of internal organization and control, the operation of personal sanctions, the traditional processes of segmentation, and the acceptance and exercise of authority based on differences of age, gender, and kinship positions still prevail. For these groups, the management of daily affairs within the kin group appears to be little affected by changes in the outside world.

Perhaps the chief reason for the low degree of perceptible changes relates to traditional processes, especially maneuverability of kinship ties and ease of segmentation, which makes the *lo* a highly adaptable social instrument. An equally important feature is that, although most men have had employment as laborers in the mines, such employment did not entail migration away from their home villages as in southern African states. Men continued to inhabit their customary homes and maintained traditional kinship norms and family lifestyles.

Each *lo* is a corporate structure composed of men who have equal rights to but not equal control over (or even equal privileges of exercising their rights to) the farmlands, trees, wild plants, and domesticated animals that belong to the group. In the precolonial period, the rights of each corporate unit to the holding and use of its designated resources in land, animals, plants, and people were exclusive—that is, they were not subject to a higher domain. Each *lo* is still responsible for protecting its rights to property against all others, and there are institutionalized mechanisms (like the informal courts in the *manjei* [ward]) for dealing with disputes, aggression, and competition harmful to village harmony operating above and beyond the structural level of the *lo* (see chapter 8).

Within each corporate group, each adult married man has nominally unchallenged heritable rights to cultivate a portion of the farmlands sufficient for his needs, to utilize fruit and oil-bearing trees and plants with the consent of his peers, and to share in the meat products gained from the hunt or from the killing of domestic stock. He maintains these rights as long as he is a member of the *lo*. Furthermore, he has obligations and duties to his kinsmen to participate fairly in the creation and use of the group's resources. If disaster should strike one of his *lo* brothers, he must share his food with him. He must use his labor as efficiently as possible to gain full measure from his portion of the land. A lazy man or a poor farmer will find himself doing without the help of his brothers, and often he is deprived of choice lands. In some extreme cases, such men have been ostracized. Should a man's agnatic ties within the *lo* be broken, he ceases to share in the rights and obligations associated with *lo* property, nor can he rely on the assistance and cooperation of his agnatic kin. The relationship of agnation is fundamentally a relationship between men in a system of property holding.[4]

Powers to make decisions over the allocation of land within the *lo*, over the use of new lands, and over the disposal of trees and other raw materials, farms, animals, and so forth are not equally shared. The oldest men, not yet senile, have undisputed authority to control the use of all *lo* property, with the representation of that authority resting in the hands of the headman (Da Lo). But even this person who holds the only recognized office of authority within the *lo* and who is permitted by custom to make final decisions is subject to the will of the corporate body. He cannot or should not dispose of a large animal, like a goat or a horse, or offer the use of a farm without the consent, preferably unanimous, of the other adult men or without at least consulting them and gaining the assent of the majority. The rights of unmarried men are prospective or potential; they cannot claim farms for themselves until they are married, at which time some garden farms would normally be given to them. Younger married men are expected to show deference to the wisdom of the older men, and while their rights to farms are not disputed, they are subject to the preferential rights of the elders. This oligarchic structuring of power over people and goods is a highly pervasive, well-entrenched custom in Birom life. It is not easily subverted even when younger men become economically independent of their "fathers," but it is the cause of many quarrels and conflict among men of the *lo* (Skinner 1961).

The chief representative of the corporate kin group to the outside world is the Da Lo. All persons who are subject to his authority and who recognize and accept his leadership are *lo* members. Many of the functions that the Da Lo performs are symbolic of the corporate nature of the *lo* group. He performs the special rituals (*kwits*) that are peculiar to (owned by) his *lo* group. He provides the material goods needed in the rites of divination and carries out many of the rituals for curing disease, he calls on the ancestors for their intercession in worldly affairs, and his powers are associated with sacred emblems like the Bato-Nyama (see the following discussion). Finally, as the headman, he makes the important decisions when his kin group moves to another area or village.

Land and animals constitute one system of property holding within the agnatic kin group, but this is not the only one in which functions exclusive to agnates within the *lo* are executed. The *lo* is also the unit in which the responsibility for paying, and privileges of sharing in, bridewealth are contained. Although other kinsmen outside the corporate agnatic kin group, such as maternal kinsmen, could help provide some of the goods that a man needs to obtain a wife, the primary responsibility rests in the agnatic group. The disposal of women born into the *lo*, either by marriage or by transfers to Buji and other northern villages, theoretically comes under much the same regulations as the disposal of any other valued property. All decisions are made by agreement among the older men although subject to the approval of the mother, and since a girl's adult brothers figure so importantly in her welfare, they too usually are consulted today in matters regarding her marriage or education.

In precolonial times, all the men of the *lo* shared in the bridewealth and gifts that resulted from the marriage of a girl of the group. There were set regulations about the division of such goods. However, since money has replaced horses, goats, meat, chicken, grain, oil, and small utensils as brideprice and gifts, the role of the corporate group is gradually being undermined. Young men earn their own brideprice in many if not most cases, and very often the cash received from the marriage of a daughter goes to the son(s) for schooling, tools, bicycles, and other material goods. Where it is not kept in a lump sum and given to a younger man of the *lo*, it is divided among all the men and used for purchasing such items as food and beer.

The men of the agnatic kin group are conscious of their solidarity in many other ways. They protect and back their fellow *lo* members in disputes with outsiders and are always ready to fight when one of their kinsmen or kinswomen has been harmed or threatened. When one of the young men of the compound where I resided quarreled with a young man of Zawang village nearby, three members of our *lo* who were living in bush wards some ten miles away arrived with knives, sticks, and spears, ready to defend their fellow agnate, although they knew nothing of the origin of the dispute. This solidarity is particularly seen in arguments arising with affines and other kin groups over women. The *lo* group maintains a united front against the rest of the village, although its members may unite with other *lo* groups for specific occasions.

Many men are quite "clannish" about their kin groups. In cases where it was quite obvious that the process of fission was occurring in a large unit, men and especially women berated me for even daring to suggest the possibility of a division in the ranks. When there were arguments and fights within a group, often both sides would come and separately tell me their versions. Somewhere in the conversation, usually near the end, the statement was made that it was but a minor thing, this disagreement. It could not be a "big" argument because "are we not brothers" or "are we not men of the house?"

Finally, the corporate and exclusive nature of the agnatic kin group is expressed through a traditionally important symbol: the Bato-Nyama, a crest or shield of animal skulls that is plastered on the side of the major storeroom of the Da Lo. All large animals caught in the hunt and some enemies killed in warfare during precolonial times were beheaded, and, in a special ceremony, the skulls were attached to this sacred crest. These heads, especially of large animals, symbolize the health and prosperity of the *lo*. *Lo* groups whose men were successful hunters were thought to be more fortunate than those who were not. Many prayers and ceremonial songs beg the deities for success in the hunt so that many heads would be taken. Several types of sacrificial and other rituals are performed at the shrine of the Bato-Nyama, and all men who participate in the rituals are members of the *lo* group for which the Bato-Nyama is a symbol.

Each kin group also has a set of rituals that it "owns."[5] Some of these rituals are more important than others, but their general significance is that they too are symbols of the corporate unity of the *lo* group. Although I have collected a list of dozens of rituals, many of them are no longer observed, and to some Birom this fact constitutes a threat to the strong ties that bind men of the *lo* together. The Bato-Nyama also has lost some of its aura of grandeur, even among some of the older men (in their forties and older). Today, when younger men start new compounds, they often do not attempt to transfer or start a new Bato-Nyama. There are so few animals in the bush that heads are difficult to obtain. It was formerly believed that to move a Bato-Nyama was to bring death to all the members of the *lo* group. A Bato-Nyama lasted the lifetime of the *lo*, but many compounds were bulldozed for mining operations over the past thirty years, and the crests that were not saved were destroyed and never again erected. However, the symbol that this crest represents is still very real to many Birom. Men express their corporate identity by the statement that they have their own Bato-Nyam, and sometimes they say this even when the crest no longer exists. Not only is it a symbol of the unity of the group, but it is also a symbol of a phase in the completion of the process of segmentation, of the separateness of a recognizable agnatic branch and its ultimate attainment of corporate status.

The Segmentation Process

Kin groups must be seen as dynamic, living entities that go through a process by which they emerge, develop, mature, and eventually disintegrate. When a kin group performs all the functions discussed previously with autonomy and has the symbols of *lo* status, it may be said to have reached its full maturity as a corporate unit. Such a unit produced by segmentation does not attain its full corporate status all at once. Segmentation is both gradual and continuous. Thus, when a group has attained full maturity in its corporate status, a new cycle of the segmentary process, a form of fissioning, will already have been started within its ranks by the spatial and social separation of its constituent branches (*nlang*). While the average fieldworker cannot be present during the many decades in which this splitting is taking place, evidence of the various phases of the process can be obtained by a study of genealogies and empirical determination of the nature of the functions and symbols that a particular group has at any one point in time.

In the genealogies shown in appendix B, I show in B1 how the various *nlang* of what used to be called Lo Shom Dong have emerged as separate *lo* units (Lo Gong Jing and Lo Rwang Shom), with the process of segmentation reflecting a separation at the sixth generational level. The two named units that resulted, when first contacted, occupied separate compounds within the original Du wards. At the same time, some of the *lallas* of both Lo Gong Jing and Lo Rwang Shom have dispersed and relocated in bush wards. Thus, each *lo* is fragmented internally already. Lo Rwang Shom and Lo Gong Jing have separate Bato-Nyama, separate Da Lo (for about ten years prior to the fieldwork period), and separate lands and rituals. The old man, Dung Shom, who provided information about the division of the previous unit, was the only person who claimed to remember the earlier name. Lo Rwang Shom was named after his older brother, and it should be noted that this brother had three sons to live to maturity, while Dung had only one.

Genealogy 2 in appendix B2 shows the process of segmentation continuing between the two groups who call themselves Lo Kwon and Lo Bwei. Marriage and brideprice responsibilities are now exclusive to each group with respect to their own sisters and daughters. Each *lo* has a separate headman, but some major rituals are still held in common and are performed by Gwom Wei, the eldest of the two headmen. Some bushlands are still held by the two groups together, and land compensation derived from the alienation of some of these farms to mining is still shared among the men of both groups. As has been shown earlier (chapter 2), the introduction of land compensation backed by government sanctions, especially during the period of World War II, has had as one effect the maintaining of group ties and delaying the process of segmentation.

There is a Bato-Nyama at Lo Kwon in the village, but the younger people of Lo Bwei have not established one, and it is not likely that they will. Gwom Wei, the headman of Lo Kwon, lives in the *lalla* of his brother, the deceased Gyang Jok. Gwom is fed by Gyang's widow for he has never had a wife of his own. The relationship with Gyang's widow is a leviratic one, a custom common among the Birom and widespread in African societies. Although I did not obtain the information from him or his "wife" (all women are called "wife of the house"), it could very well be that he is the genitor of some of Gyang's children, and this might explain his alliance with Lo Kwon and not Lo Bwei, with whom he shares closer genealogical ties. Recently, most of the younger men of Lo Bwei moved away to bush areas. Note that the splitting in this case is not a split of equal parts but rather the separation of a genealogically inferior unit from an original senior unit. This is not an uncommon form for segmentation to take; some *lo* names have a longer life span than others, but all must change in the end. In the contemporary situation, however, this fissioning process involving a younger generation of men may portend an even more drastic change in the structure and function of this larger kin group.

A third case, illustrated in appendix B3 (Lo Chang), shows the process of segmentation taking place along the cleavage provided by descent from separate mothers, with brothers "of the same womb" remaining together. The unity of siblings of the same womb is an important value among the Birom and is often in conflict with the principle of agnatic collaterality. I frequently witnessed arguments between men who were brothers, and the explanation very commonly given for constant bickering between these men was that they were "not of the same womb." The Birom say that men of the same womb will not fight among themselves but that brothers of different wombs sometimes do. The contradictory nature of some social principals has been well analyzed by Gluckman and others (Gluckman 1955a, 1965b; Mitchell 1956; Turner 1957). It should be clear also from the previous description of Birom agnation and in earlier chapters that these principles operated in different circumstances. Which will take precedence in any particular situation depends at least partly on the phase in the process of segmentation that the total structure is undergoing. When a new *lo* is just emerging, consolidation may be important to the functioning and identification of the new group, in which case the solidarity of the "brothers" has primacy in all affairs. At the same time, the new group may take its origin from the cleavage that separates descendants of two brothers or the offspring of different mothers.

Lo Chang is a large *lo* that, because of its wealth in land and its numerical strength within a short genealogical depth, has remained fairly intact in the village. This unit illustrates how segmentation is a function of generational depth as well as the size of the agnatic group vis-à-vis the amount of land held. There are seven bi-*lallas* still in the original Du wards and another seven that are widely scattered in bush areas and mining settlements. Yet the initial actions of the segmentation process, recognized overtly as verbal claims to *lo* status, are just beginning. There is still a single Da Lo for the entire group. There is only one Bato-Nyama at Chollom Tok's compound, and all the men share in common rituals. But some of the descendants of Tok Chang are now calling themselves Lo Tok Chang, though they did not so classify themselves in the 1955 tax records, and they stated to me that they have separate lands from the others of Lo Chang. By this they meant garden farms (*bwi*) because in 1960 they were still farming bush farms together and claiming that all farms belonged to Lo Chang. When an argument over the engagement of the daughter of Pam Davou Chang arose, the older men who were consulted—Zi Tok, Gyang, and Nyam Davou—gave way to her two brothers, Dung and Gyang Pam.

This illustrates another feature of the kin groups and their development over time. In each event in which the corporate unit as a whole must act, there appears to be much discussion of the limits of responsibility. It is through the setting of the responsibilities of men on each occasion that one comes to have some understanding of how segmentation must take place. As long as there is no question of the genealogical limits of rights and obligations in each situation, the *lo* is intact. We can presume that segmentation is occurring when, for some particular corporate event such as a marriage arrangement, there is some question whether certain members have rights to make decisions or whether the rights and obligations of some prevail over those of others. When such questions are raised, particularly at an event of major importance to the group, there is usually some issue of conflict among the men of the kin group. The quarreling may seethe for a long time, sometimes years. Ultimately, a decision is made that separates some men from others of the kin group. Each group of men then takes on separate responsibilities and obligations, and members of each group begin to see themselves as an entity distinct from the others.

Segmentation for the Birom means a recognition of increasing pressures on the available resources. But it also means an awareness of unequal interests and claims that persons have over one another within the common group as well as recognition of divergence of interests and aims set partly by genealogical distance and partly by loyalties and allegiances of a personal nature. The main arguments, quarrels, or disputes that pinpoint the process of segmentation and that serve as the overt causes for division in a kin group usually are over land—the use or disposal of certain farms—or over bridewealth and/or the marriages of daughters. Disputes over other matters, from minor issues to such grave ones as the attempted seduction of a brother's wife, may or may not have a clear-cut effect on the process of segmentation for they are not always considered corporate matters. They may pertain only to individual disagreements that are resolved within the group or by resort to mediation by a ward head.

To summarize briefly, with the passage of time, a *lo* group fluctuates in size, in specific membership, in internal arrangements and external relationships, and particularly in the performance of certain corporate functions. At some point in the history and development of the *lo*, some of its members must separate from a common household and, in doing so, form the nucleus for the establishment of a new *lo*. This is, we might say, the beginning of the process of segmentation seen from a structural point of view. Both spatial and social distance become significant and are necessary counterparts of the process by which a corporate group divides. Internal segmentation, which may signify the eventual demise of the earlier or original *lo* group, is not just an integral part of the social system; it is a most fundamental economic characteristic because of its close connection with the holding of property and the manner in which the Birom exploit the plateau.

Now such segmentation means, in the course of time, the ultimate termination of former agnatic kinship connections between men at the level of the *lo*. More specifically, it means the breaking of those kinship ties that are founded on recognized genealogical links by way of patrilineal descent. Segmentation replaces the kinship of the *lo* with a new sort of kinship—that of *yere* and, in time, *chang* (see chapter 3). A former subunit that has acquired *lo* status and is fully matured in the performance of its corporate functions is the equivalent ("brother") of all other such units that have evolved by fission from one another.[6] Its relationship with members of the other *lo* is no longer seen in terms of the individual connections of its members, although personal kinship terms of a classificatory sort may still be used for individuals in both groups. The relationship is that of a structured, generalized agnation between two groups, and men speak of themselves in the plural as being *yere* to one another. Thus, Lo Rwang Shom and Lo Gong Jing are *yere* to each other, as are Lo Gyang Bagei and Lo Dam (appendix B4), who are separate entities with respect to all the previously noted features (Da Lo, lands; Bato-Nyama, marriage rights; and so forth). And the three *lo* groups in appendix B5 (Lo Go Zang, Lo Kwon, and Lo Bwa) are also *yere* to one another.

Within the village, there are many sets of two or three *lo* units (none more than three) that are related, for the time being, at the level of *yere*.

At some point several generations later in time, in the long-range processes of growth, expansion, fission, and segmentation, a new level of relatedness is reached, that of *chang*. We have already seen that this term refers to the most remote of kinship ties among groups and also to the relatedness of *lo* units in a ritual group. For groups that were once *yere* to one another, this new order of relatedness means essentially that the two independent *lo* may now intermarry and that agnation is completely severed. Marriage creates affinity and thus totally transforms the patrilineal kinship connections. Some of the genealogical data suggest that a single calculated marriage (for indeed all marriages are calculated) between groups that were *yere* to one another serves to produce or reflect this *chang* relationship; that is, it serves to sever the *yere* relationship. Marriages of this sort, when viewed from the genealogies, were too obvious to be accidental. They seemed to appear at crucial points after the process of segmentation had created two clearly mature units.

An old man of Lo Kwei (not illustrated) claimed that long ago the people of Lo Kwei and Lo Go Zang were *yere* to one another but that now they are only *chang*. This is an explicit recognition of the process of movement from one order of structured kinship to another. Of equal significance is the fact that three generations ago, according to the genealogies, there was a marriage between a girl of Lo Kwei with a man of Lo Go Zang. In addition, there are two marriages between Lo Kwei and another group to which it is *chang*, Lo Pam Teng, recorded in the second and third generations from the younger living today.

It seems clear then that beyond the *lo*, the relatedness of individuals from a structural point of view loses its force and becomes the relatedness (*yere* and *chang*) of corporate groups to one another. Actual genealogical connections of the members become irrelevant. It is not important *how* units are connected, only that they *are*. The connecting links are no longer familial, personal, or even genealogical but become largely ceremonial and political.

Young men and boys are not specifically taught information about their individual ancestors. Knowledge of names is picked up through hearsay and the gossip of older people, and older men particularly always seem not to know very much about their immediate ancestors. Nearly every one of my genealogical charts was collected under circumstances in which there was a great deal of vagueness and consequently disagreement and debate among informants about the relationships of deceased ancestors. There was a tendency to make "brothers" out of all sorts of relationships where actual connections were unknown (compare Colson 1958, 45) and much indecisiveness as to who were "fathers," sons, and/or "brothers." Many old men simply got up and left after a long harangue, pleading only that they did not recall the men of the older generations. This myopia of remembrance, what Barnes (1955) has called "structural amnesia," is practically universal at the level of from five to seven generations in the past (compare Bohannan 1952, 312 ff.; Evans-Pritchard 1951, 199; Peters 1960, 40–41). The absence (or avoidance) of memory is critical to the process by which new kin groups can emerge.

However, I found that it was the women who knew more about their husbands' kin groups at the higher genealogical connections of the male members than did the men. When the men would leave, older women would come and tell me details of the genealogical relationships, and almost always there was greater agreement among the old women than among the men. The reason for this now seems obvious: Women bear the sons for the kin group, and their greatest concerns have always been the welfare of their children, particularly protecting the inheritance rights and privileges of their sons within the kin group. Individual women may use their knowledge of their husband's kin group to delay the process of segmentation or to manipulate and accelerate existing divisions. As this analysis continues, it will show that women are major agents for protecting and perpetuating many of the values of patrilyny in this society (see the story of Bus in chapter 9). Their influence can be incalculable; it can be both subtle and powerful, impacting the long-range future of the kin group. When we consider the interests of women whose priority is the welfare of their children, we begin to have some comprehension of why this is so.

Notes

1. The Birom *lo* is much smaller than the minimal Tar of the Tiv (Bohannan and Bohannan 1953), the Ngombe *etuka* (Wolfe 1959), and the Konkomba minor lineage (Tait 1956). The Tallensi nuclear lineage is smaller than the Birom *lo* on account of its brief genealogical span, although we are told that "there is land owned by lineages of larger span than the average nuclear lineage" (Fortes 1945, 178).

2. There were no compounds bearing the name of a woman, although in several instances the founder bore his mother's name affixed to his own to distinguish him from other classificatory brothers with the same name.

3. In this study, the term "segmentation" is used with the same meaning as Firth's (1957) "definitive segmentation," which he defines as "the irreversible process leading to the formation of new groups which do not then recombine" (7).

4. For a theoretical discussion of this very important point, see Gluckman (1965a, chap. 2).

5. Compare Meek (1969, 72, 74, 85).

6. Compare similar processes among Tallensi (Fortes 1945).

Ritual and the Distribution of Public Power   6

I<small>N CHAPTER</small> 3, I described the organization of sodalities and the significance of these groupings in the performance of rituals that I called the Great Ceremonies. These rituals and what can be identified as the exercise of public power or authority were interconnected in the Birom traditional polity and continue to influence behavior in a modernizing context. All public, purposive activities and decision-making events in the traditional culture have as one component the performance of ritual. What is predicated in all such ritual is an acknowledged potential for appealing to (via symbolic and direct forms of communication) and influencing superhuman agents and, by so doing, effecting desired changes in the human condition. An element in the ritual process is the conceptualization of a social order in which only a selected number of individual men can claim such interlocutory powers. Since most of the occasions for ritual supplications arise out of secular concerns (the provision of resources, health, and elimination of disease, defense, warfare, success in hunting, decisions on whether to move or migrate, internal conflicts, and so forth), the men holding such positions come to exercise what are essentially economic and political functions and powers. A study of those rituals that pre-date the colonial period reveals that certain rituals functioned as mechanisms of social control and as political devices for organizing and controlling groups of unrelated people.

The Birom have or had a highly intricate system of rituals, some of which, performed at certain times of the year, served to temporarily override village and sectional boundaries and bring far-flung groups together for ceremonies involving the common good of all the plateau peoples. There are two major types of rituals: public rituals, involving many kin groups or the entire village, and private rituals, pertaining to only the members of a single kin group or related kin groups. In this chapter I will be concerned only with the public rituals. These can be conveniently classed into two categories: those that entail the invocation of "Da Gwi" (which can be translated as Sun God, Father Sun, or Father of the Sun) and those rituals, generally called *kwit*, that are performed to propitiate the *chit*. *Chit* is a spiritual force that has no constant or definable characteristics; it is not an anthropomorphized power, having no gender or other human qualities. It can be a force behind both good and malevolent events. Some Birom say that there are many *chit*; others claim that there is only one power that can manifest itself in many places and in many ways.

Rituals of the first category always involve the entire village. They consist of special shoutings or pleadings to Da Gwi, are held in special village locations, and are led by a traditional priest-leader known as "Gwom Gwelle," or "Gwom." Da Gwi appears in most descriptions as a deity who created and placed all things in the universe and then left humans pretty much to their own devices. Except for sometimes preventing the rainfall, Da Gwi does not cause misfortunes but can intercede with other powerful supernatural forces to alleviate the suffering of the people. When the villagers are called on to congregate to make pleadings to Da Gwi ("wok Da Gwi"), it is almost always in response to widespread adversity such as famines, extreme drought, epidemic diseases and death, or other catastrophic "acts of God." In Du village, the last great meeting of this sort ("Badu") was called several years prior to my arrival because of the disastrous results of an invasion of locusts.

Rituals of the second type, involving the *chit*, include the greatest number and variety of all religious events. They are led by leaders called "Gwom Kwit," and there are a number of such positions in each village. The term *kwit* refers not only to the rituals themselves but also to the entire body of beliefs and practices associated with the varied rites. As Baker (1954, chap. 4) also points out, the term is additionally used in an adjectival form to refer to sacred places, sacred objects, things that are considered to be taboo, and other matters for which there are supernatural explanations or adhesions.

The term *Gwom Kwit* has both wide and narrow meanings. Each of the sodalities has its own special priest-leaders for the rituals that they command. A headman of a kin group, for example, will serve as the Gwom Kwit for a special First Fires ritual, or the "kwit re Botonyama," the naming ceremony of a newborn child, or the "Kwit re Chun Pyas" (new *acha* harvest). On the other hand, there are the Bi-Gwom (plural) Kwit of the large public festival occasions that for simplicity I call the Great Ceremonies and the Little Ceremonies. Mandyang, Ngasang, Tyi, Pe, Bwuna, Kwit Behwol, and Mado, for example, are the Great Ceremonies, and their adherents cut across kinship, sodality, and even village boundaries.

The Little Ceremonies and some of the Great Ceremonies are connected with economic activities, or, to put it another way, virtually all economic activities have their ritual counterparts. No important event (the first planting of all major crops, harvesting, hunting, cutting of bamboo, firing of brush before the planting season, and so forth) can take place without the prior and proper performance of its special rites and therefore with the consent of the Bi-Gwom Kwit who are the leaders of these rituals. Thus, what is extremely significant in the Birom sociopolitical system is the great amount of power or control over the economic life of the village that is deposited in the hands of a limited number of ritual leaders. These positions of leadership are dispersed traditionally among certain groups in the village. In order to understand the mode of distribution and operation of the social power that these men have, we must take a look at the nature of the varied types of ritual alliances (compare Fortes 1945, 98 ff.).

Ritual alliances can be seen on several levels. At the lowest level, there are the bonds among closely related kin groups, as, for example, where several groups who consider themselves *yere* share in a special First Fire ritual together. The alignment of kin groups involved in these rites appears to be fairly stable, but in fact they constantly shift as generations pass in response to the changing composition of *lo* groups. Moreover, as there are many rituals and the composition of the congregation concerned varies with each type of rite, there is a certain overlapping of groups for different ritual purposes.

Second, there are the rituals, many of which are the Great Ceremonies, that pertain only to the sodalities as ritual groups. By way of illustration, Mandyang is a ceremony brought to Du by some Bi-Bwata peoples. But not all Bi-Bwata groups perform Mandyang. Neither do the Bi-Lei or Bi-Kabong. Ngasang (a rite of passage for teenage boys) is done only by the Bi-Gabong and some Bi-Pyomo, together with related groups at Forum village. It is not done by the Bi-Lei or Bi-Bwata. All groups in the village participate in the great Pe ceremony, which requires taking the heads of large ferocious animals, but only the Bi-Lei (Lo Du) elders can be leaders in the ceremony. Tyi, the great hunting ceremony, is also a ritual done for and by the entire village. Four Bi-Gwom Kwit from different sodalities are the leaders of this ritual. The failure of any one of them to perform his special functions or bring the special medicines that his post alone controls is seen by the villagers as constituting a grave threat to the prosperity of the entire village.

Finally, at perhaps the highest level, there are alliances among sodalities in different villages, as mentioned earlier in the first chapter. Throughout the high plateau, peoples like the Bi-Bwata who hold Mandyang carry out this elaborate ceremony in conjunction with homologous groups in other villages. The ceremony begins at Riyom, a place that some consider their village of origin, and continues through about seven or eight villages. In Du village, the multifaceted ceremony for installing a traditional "Gwom Gwelle" must be performed by representatives of certain groups from the villages of Forum, Heipang, and Du. Representatives of the Lo Gwom sodalities in Du, Shen, Forum, and Zawang villages also participate in a pan-village ceremony called Mana, which is one of the formal invocations to Da Gwi performed during periods of plagues and disease to restore the people's health.

The most important of the intervillage rituals are connected with shrines, focal points around which member groups can gather. These shrines are specific features of the land, such as rock formations imbued with a sacred aura, so that fighting or any form of conflict is prohibited near them.[1] Shrines can be located anywhere around the village area or out in the bush. All are thought to have some historical significance, being the site or locale of some important event in the lives of ancestors. But their most important feature is that they serve to give identity to the specific arrangement of kin groups that constitute the ritual group or association. Both the Bi-Lei and the Bi-Kabong have such shrines located in Gabong, near the town of Jos, and in Buji lands (Gwon District). Annual pilgrimages are still made by some of the older men to these sacred places. The men who held the positions of Gwom Kwit in the old days are even today judged to have been the most powerful among the Birom. They determined the nature of all intervillage relationships, making decisions as to whether relatively minor conflicts should be escalated into full-scale warfare, when and how fighting should take place, the penalty for failure to observe ritual taboos, and the forms of retribution and vengeance for raiding.

Ritual pacts at this highest level seem to have had two other vital functions in precolonial times. First, they enabled small groups of men to have a maximum of mobility in an area where, as we have seen, men perceived themselves as being subjected to external hostilities and personal danger. Despite slave raiding and warfare, people did move from one village to another and managed to find someone to whom they could relate and from whom they could acquire lodging and assistance. The ritual groupings provided a form of pseudokinship connection that facilitated this kind of mobility. A second function was the means by which certain goods were distributed throughout the plateau and surrounding areas in the absence of a well-developed and specialized trading organization.

Considering the first function, one feature of the ritual group was the obligation of members to offer hospitality and protection to one another. Another feature was that during certain times of the year, fighting must cease between villages where there are ritual alliances among the member sodalities. At the time of Bwuna, a harvest festival, six villages around Du are at peace and visiting between villages was common. Similarly, at the time of Mandyang, those groups who participate in the pre–farming season ceremonies can expect safe conditions for traveling back and forth. For people who because of land shortage or other reasons desired to move to another village and establish residence, the existence of alliances with groups in the other villages facilitated entry. There are, for example, many Bi-Bwata from Vom (Vwang) in Du village, and their description of the cause and mode of their immigration is consistently underscored by the existence of ritual ties.

The second function is quite readily understood in terms of specific types of commodities peculiar to certain areas. The plateau peoples were tin and iron smelters but only in certain areas, and only certain peoples were involved in the occupation. Pieces of flat iron called *yere* were widely dispersed throughout the plateau and into other areas, being used as media of exchange. Tin from the plateau and copper from off the plateau were traded back and forth. In addition, clay pots were made by women in areas where suitable material was found and subsequently spread by a kind of informal trading into other areas. Meat as well as other foodstuffs were also dispersed in the exchanges that took place among groups engaged in ritual alliances. And, in the background orchestrating these interchanges, directly and indirectly, were the Bi-Gwom Kwit, leaders of the sodalities and of their own kin groups.

Leadership and Power

There clearly were developed in the precolonial period certain offices in which socially accepted and recognized power was exercised, backed by supernatural sanctions. There were priests (Gwom Kwit; Bi-Gwom [plural]) whose functions included the control of planting and harvesting activities, military leaders who organized offensive and defensive undertakings, and other leaders who coordinated and managed villagewide ceremonies and acted as chairmen for the meetings of the elders (*tula*) when, as the Birom say, things needed to be discussed. When older informants recalled the history of the pre-European period, they invariably gave details of the relationships among the core groups. All recognized the Bi-Lei and Bi-Gabong as the repositories of hereditary titles to the most important offices and positions within the village. Only men of these core groups could compete for the positions of highest status and influence. According to traditions, there were three "first families" of Du: Lo Gwom (Bi-Lei), which holds the rod (*gwelle*) of what has now evolved as the village chieftainship; Lo Du (also Bi-Lei), who supplied the powerful priests, especially the Gwom Kwit called by the title "Mwad Shi Chun"; and the Lo Kwei (Bi-Kabong), who were the military leaders, strategists, advisers, and protectors of the people. Under special circumstances, they could impose the death penalty for certain types of offenses.

It is not wholly clear what the functions of the Gwom Gwelle were traditionally or the extent of his powers in the century prior to British contact. Given the wide range of powers held and exercised by other men, also called "Gwom," it is

difficult to identify the Gwom Gwelle as the highest chief in a typical chief-
domship. Knowledge of other societies with hierarchical positions of power and
a formal high office was certainly present among the Birom at the time of European contact, but few of these villages appeared to have had strong chiefdoms
supported by a redistributive economic system.[2] Old men say that the Gwom was
a leader who officiated at certain meetings, Mana and Badu, and he was an arbitra-
tor who was called on to intercede in disputes that threatened to disrupt the
village. He was also the functionary who had the duty of calling on Da Gwi for
the general blessings for which the villagers prayed in unison. Some of the early
ethnographic notes written by touring offices state flatly that the Birom chief was
the "owner of the land" and had ultimate powers of life, death, and/or enslavement over the villagers.[3] Yet the Du people, including the present Gwom and two
ex-Gwoms, deny this. Along with elders in other villages (Forum, Vwang, and
Gyel), they stated that it was impossible; the chief (Gwom) was a wise and
respected man, but as "primus inter pares," having no such autocratic powers. He
could not, for example, command goods and services (taxes or tithings) from
people as a privilege of his office. The only farmlands over which he had control
were those of his own kin group.

The men of Lo Kwei and other Bi-Kabong groups were the leaders of the
"ferocious" horsemen whose reputations had spread among the Hausa and Fulani
long before British occupation. As advisers to the Gwom and controllers of military power especially in the defense of the village, they may very well have wielded
enormous influence during certain periods of time. They could, for example, call
into active warfare the militia of other villages with whom they had ritual ties.
The leader, called "Mwad Lo Kwei," had a determining voice in the selection of
chiefs from the Lo Gwom group. No Gwom Gwelle could be installed without
his concurrence and active participation in the rites of installation.

Finally, the functions of the ritual offices held by the other priests of Lo Du
must have been a not insignificant field of influence in the village polity. Many
elders said that in the old days the Mwad Shi Chun (some said he was the highest
Bi-Gwom Kwit) was as powerful and important as the Gwom. Others thought
that he was even more important because of his control of farming activities. He
determined the propitious time for preparing the ground and planting the most
valuable crop, *acha*, which in turn initiated the entire planting season. It was he
who communicated with the supernatural forces that controlled the prosperity of
the village. These Bi-Gwom Kwit of Lo Du conducted the great Pe and Tyi ceremonies, and their reluctance or failure to perform would incur the wrath of the
chit and disaster. Even today, when most rituals have lost their former force and
significance, fear and anticipation grip the older people when no one from Lo Du

is present to conduct a ritual. In 1961, one Gwom Kwit from Lo Du refused to take part in the Tyi ceremony on the grounds that land compensation monies from one of the sacred areas had not been divided with him. Since he and his special medicines were required, the rituals were delayed one whole day until, after he had been pacified with a goat and some money, he agreed to come. During the interval, many people were visibly upset and anguished by his behavior, and they predicted imminent disaster for the village.

Some rights, duties, and prerogatives of office were institutionalized in these titled positions. But the power that these traditional leaders had appeared not to have been backed directly by the sanction of force. What it did carry were the sanctions provided by fear of supernatural retribution and the collective reprobation of fellow villagers (Maquet 1971). However, there were some rare occasions in which socially sanctioned or legitimate physical force did apply. During the great Tyi hunting ceremony, in a series of rites performed over a three-day period away from the village, men who were accused of great transgressions would be judged by their peers. In a special dance involving all the men of the village, their names would be sung out and their heinous offenses named (such as incest with a sister or sister's daughter, beating of one's mother, or habitual stealing from other than one's own kinsmen). If there was consensus among the elders regarding the guilt and general undesirability of the offender and if no possibility of rehabilitation seemed available, then such offenders would be put to death by beating with bamboo sticks. Also, if on occasions not involving the Tyi ceremony a young man was found guilty by his own relatives of extreme misconduct and they could not or would not punish him, the Da Lo (headman) of his kin group could call on men of Lo Kwei to capture him and sell him into slavery to Hausa traders.

Many events described to me indicate that the relationships among the men who held positions of traditional power and the kin groups that were the repositories of these influential positions were far from static. The wielding of influence and the exercise of power existed in a state of flux, subjected to oscillations that may have been of a cyclical nature or, on the other hand, the precursors or mechanisms of evolutionary changes within the social system. Shortly before the coming of Europeans and during the early years of colonial administration, a man by the name of Chunung Nyap held the title of Gwom Gwelle. He was known to have wielded unusually large personal powers that were not considered legitimate or appropriate to his office. Informants said that it was he who started the practice of confiscating the lands and property of certain kin groups that had the misfortune of being caught and sold into slavery. He made their farms and livestock part of his personal domain. Several old men knew such families by name and fully remembered some of the people. They pointed out areas of their former

compound sites and farms. As if in additional proof, a survey of the farms of Lo
Gwom people in 1960 showed that they are more widely scattered than those of
any other kin groups and in areas that did not originally belong to the Lo Gwom
people. One basis for these acquisitions lay in the fact that at some point in
Chunung Nyap's long "reign" of nearly forty years, he appropriated for himself
the duty (or right) of enslaving whole kin groups for the witchcraft practices of
one member. He also began imposing fines on wrongdoers in the form of whole
storerooms of foods, fields, horses, houses, and livestock. In some cases, he had
his kinsmen and followers tear down offenders' houses. There appeared to have
been little opposition and few social barriers to such appropriation of power.
This situation suggests that perhaps some developmental modifications in the
nature of the office of the Gwom Gwelle were occurring before the coming of
Europeans, and Chunung Nyap might eventually have been able to establish a
strong chiefdom as his power became more concentrated and he gained more
followers.

What was the source and basis of Chunung Nyap's power as well as that of
the other traditional leaders? And how did it happen that the village accepted
such dominance and autocratic behavior on his part? The story of another man
of Lo Gwom provides a key to part of the answer.

Da Jang da Gwong Go calls his kin group Lo Dagbwan. He is the sole adult
male of the group and has three wives and three small sons to succeed him. He
once had many older sons, he said, but they died. As a man of Lo Dagbwan, he
is said to represent a line (*nlang*) of the Lo Gwom peoples who lost face, status,
and influence in the village for a number of significant reasons. At one time,
according to Da Jang (and other elders agreed), his ancestors held the staff or
rods (*gwelle*) of the Gwom. But as time moved on, the men of Lo Dagbwan
became fewer and weaker. They did not prosper or produce many sons to stand
up for and protect their domain. Other lines of Lo Gwom overran them and
finally captured from them the sacred emblems (the rod, drums, and calabash).
At the time of Chunung Nyap, the emblems were sealed in his house, thus fortify-
ing his position of leadership. Chunung Nyap was strong, and he had many loyal
supporters; that is why today his descendants claim the right to the chieftainship.
Da Jang makes a limited active claim to the position of the Gwom, and he is
bitter about his present weakness and inferiority in the village polity. A man of
about sixty years old, he has memories of at least the latter part of the rule of
Chunung Nyap and the events that took place around him. He pointed out other
lines of the Lo Gwom that had suffered the fate of total extinction (by witchcraft,
ostracism, or enslavement for false reasons) in a struggle with stronger units of
the Lo Gwom.

First, these events show strong internal competition for the office of the Gwom within a restricted unit of people, the Lo Gwom sodality. Second, they show that men competed for the weapons and symbols of power through the accretions of personal followers and prestige: wealth in the form of land, horses, and other livestock; prestige in the form of the acquisition of many wives and mistresses (Chunung Nyap had nine wives and twelve mistresses in the "Njem" relationship [see chapter 10]); and personal strength and wealth in the form of large numbers of followers, including a large kin group with many sons. Third, the events underscore the progressive ascendancy of the position and power of the Gwom (and the Lo Gwom sodality) vis-à-vis the other leadership positions held by the Lo Du and the Lo Kwei. A clear-cut recognition of the superior position and power of the Lo Gwom was succinctly and fairly rapidly effected by the coming of Europeans and their later selection of a man of Lo Gwom as the official chief of Du village with formal powers buttressed by the might of the colonial government.

The other traditional leaders did not accept the elevation of the power of the Lo Gwom without some degree of resistance. They hired letter writers and sent numerous petitions to the colonial government protesting the selection and arguing their own cases. They still see themselves in competition with the Lo Gwom for eminence and power in the village, and the conflicts among the Lo Du, Lo Kwei, and Lo Gwom men smolder strongly under a modern facade. The political tactics utilized now include attempts to manipulate individuals in the colonial administration plus maneuvering to increase their number of followers. They also include petitions of complaint about such ordinary misbehavior as lying on the part of their opponents, theft, or misrepresentation.

The principal issue of active dispute between the Bi-Lei and Bi-Kabong at the time of this study concerned the highest position of all, the chieftaincy of Jos, a second-class chiefdom and political office created in 1947 by the colonial administration. The chief of Jos was established to be the chief of all members of the Birom ethnic group and of all the villages of the high plateau. The man selected, on the basis of reputation and educational background, for the first chief of Jos was Rwang Pam, formally the headmaster of a primary school at Riyom and at that time one of the best-educated men in the area. He is a man of Lo Boggom in Du village and therefore from the Bi-Kabong core group. His selection brought increasingly loud opposition from the various sectors of the Bi-Lei who felt that one of their own men should have been chosen. Since that time, opposition to Mallam Rwang Pam had reached great intensity because of alleged favoritism that he had shown his son-in-law in a dispute over land compensation in the village. The incident was widely scandalized in the province, and there was particular concern at higher political levels, involving members of the national political parties, about who should be Mallam Rwang's successor and whether the office of the chief of Jos should be made hereditary.

In the village context, the issues and arguments were couched in familiar terms relating to the competition among the core groups: which of these sodalities was the most powerful in precolonial times and therefore should hold by virtue of hereditary rights the village and district leadership posts within the modern state.

The historical and ethnographic materials discussed in this chapter reveal a complex political kaleidoscope in which traditional forms of social power were diffuse and decision making was divided among a wide range of people and positions. Both group alliances and ties among individuals were the mechanisms by which plateau societies managed to organize political relationships and thereby maintain a system of order. Such alliances and interconnecting links were dynamic and fluid, but stability and continuity were built into the system and regulated by such features as the Great Ceremonies and the enduring relationships among sodalities. Even before the coming of Europeans, the Birom and other ethnic groups on the plateau had evolved a system in which groups could maneuver into and out of (pseudo)kinship relationships by the manipulation of genealogical connections at the fourth to seventh generations. The relationships expressed by the terms *jere* and *chang* have no counterpart that I know of in most other "tribal"-level kinship systems. However, it is clear that they are political relationships necessitated by the complexities surrounding the peopling of the plateau area.

I suggest that these ritual relationships, along with the structuring of relatively small patrilineally ordered kin groups and the various mechanisms of maneuverability along with patterns of alliance and stability associated with them, may have had long historical depth. Structural myopia permitted kin groups to move in and out of alliances with one another. In these circumstances, the ascendance of one sodality to a position of power, albeit temporarily, gave it leverage that could have magnified its influence in a wide area and could have led eventually to the establishment of a statelike structure. In the reading of West African history, these local processes may very well have been the mechanisms by which some large-scale empirical forms, such as ancient Ghana, Mali, Songhai, and to some extent Kanem-Bornu, were able to be consolidated.

These are levels of political activities that involved and still involve only men. Yet as we will see in later chapters, much of the decision making, particularly those having to do with the scheduling of economic activities, took place only with the compliance of women.

Notes

1. For a discussion of similar shrines among the Tallensi, see Fortes (1945, 80, 104, 108).
2. The stages of sociocultural evolution postulated by evolutionists in the past obviously

do not encompass all the variations and complexities of sociopolitical systems found around the world. The possibilities of systems found in West Africa where populations moved into and out of large empirical structures but maintained their own integrity over long spans of time have not been well explored and do not fit neatly into the "bands," "tribes," "chiefdoms," or "states" categories. See Fried (1967) and Service (1971).

3. One of the first reports was that of Monckton (1929). Ames (1934) concurred in this assumption, although it is obvious that he knew very little about the cultures of plateau peoples.

Village Wards and Other Forms of Social Control

7

ALTHOUGH IT WAS FROM THE membership of the core ritual groups that the most important positions of public authority and prestige were filled, the powers exercised by holders of these offices normally affected individuals' daily lives primarily through the ritual regularization of economic activities and the persuasive power of appeal to supernatural sanctions. Traditional leaders had the threat of physical force at their disposal in only one instance, as we have seen, a fact that emphasizes the limitations of their political power. They could not, for example, establish and uphold values regarding group and individual conduct in public by coercion, nor could they deal with the many quarrels and disputes that arise among kin groups. Moreover, political and ritual authority was held by rival sectors within the village and thus was decentralized and diffused.

There were areas of daily life that could not be guided, controlled, and maintained by these limited institutions. In the absence of a centralized political system, the fluidity and heterogeneity of personnel within the traditional Birom villages suggest that some other principles of social control and cooperation operated in the autochthonous setting. There was and is a domain that bridged the gap between small, restricted kin groups and the rudimentary or quasi-political structure provided by the leadership positions held within the core groups. This domain centered on the role and status of the headman of the *manjei*, a traditional position tolerated as peripheral to the colonial government and having no official recognition or status.

In chapter 3, it was pointed out that the official boundaries of the colonial "ward," whatever they may be for tax and census purposes during any one year, corresponded little or not at all to the Birom *manjei*, although in tax records the wards are given the same names as those of the original *manjei*. The traditional *manjei* did not so much refer to delimited geographic areas as to social units, with spatial proximity as just one basis for membership. The ward and *manjei*, then, are not homologous units but rather emerge out of different conceptions, functions, and values. At the time of this research, the activities and functions of the *manjei* were still carried on side by side with those of the modern ward.

It is the traditional *manjei* that I identify as the important intermediate domain of sociopolitical action in the village. In the precolonial world, there may very well have been a number of dimensions that defined the *manjei*. In the early 1960s, it appeared to be based fundamentally on that most ancient of principles: social grouping by proximity. Present in most of the activities associated with the *manjei* is the notion that people who reside in a common spatial area share a higher degree of common interests and values with one another than they do with people of greater distance.[1] The social and spatial product of the operation of this principle is the local community or neighborhood. In the Birom case, I prefer the use of the term "neighborhood" for the *manjei*, as it does not connote sharp physical distinctions or aggregation of residences.

In its most elementary meanings, the *manjei* encompasses those people who live in contiguous compounds, who usually associate with one another, and who are conscious of their common interaction and mutuality of interests. But I stress that the *manjei* as neighborhood is not solely a territorial concept. Its boundaries, if they can be said to exist, are fluid and overlapping, expanding under certain conditions and retracting in others. That the principle of the neighborhood is still maintained despite increased mobility of individuals and some atrophy in the operation of kinship principles attests to its strength and adaptability to modern conditions.

Characteristic Features of the *Manjei*

Earlier, I pointed out that the values for maintaining the proximity of male agnates frequently results in the appearance of clusters of related kin groups concentrated in certain areas of the villages (as seen among the Bi-Lei and Bi-Kabong). Nuclei of groups that are *yere* to one another are found throughout the village. At the same time, other, similar groups can be found dispersed in several *manjei*. Sometimes this spread was the result of recent moves; in other cases, several generations of dispersal can be shown. Older informants denied that the *manjei* ever corresponded with units defined by kinship. They always pointed out that a man could build his compound anywhere in the village where there was vacant land and that even a stranger could be given a place to settle by anyone who had sufficient lands. Records show that there has been no one *manjei* in which all or even a vast majority of the kin groups are related to one another or thought to be ultimately descended from a common ancestor.[2] The *manjei* is neither bound into fixed territories nor associated with genealogically determined kinship groupings. It can and does cut across other lines of distinction.

There is, however, a situation or place dimension to the concept of the *manjei*, so that villagers speak of Nadu (literally, "back of Du") as being east of Lo Ku Lo Du and of Le Chom as being "near" or "on the other side" of Shei. But they cannot tell you precisely where Shei becomes physically separated from Le Chom. Moreover, it does not disturb them that some people are placed in one ward during one tax year and in another the next year. Thus, more crucial to the concept is a social but not a group parameter; the view is that of the *manjei* as a discernible arena of social interaction, associated with particular activities and functions.

Every *manjei* has a headman who is appropriately called the "Da Manjei," ("Father of the Manjei"). This office unquestionably dates from precontact times, and it is a position of considerable prestige and influence. The responsibilities of the office include primarily advising the people on all matters of public concern as well as private or personal matters. They also include settling disputes among members of the *manjei*, arbitrating claims and mediating quarrels among the various kin groups, and apportioning fines for damages. Although the Bida Manjei (plural) are not judges in the formal sense and are unable by tradition to impose punishment on malefactors, they are empowered to make decisions, subject to agreement by the people, concerning the amounts of restitution to settle claims. The Da Manjei also performs certain of the many special rituals in his community, such as the First Fire rituals each year before the burning of the bushlands.

Together, the BiDa Manjei constitute, in modern times, the highest-ranking members of the informal group of elders who act as advisers and consultants to the Da Gwom in court sessions. Some of the BiDa Manjei may serve as appointed members of the court from time to time. However, the degree of their influence within Birom society may best be judged from the fact that all internal disputes, actions of both civil and criminal nature, are brought to the Da Manjei before they ever reach the legally constituted court of the district, and most are settled at this stage. As headmen, the BiDa Manjei handle conflicts through calling gatherings of elders who hear cases and inspire solutions. This is particularly true of domestic disputes between husbands and wives that do not reach the Da Gwom unless a definite divorce is sought by one party, a major conflict ensues, and no reconciliation seems possible. Very many arguments over land, crops, women, livestock, and claims to cash are settled by the wise handling of the Da Manjei. It is to be noted in these cases, as we will see later, that the basic values of Birom society are not threatened. The cases that become part of the litigation of the district court are those in which it is fairly clear that not even the appeal to the most fundamental Birom values will provide a resolution. Thus, the position of the Da Manjei carries the obligation to uphold customary law and practices and the traditional rights and obligations that individuals have vis-à-vis one another as established in an older social order.

According to all informants, the position of the Da Manjei was not hereditary in the past, as appointment was made by consensus of the elders. It was quite common, however, that a man of the same kin group might succeed to the office. Today, as in the old days, men who hold these positions are important men, thought to be of impeccable reputation and prestige. They are men who have been able to acquire substantial followers by their wisdom and integrity and their knowledge of Birom customs and values. More important, in the competition for eminence and status in the village, these are the men who have emerged victorious in part through the achievements of their kin groups. Most of the BiDa Manjei are members of kin groups that through the acquisition of land, through their productive efforts and the relative prosperity, and through good marriages and the birth of many sons have gained high status in the village.

Thus, many BiDa Manjei have dominant or supporting roles in the most important village rituals. Lo Ja is or was such a dominant kin group in a sodality that includes eight or nine other kin groups. Gyang Chun Ja, the Da Lo of Lo Ja, is also the Da Manjei of Ropwang. His kin group includes some twelve bi-*lalla* and sixty-seven people, some of whom are quite scattered today in other districts and in the towns. His predecessors were all men of his kin group or related kin groups, and they are all Bi-Pyomo, participating in some of the rituals of the Bi-Lei, and also in Ngasang, which is done only by the Bi-Kabong. Although the process of segmentation during the past two generations has fractured the kin group, Gyang has retained the respect of all the members.

Today, BiDa Manjei are at least formally appointed as ward heads by administrative fiat. While the appointment is the legal responsibility of the Da Gwom, the chief of the village, it is in fact the elders of the *manjei* who select the ward-heads, as is well brought out in the records of administrative officers in Jos. In all except one instance that came to my attention, the appointments coincided with the traditional Da Manjei. The one case concerned a conflict between two men who were supported by quarreling factions in the *manjei*. It was resolved when the man who best reflected traditional customs was finally appointed by the chief of the village.

There seems to be no occasion when all the adult members of a *manjei* meet together as a unit for a common action. The *manjei* is not a group counterposed against other like groups, nor does it have an internal hierarchy or structure or policies by which it is differentiated from other *manjei*. What is conveyed to its members is a common sense of community based on their territorial contiguity and the intimacy of daily relationships. The contexts in which *manjei* membership becomes explicit, at least to an outsider, are not frequently or easily observable. Individuals are not normally identified by their *manjei* membership with the exception of incidents where it is desired to convey remoteness of relationship. In other words, where social and spatial distance are significant (and there is a positive correlation between the two in Birom values), a man will be identified as "a man of Madu" or "a man of Janda" rather than by the name of the *lo* group to which he belongs as is the more usual custom. As will be seen in the description that follows, the *manjei* was and still is a very important sociopolitical entity in whose limits specific mechanisms concerned with the maintenance of social order operated.

One first becomes aware of the importance of neighborhood association, that is, the reality of the *manjei*, through the farming activities of the villagers. The major grain crops—*acha*, bulrush, and finger millet—are sown by individual men in bush farms. If the requirements for labor are small, a single household, the members of a single domestic unit, can perform this activity efficiently. But there are two major activities of the farming season that require larger numbers of men and therefore the aid of individuals outside the domestic unit. These are hoeing and preparing the ground for the sowing season and the harvesting and particularly the threshing of the grain. Both activities require tremendous physical exertion. The group of men who engage in these major tasks never consists of a single kin group, although kinsmen will help out, but is always a spontaneously organized work group (*yat*) composed of neighbors, kin people, and friends.

Each individual farmer, before starting to cut the ground or to harvest his grain, has his wife brew a large amount of beer and lets it be known throughout his area that he will be holding a work party in a few days' time, or he may reverse the procedure and give notice before the beer is brewed.[3] Everyone is invited to come, and on the appointed morning the neighbors gather at his compound, although some individuals may appear later in the day on the farm. The work party spends the entire day at work, stopping only to eat and to drink beer later in the afternoon and evening. There is much camaraderie, laughter, and teasing, all of which seems to be designed to encourage as much work as possible by the individual members. The only reward for the workday is the beer. But every farmer is bound in a reciprocal arrangement to help not only those neighbors who showed up for his work but also all other kin groups in his neighborhood.

A work group normally consists of about ten or twelve persons, although I have recorded work groups of more than twenty. Although it seems to be the ideal, not all members of a neighborhood participate in all work groups. But every work group will be composed of at least representative members from a number of compounds. In nearly all cases recorded, five or six compounds were involved through at least one member. In some cases, it appears that year after year the same compounds are involved, although the individual members may vary, as some get too old and others come of farming age. It is rare that a person who is outside the neighborhood offers his services. In most of the cases of which I have knowledge, such a person is either a *bwong sa* ("Big Friend") or a kinsman who happens to be present on a visit or in some cases comes from far away specifically to help with the farming. People outside the *manjei* are not expected to volunteer, and I have heard occasional snide remarks that such people will come and do very little with the expectation of getting to drink beer. There is also the very real factor that too great a distance would make people reluctant to work, as they would not have strength to return home.

There is a great deal of sociability on these occasions and within the *yat* a strong sense of social unity. Members depart each evening with the satisfaction not only of having done a good day's work but also of having performed the most important neighborly duties and of living up to the ideals of cooperation and good neighborliness. Each occasion strengthens the bonds among neighbors—a factor that often makes individuals reluctant to move away or to behave in a manner disruptive of the relationship.

Accompanying the sociability of the work group, there is another feature of the neighborhood that has important consequences for individual behavior. This is the fact that the neighborhood is the primary unit of social control by gossip. People who gossip about one another are members of a common community (Gluckman 1963). People outside the neighborhood are not ordinarily subjects of gossip unless their transgressions are very great. But ordinary day-to-day gossip is centered on the members of the neighborhood. It is considered somewhat improper for someone outside the neighborhood to gossip about an individual within the neighborhood or with the latter's neighbors. While there seems to be no exact boundaries, either social or geographical, to the neighborhood, the circle of gossip and gossipers as well as the work groups over a span of time serve to delineate the reality of membership within a *manjei*.

A third characteristic of the neighborhood that helps define it concerns the involvement of its members in debt and credit relationships. Thus, the lending and borrowing of land, of personal goods such as clothing and decorative items, and of money seem to be confined to the circle of relationships that I have described as the neighborhood. The evidence for this is somewhat elusive, as some people may be reluctant to disclose their actual debts or may distort their debtor–creditor relationships. (In addition, there were probably some people who were not involved in debts at the particular time of this research.) Not all borrowing, especially of cash, is confined to the village.

Still, indebtedness is one of the most ramifying and complex of all relationships in the village. It cuts across lines of age, gender, affluence, occupation, and other circumstances and provides an almost impenetrable jungle of links among individuals. The multiplicity of debts has such a wide range that I would unhesitatingly assert that all adult persons are involved in debts for some periods in their lives. One might even argue that indebtedness per se is an institutionalized feature of personal and social relationships and provides a social glue that binds people together.[4] It characterizes the events and activities surrounding most marriages. Some men, for example, have loaned or pawned fields to obtain the horse and six goats (£16) for the brideprice with the debts often lasting nearly two decades. Until a man could accumulate enough goods to regain his land, he would commonly be involved in multiple debt relationships occasioned by his borrowing "from Peter to pay Paul," ad infinitum. Thus, complex cycles of indebtedness are created involving many men, and especially women, who are not kinsmen.

During the farming year 1960–1961, I recorded 147 instances of farms that were loaned, borrowed, rented, or pawned, although the differences among these processes in terms of what actually transpires is often a matter of fine definition. When a Birom speaks of pawning, he or she uses the Hausa word *jingina*, the common definition of which is found throughout the north. It refers to the giving of a valuable security in order to obtain cash. In many cases, the item put "on deposit," so to speak, is a piece of land, and what is borrowed is money. The initiator of the transaction must return the borrowed money or its equivalent in order to regain his land. Renting, on the other hand, is initiated by the person who wants or requires the land for a period of time and has some cash or some other valuable (such as a goat, part of the crop, or sometimes money) to give in exchange. The rental period is rarely precisely defined among the villagers. There is only the understanding that when the renter is through with the land or the owner requires it again, the former will discontinue his cultivation at the end of the season. Borrowing and lending are distinguishable from pawning and renting in that normally there is no consideration involved, that is, no direct exchange of valued goods. However, both the lender and the borrower expect as a matter of custom that the latter will reciprocate the favor at some time in the future by one of several possible methods. He may give the lender some produce, though not necessarily from the particular farm borrowed; he may lend him some other goods, such as cash or clothing; or he may give some personal service, such as helping with house building, farming, or the like.

Because the vast majority of these transactions are among neighbors, they are informal and usually have no stated time limits. Agreements with regard to borrowing, renting, or pawning may last indefinitely so that the terms of the original agreements may become obscure. In fact, this is such a common occurrence that many such arrangements appear to end up as the cause of disputes over who has what rights to the land at some point much later in time. Men sometimes told me as we were going over their lands that they were working some farms whose ownership was in dispute or of which they were not certain who were the owners. There are instances of renting, lending, and borrowing that have persisted for more than a generation, a condition that serves further to confuse the relationships of men with one another and to the land. This is particularly true when the two parties to the original transaction have died and the verbal agreements, frequently sealed by the sharing of a common calabash of beer, are either not known or are remembered from secondhand reports. Occasionally a transaction such as pawning will amount in time to outright sale.[5] In one such instance, the borrower never was able to regain his land because he never obtained sufficient cash, which in this case was a considerable amount. He died, and the land continued to be worked by his creditors. Although the sons of the deceased tried to regain the land by claiming that it was "stolen" from their father, the creditor, in a rare instance, was able to produce a witness to state that the exchange was a fair and outright sale since the luckless debtor did not make an attempt to regain it and moreover forfeited it before his death. The tradition that selling of one's agnatic land is never done among the Birom served little use in this case because everyone knows that in modern times the permanent alienation of farmland sometimes occurs.

Disputes over lands involved in these transactions are so frequent that they are accepted as part of one's way of life. Most simmer as arguments until they flare up when provoked by some incident. Open breaches and actual physical hostilities are prevented when the disputants are members of the same neighborhood. Restraining the overt expression of conflict is the feeling of the permanence of both the land and the neighborhood relationship of men to one another. Some day, it is thought, we may settle the disagreement, that is, when one of the opposing parties gives in. In most cases of intense dispute, some arbitration by other neighbors or the Da Manjei occurs, and deep wounds may be healed by setting new conditions that may be acceptable to both parties. This happened when an old man, Da Jang of Lo Jang, gave three farms to a younger man, Davou Lo Chun Yo, who had moved away from his natal compound twenty years earlier and built a house in the neighborhood of the people of Lo Jang. The terms of the original agreement were lost in numerous accusations and the fact that both men were twenty years older and had long accepted the arrangement. In 1960, Da Jang wanted his land back for a young son, and Davou refused, claiming that he bought the land from Da Jang. Since there were other people involved and some of the younger men threatened to "fight it out," several members of the neighborhood tried to negotiate a settlement in the matter for several weeks. It was finally agreed that Da Jang would accept a settlement of seven bags of grain and a gift of one portion of the land that had been lying fallow for two or three years. All the land involved consisted of several garden and intermediate farms on which mainly grain crops were grown. Davou, subsequent to this agreement, "rented" a garden farm for growing guinea corn and beans from one of Da Jang's "brothers."

The majority of transactions cut across kinship boundaries. Moreover, when plotted on a map of the village, these transactions showed clear differentiation of circles of people who formed distinct neighborhoods. The circles overlapped on their peripheries, and on occasion one or two transactions would involve men of distant neighborhoods, but these were so rare as to be the exception to the rule. Not all people who live in the neighborhoods were involved in transactions, and there were some men who were involved in five, six, or more debtor arrangements. The complexity of debt relations is indicated by the following examples of transactions that were recorded for one neighborhood unit:

1. Lo Matta owns garden farm 10, about half an acre, but yams were grown there this year, and Lo Matta men do not yet know to whom they belong. It is certain that as the yams are harvested, someone will discover their owner and the latter will in turn compensate Lo Matta people for the use of their land. This is considered to be a type of "borrowing."

2. Manga Bot Tiri (Lo Bot Tiri) lent a farm three-fourths of an acre in size to Davou Matta, who returned it this year. Davou did not give Manga any of the produce.

3. Manga Bot Tiri pawned a plot of one-half acre to Davou Matta for one bag (*chit*) of *acha*.

4. Many years ago, Manga Bot Tiri had borrowed one bag of *acha* from Musa (Lo Matta) but had not repaid it during the years. So this year he gave Musa a quarter-acre plot of land to discharge the debt. The *acha* borrowed originally belonged to Musa and to his Bwong Sa (best friend). Thus the land rightfully should have been divided with the latter. Instead, Musa gave his friend £2 for his share of the small farm.

5. This year, Gyang (Lo So) gave a one-half-acre farm to Manga Bot Tiri.

6. Manga Bot Tiri lent a one-and-one-fourth-acre farm to Bwang Da Ling of Lo Bo.

7. Gyang (Lo So) pawned a farm of one-fourth acre to Manga Bot Tiri for ten shillings.

8. Lo Gan gave a one-half-acre farm to Musa Lo Matta to grow *were chun*, a special type of *acha*.

9. A one-half-acre farm belonging to Lo Nyap was given to Chuang Gyang Ja, Lo Bo, for no consideration.

10. Cholom Pwajok (Lo Gyang Bang) used a one-fourth-acre farm of Lo Bo for two years, first planting yams and leveling with *acha*. It was returned this year.

I collected a list of transactions that includes all known transfers of farms from one person to another where the individuals involved were not members of the same agnatic kin group. When the twenty-two houses named are plotted on a map of the village, their locations and arrangement give a graphic picture of the approximate spatial extent of the neighborhood.

Any act of indebtedness, through pawning, renting, or lending, is never a simple transaction. It is always invested with additional circumstantial obligations, anticipations, and prescribed patterns of behavior. Moreover, every debt is usually the focal point of much intrigue and manipulation of social roles. The complexities appear to be even greater when the transactions involve personal items and/or cash, perhaps because they are portable and easily concealed.

The intricacies of indebtedness require sustained social contact, a fact that is essential to the idea of neighborhoodship. Many kin groups involved in these dealings may be linked already by ties of affinity or by distant kinship (*chang*) ties, but such links are neither necessary nor important to the situation. Kinship ties may bring an additional dimension to the social context of the event in which the indebtedness is established. But Birom values normally operate against indebtedness among kinsmen, especially of the *lo* or *yere* type. Indeed, the obligations and privileges of kinship, as among many peoples, are never seen in the same framework as debt and credit arrangements, and the latter are precluded, at least verbally, from the setting of kinship.

Many other varied types of events occur that serve to delineate the notion of the neighborhood as a very real context for certain types of social interaction. One such event illustrates some of the multiple facets of the neighborhood concept and the kinds of functions that are prescribed within this social setting. It is described very briefly here to pinpoint these features.

Dauda Chuang, the enterprising twenty-two-year-old son of Chuang Matta, of Lo Matta, had a long-standing argument with Choji, of Lo Pam Mo. Choji is a brother of the dead husband of Pwachom, a younger sister of Chuang Matta. Choji inherited the care of his brother's wife (Pwachom) through the levirate and has never had a wife of his own, although at least two of Pwachom's children were begotten by him, Choji is thus of a senior generation to Dauda although only about ten years older. Because of his treatment of Pwachom, he is not held in high esteem by the men of Lo Matta with whom he has had frequent quarrels. The argument that he has with Dauda concerns a shirt (*riga*) and trousers that he agreed to sell to Dauda. (He has previously borrowed money from young men of Lo Matta and has pawned personal items with Dauda for small cash.) Dauda reluctantly agreed to purchase these three items after several weeks of haggling but was unable to pay the full amount finally agreed on: six shillings and six pence. Weeks of bickering back and forth led to a point at which Choji returned some of the money already paid him and demanded his clothing back. (By then the debt had been increased by two shillings that Choji had borrowed for drinking beer.) Dauda refused, arguing that the money he had paid for the clothes was what he normally used to buy goods to sell in a small canteen nearby. If he had kept the money and used it in this manner, he would have gained a profit. He demanded that ten shillings be returned to him to compensate for his loss.

An argument ensued during which a number of other individuals became involved. Both Choji and Dauda stopped some men passing on the road and invited them to help settle the dispute. They came: one man each from Lo Bwengi, Lo Kwon, Lo Jok, Lo Chang, Lo Nyap, and Lo Chun Yo and two men from Lo Gwang Bagai. During the proceedings, a man from Lo Gyes on the other side of the village sauntered into the compound area apparently out of curiosity. His entry occasioned some unusual attention and discussion, and I heard the comment that this was not a matter for a man of Beg, a *manjei* two miles distant to the southeast. In this manner, the man of Lo Gyes was excluded, although he stood around at some distance and watched the proceedings. He did not, nor would he have been allowed to, participate.

Eventually, there were twelve men—the two disputants, Davou Matta, the headman of Lo Matta, and nine outsiders—gathered in a sort of semicircle outside of which about fifty other people, including many children, were standing. Everyone was asked to be silent, and Davou Matta, by virtue of his senior position (he is the Da Manjei of Rugut ward), began to speak, presenting the facts of the quarrel in impartial tones. Occasional interruptions were immediately halted, and each person involved in the dispute was allowed to have an opportunity to describe his version of the situation. The nine men who were seemingly functioning as a kind of jury repeated the essential facts among themselves and called on traditional values of members of close families not to argue but to settle disagreements among themselves. Dauda, being Choji's junior, was chastised for his abrupt and disrespectful behavior toward his elders. In the end, each man who had been called in or who had wandered in from nearby areas, having seemingly decided on the merits of the different positions, said his piece, and each gradually started drifting back toward the road. The main decisions were that Dauda should accept back a total of seven shillings and six pence, already paid, and that Choji should regain his clothing. The only men who did not participate fully in the proceedings were a half dozen young unmarried men, two young married men, the man from Lo Gyes, as well as several other strangers (one a Hausa man) whom I did not know.

This case demonstrated first the essential characteristic of the *manjei* (the neighborhood), namely, its exclusiveness in a matter of common concern. This was stated in the explicit exclusion of the man from Lo Gyes who had walked into the center of things. Other men not of the neighborhood or young men who were not invited to participate (nor were they expected to because of their youth) stood around in the background. The man of Lo Gyes, by his somewhat bold obtrusiveness, made it necessary to put some definition on the boundaries of the neighborhood, an event that rarely occurs, as the vast majority of people take for granted without verbalization the concept of the neighborhood and their membership in it.

Children learn that they are members of a specific *manjei* undoubtedly through experiences of the sort described here. In the area of Lo Matta and Lo Pam Mo compounds, there are certain people who consider themselves as having common interests. Some live in Rugut ward, some in Janda, and a few in She in the formal wards recognized by the government. In any case, most compounds are more or less contiguous territorially, and their members have frequent social interaction as a result of inhabiting a common neighborhood. They resent the intrusion of outsiders, such as the man of Lo Gyes.

Another element in this case that is an important feature of the concept of the neighborhood is the existence of a marriage between a woman of Lo Matta (Pwachom) and a man of Lo Pam Mo, the location of whose compound was about 150 yards from Lo Matta. The Birom prefer that their daughters be married within the neighborhood, and women desire to remain close to their brothers and fathers. Specifically, as indicated by the situation between Lo Matta and Lo Pam Mo, men feel that such marriages are better from the standpoint of their being able to watch over their sisters and daughters. Who will look after them and protect them if they marry strangers far away?

The levirate is seen as a relationship of "suffering" because it is anticipated that sometimes the brothers of deceased husbands will treat such widows cruelly. Many times during my stay in the village, I heard complaints regarding Choji (Lo Pam Mo) to the effect that the reason why he beat Pwachom and refused to feed her was that she was not "really" his wife. The Birom thus recognize the important distinction between the levirate and an original legal marriage in the identity of children born to a woman. A brief survey from the genealogies of marriages in this neighborhood area shows that slightly under 50 percent of the marriages in the past two generations have been within the neighborhood and that over 65 percent of all marriages were between persons of nearby areas, that is, closely associated bi-*manjei*.

Finally, this incident and the case of Da Jang described earlier denote a highly significant aspect of the neighborhood. Individual men, elders acting in concert, frequently serve as a "moot," or an informal court that hears cases.[6] Although there is no single meeting place and no court organization, decisions made and conclusions rendered by the older wiser men in a neighborhood carry more weight than decisions by the proper jural body headed by the chief, making up the Grade D Native Court. These informal and local moot have no legally recognized authority in the colonial government, but even the chief himself respects and is influenced by their actions. The unstated power that they hold is that of custom, strengthened by social disapproval and the threat of ostracism. Within the neighborhood, with its informal lines of communication, talk, and gossip, such "penalties" as ridicule and other forms of social reprobation are highly effective.

An extremely important difference between the sessions of the district court, as established by the administration and the informal moots, is the latter's distinct influence on and connections to all levels of the social system. Women and children, for example, never attended the regular weekly sessions of the district court, but they are always present in the background of the moots and are able to observe, influence, and learn from the events that happen in them. All such sessions normally take place in and around the compound of a Da Manjei. The Birom claim that this is because of the position of respected elder that these men hold and because it is the Da Manjei who settles disputes. They also say that any older wiser man may be called on to mediate in cases of argument and disagreement.

Moot courts deal with the complexity of the various sets of relationships in which all Birom participate. They are not impersonal; on the contrary, it is the intimate knowledge of one another's lives that enables their members to "judge" their fellows and to exercise control over individual behavior in the interests of social order and peace. Thus, members of the court are not confined to consideration of just the facts of an occasion of dispute or a crime; they know the full social context of all events that disturb the social order and the peaceful relations between people. It is perhaps for this reason that they are still so effective (Gluckman 1965a).

The chatter of women during and after the event may seem to be merely "noise" in the background. Women do not overtly participate in the proceedings of the moots. But on many occasions when men cannot come to a consensus or resolve the issue, it is the women who will suggest a course of action that results in a compromise or other solution. After sessions are over, women always come out to discuss the situation among themselves. While they may have little to say about some of the conflicts among men, in virtually all cases where a woman is involved, the women of the neighborhood will have much to say (see chapter 10).

In summary, the social and spatial limitations of the *manjei*, or neighborhood, can be discerned 1) by the extent of debt and credit arrangements; 2) by the frequent transfers of property through lending, borrowing, and pawning; 3) by marriage arrangements; 4) by the recruitment of work parties; 5) by sustained social interaction predicated on gossip; and 6) by the social exclusiveness and socially effective perimeters in the operations of informal courts. The *manjei* most certainly operated in the past pretty much as it does today. It is still a prime mechanism by which unrelated persons and strangers are fused together into a cohesive body by virtue of a common acceptance of the controls and functions of the "neighborhood." Although numerous marriages may take place within the neighborhood, the Birom do not see their neighbors as kinsmen except where there are specific agnatic, affinal, or cognatic ties. None of the terms used for general kinship are ever applied to the neighbors as a body, nor are neighbors ever spoken of as being different from other people in the village.

Changes during the colonial period did not necessarily diminish the role of the Da Manjei or the significance of the relationships and processes pertaining to the neighborhood. While the functions and importance of the ritual groups and ritual leaders declined, yielding to the superior superstructure of the colonial presence, the intermediate political role of BiDa Manjei tended to expand. For example, allocating the collection of taxes to some of the BiDa Manjei via their appointments as ward heads tended to enhance the reputation and stature of the Da Manjei. Older people still relied on his position as a repository of traditional Birom values, and younger people combined respect for this position with their sense of his importance within the greater government structures. Unlike the newly created chief of the village, the Da Manjei cum ward head had a base in both traditional and colonial imposed systems.

In some cases, modifications in the traditional political format had the effect of eliminating some of the constraints on the power of the Da Manjei and provided scope for channeling new ideas into the community. This was particularly true of those BiDa Manjei who were men of vision or perceptive enough to grasp the realities of social and economic changes. In one case, a highly active Da Manjei encouraged some families to send their children to the mission school. He also paved the way for some of his own kinsmen to be appointed to the native police force. By his presence and actions, other members of his *manjei* have also benefited within the colonial context. In other cases, such material changes as in house structures and household implements have entered village culture often via the receptivity and inspiration of the Da Manjei.

In the development of the character of the *manjei* during the colonial years, its role and functions have been enlarged by the emergence of two of the factors that were used to identify it. Debt and credit arrangements and various devices for the transference of land (pawning, renting, and so forth) between individuals and kin groups are not traditional processes. They came to be associated with *manjei* relationships in the colonial period, appearing in part as consequences of the introduction of general-purpose money. Principles already operant within the existing *manjei* made it possible to use this arena for monitoring the structuring of debt relationships and land transfers. Likewise, conflicts over debts and alienation of land came to be handled and resolved by mechanisms extant in the traditional *manjei* structure and functions.

Notes

1. Compare, for example, the "parish" of the Arusha (in Gulliver 1963), and to some degree the Ndembu "vicinage" (Turner 1957, 1966). The Birom *manjei* tends to be more stable in composition than the vicinage, and the circumstances of its emergence are pragmatic and secular rather than ritual.

2. This is in contrast to, for example, the Tiv Tar, which is composed of "all the agnatic descendants of a single ancestor" (Bohannan and Bohannan 1953, 20). The Birom do not today recognize agnatic segments as necessarily correlative to territorial segmentation, and there is no evidence that such a principle ever obtained in the past.

3. In reality, it is the women of the compound who brew the beer, so that a man is dependent on his wife (or wives) both to acquire the grain and to brew the beer.

4. Gluckman (1965a) has dealt with the nature of debt relationship (see particularly chaps. 7 and 8). See also the classic earlier work of Mauss (1954).

5. Davies (n.d.) has also recognized this as apparently a common occurrence. "A difficulty always arises over selling as it is not easy to define selling especially when the system of 'pawning' . . . occurs, as the two are apt to shade into one another" (4).

6. This term is frequently used by anthropologists because it is reminiscent of town meetings in medieval English history.

Gender, Marriage, and the Establishment of the Domestic Unit

8

O VERALL, THE RELATIONSHIP of gender roles in Birom society can best be understood as complementary (Smedley 1974). The differentiation of gender roles and their essential complementarity was, I argue, crucial to the adaptive success of the Birom in the difficult environment of the Jos plateau. All African societies maintain some form of sexual division of labor, but the contents of such customs vary widely, and this results in diverse patterns of gender activities and varying ideologies about gender differences.

There is another sense in which complementarity exists. From the standpoint of women, the tasks that men do complement their essential reproductive function. Birom women have a clear answer to that proverbial Freudian query, What do women really want? All women desire to have children and to have them cared for so that they can be healthy and grow to maturity. This is the basis and substance of all prayers to the Da Gwi (high deity) and to lesser deities and ancestors. When men and women gather for any of the Great Ceremonies, they have a uniform request, a standard prayer, heard at every gathering: "Give us meat (food), give us children, give us health, give us protection." Their reproductive roles give women special status and special rights. For the most part, women see the activities of men as complementing and supporting their essential role as mothers (Mikell 1997).

Men and women developed as economic specialists. Each supplied inputs in terms of energy, time, and knowledge to distinct sets of tasks, and each contributed different kinds of resources to the village community. Before the coming of Europeans, the division of labor by sex was much more clear and rigid. Men did all the heavy, backbreaking work of clearing the land in all the different farming zones and burning the brush materials. They prepared the ground for cultivation, did the hoeing and building of yam and cassava ridges, constructed all housing, and enclosed both housing and garden farms with euphorbia and other materials to keep out animal and human predators. Out on the bush farms, men in groups prepared the ground and sowed and harvested the grain foods: the high-status *acha* and millets.

Such a pattern continues into contemporary times, and some activities reveal much about the cultural construction of gender. At harvest time, men cut down the grain stalks, and women transport the bundles back to the village area. The grain is deposited in a central area, a huge rock depression about eight feet in diameter, where the threshing is done. (The physical characteristics of the threshing areas bore evidence of decades of use.) Here, men using long, heavy poles pound the *acha* for hours until the seeds are separated from the stalks. Then the seed is gathered and placed in bags made by men and stored in the men's storerooms.

It is during the threshing process that we begin to see clearly some of the dynamics in the cultural definition and expression of gender roles. From early morning until late at night, until all the grain is threshed, men stand around the basin pounding until they are exhausted. Women and girls, meanwhile, dance and sing around the men, urging them on, laughing, joking, mocking the way the men work, and calling out to them to pound harder and to use more strength. With salacious songs, they jeer at and ridicule individual men who appear weak, stop too soon, or take time out. The symbolic meaning expressed in nearly all the songs is that of sexual strength. A man's masculinity and sexual prowess are manifest in his threshing strength; one becomes the metaphor for the other, and the bonding of maleness with the production of *acha* becomes overt and unambiguous. Little boys and girls watch these activities and learn very early what constitutes the bases for a man's reputation and status and the measure of his manhood.

The association of men with the *acha* crop is no minor value construct. A man is considered well off if he is fed *acha* every day. Poor men express their social and economic status by the expression that they eat little or no *acha* or that they are eating "only yams." When women are evaluating men as marriage prospects, they speak of the *acha* farms of their kin groups. *Acha* indeed is the high-status food par excellence; eating *acha* is an indicator of health and wealth. But the reality is that women have made it so, and they continue to place emphasis on *acha* production as if there are no other foods worthy of mention.

The harvesting of garden crops by women receives no such attention. Cassava and yams can be stored or left in the ground and eaten as needed; vegetable crops are generally consumed as they ripen. Much depends on how much was produced and whether a crop can be stored for a while. Beans and peas can be dried and stored high off the ground. Weeding and watering and eliminating insect and other pests are done on a daily basis and are activities that are clearly compatible with women's housekeeping and child care roles (Brown 1970). There seems no objective reason why these foods should be considered low-status foods, but we will see shortly that women have had good reasons for the valorization of some foods over others.

When women speak abstractly about the tasks that men and women do, they often observe that men's work is very hard. No woman in the village expressed the idea that she would like to change roles with men. Women also admit that their work is difficult, but the most painful aspect of women's work rests not in the work itself but in the circumstances of watching their children go hungry or die. As Birom women see it, the work of both men and women contributes to the ultimate objective of keeping their children alive and healthy.

The finely honed complementarity of gender roles was still operating among most kin groups at the beginning of the postcolonial period. However, changes in subsistence activities, the introduction of mining and mine work, money and the attractions that it buys, and the alienation of many farms to mining have impacted sex roles. For some kin groups, the balance in the complementarity of sex roles has been disturbed, and new patterns of behavior are emerging that carry in their wake frustrations and conflicts. We see this best in the institution of marriage.

Marriage

I have shown that some marriages are inspired as the terminal event in the process of segmentation and thus constitute a social mechanism in the emergence and proliferation of kin groups (chapter 5). Simultaneously, all marriages are seen as uniting two kin groups and establishing new kinship relationships. The ideals and behavioral expectations that define the new relationship are different, and sometimes radically so, from that of the previous relationship, that is, whatever form that might have been before they became affines to one another. The Birom data also suggest that the linkage is not truly complete until the birth (or, more aptly, the naming) of a child. This is what binds separate kin groups irreversibly together as affines.

All arrangements are designed to prevent marriages between persons with too close genealogical connections (within three generations). Prospective marriage partners and their family connections are carefully scrutinized to avoid infringement of incest regulations. In this way, as people enter into new relations with a newly married couple and later their offspring, there is no confusion of kinship roles and their anticipated behavior patterns.

Marriage is also the basis for the establishment of new and independent domestic units (bi-*lalla*). Proper marriage, involving full payment of an agreed-on brideprice, is the only means by which an enduring domestic unit may be established, although an original domestic unit may be modified by circumstances and practices that do not involve marriage. No single individual can set up his or her own domestic unit, as he or she would be considered incomplete in terms of specialized economic roles. The complementarity and interdependence of economic roles are perhaps the foremost factors in marriage.

Stable domestic units are important to the economic well-being of the Birom because of their functions as the primary units of food production and as the only units in which food preparation, distribution, and consumption take place. The key element, then, in the domestic unit is a woman who is or has been married. A domestic unit is considered stable to the degree that its functioning is not altered or permanently disrupted by the absence or incapacity of this central figure: an adult married woman. Aside from the death of a wife, which naturally disrupts the domestic functions, the greatest danger to the stability of a household is divorce, which always means the separation of the wife from the domestic unit.

Given these conditions, it is not surprising that evidence indicates a high degree of both conjugal and jural stability in marriage, although temporary separations early in marriage will affect the former but not the latter relationship.[1] Jural divorce is brought about when a husband accepts a return of his bridewealth from his wife's kin group or from another man who agrees to marry the wife. The latter is nearly always the case since a young woman is usually remarried. In a sample of 253 women over twenty years of age, only forty, or approximately 16 percent, had ever been divorced.[2] Of these forty, three women were separated from their husbands but not yet remarried. These were all young women, living temporarily in their natal compounds, and only one had a child (a girl). Seven of the women had divorced twice, and one had been married and divorced three times. Five of these women with multiple divorces had divorced because they failed to conceive children in their previous husbands' homes. Four of these women had had no children at all, although all were in their late thirties or older. Birom greatly desire children, so that barrenness or the deaths of many children are among the most common causes of divorce and remarriage. There was no barren woman who lived all her married life with one husband.

In this sample, there were 129 women estimated to be over thirty-five years of age. Of these, nineteen had been divorced. All except one of these divorces had taken place when the women were quite young before the birth of children. From this data and intensive personal interviews with older women, it became clear that after the first three or four years, women do not divorce their husbands or live separately from them where there is a legitimate marriage, nor do they divorce them when there are children. Many women of thirty-five years of age and older are widows, and the majority of widows remain in their husbands' compounds, often going to a brother of the husband in the levirate relationship. The death of a husband does not dissolve a marriage or the obligations entailed in this relationship; only the remarriage of a woman does this. The kin group that paid the brideprice continues to be responsible for a wife and to have jural rights over her and her children.

In addition to the forty women who had proper legal marriages and had been divorced, there were eight other women who had lived as wives to men for a period of time but subsequently left them because these men failed to pay the full bridewealth. Today, sometimes a domestic unit is established by a man and woman living as consorts even though a proper marriage has not taken place. In all such cases, some property had exchanged hands—a down payment on the brideprice with the understanding that the full amount would be forthcoming later. The Birom do not identify this as a true legal marriage (*wining*) but express the situation with the terms *vog bwong* (taking the girl). Such a situation is normally considered preliminary to the true marriage, but these unions are considered very unstable until the full payment of bridewealth. In the cases of the eight women cited previously, their fathers or guardians had grown impatient with the delay and, with the consent of their daughters, had subsequently married them to other men.

These data give some indication of the general stability of the marital relationships (see Barnes 1949). (In the next chapter, dealing with relationships within marriage, I provide some further data on the nature of divorce.) There are a number of factors that operate together to produce this kind of stability in Birom marriage; these relate directly to the functioning of the domestic unit. What I will demonstrate in this and the next two chapters is that the stability of the domestic unit is far more important to the Birom than the stability of marriage per se. In view of this, it seems that the stability of marriage is quite possibly an unanticipated consequence of the stability of the domestic unit, all of which rest primarily in the hands of women.

The significance of marriage lies in three fundamental aspects of the institution: (1) in the notion of the exchangeability of women, (2) in the traditional patterns by which cooperative effort is obtained for the performance of economic tasks (that is, the traditional division of labor by sex), and (3) in the creation of kinship and its resultant ties, duties, rights, and responsibilities.

In analyzing these aspects of marriage there is a twofold objective. First, I attempt to demonstrate how these aspects are separately or together related to certain other specific features of social and economic life that are part of long tradition. Second, I discuss some of the conditions of marriage in the contemporary setting as they appeared in the early 1960s. In doing so, I point out how these three aspects have changed or been influenced by modifications within the total economy. There are numerous elements to be included in a study of marriage that I have considered to be irrelevant for the purposes of this work. I have not, for example, included a discussion of such matters as the sexual life of married (or unmarried) partners, and I have only briefly touched on child rearing, which is generally regarded as one of the functions of marriage but which in the African setting is never relegated solely to a married couple.

The Exchangeability of Women

In chapter 2, I outlined the three separate spheres in which goods were exchanged in the traditional Birom economic system. I noted that the highest sphere of exchange was that which contained horses and women and that the supreme context was that of marriage. However, marriage is not the only institution by which women may be exchanged for valued goods. Two other mutually distinguishable practices serve to emphasize the notion of the exchangeability of women for important material items. There is a custom called "Njem," which has been classified in the anthropological literature as "cicisbeism" (see later discussion). And there is the practice, previously mentioned, of transferring young girls to non-Birom villages in the north, a custom that the Birom call "Pyomo" marriages or exchanges.

From one point of view, this belief in the exchangeability of women can be seen as an element of a more general body of practices in which some aspects of human beings can be exchanged for valuable goods. Slavery is another such practice (and so, for that matter, is wage labor). Among the Birom in precolonial times, a man unfortunate enough to have had no sons could obtain a son through purchase, usually from a distant kinsman. Young boys as well as fully grown men were at times exchanged in this manner for a horse. In some instances of extreme privation, men were known to have "sold" themselves for food, acquiring a status not quite that of a slave who was by definition an outsider and stranger. Such a man became rather a "client" attached to a "patron" via fictive kinship ties carrying stated obligations of mutual aid, dependence, and loyalty.

The exchange aspect of marriage, then, is part and parcel of a widespread ideology and custom that equates some aspects of human beings with material goods. It is a necessary ingredient in the institution of marriage inasmuch as marriage involves the transmission of specific rights in persons from one group to another. There are important differences, however, between true marriage and the two customs, "Njem" and "Pyomo" transactions. Njem is a custom by which a married woman takes a "lover" who acquires the right of sexual access to her through the payment of a goat. The lover also accepts obligations to perform economic services for his "mistress" and to bring her gifts from time to time. A description and analysis of this custom is given in chapter 10.

The practice of sending prenubile girls to Buji and Jerawa (Pyomo) lands was and probably still is to some small extent of economic importance to some Du families. There are two reasons why a kin group would send a girl to Pyomo. The first is considered the most powerful and most honorable one, and that was simply to obtain food for the members of one's family. This is the reason given in three out of four cases. In addition to a storeroom of grain (twenty-four bags), all transactions were accompanied by much gift giving of beer and meat. Indeed, part of the often nonverbal but clearly understood contract was that the Pyomo family that received the child must once each year until her marriage supply the Birom donor family with a freshly killed goat and other goods (such as beniseed and salt) according to their circumstances.

The second reason, more common in the precolonial period, was to obtain sufficient goods to comprise bridewealth for a man or his son. In these cases, the arrangement meant that there was no other way of acquiring bridewealth and/or there were many daughters, none of whom were of marriageable age. Under the precolonial situation, if a man had large debts and faced desperate circumstances, he might pledge or give a young daughter in marriage in exchange for payment of his debts, or he might give her to his creditor to erase the debt. Generally, the girls grew up and were married into the villages of their recipients. The practice was widely accepted, so much so that a number of positive sentiments arose about it, such as the belief that Birom girls are more fertile than Jerawa women or that they are easier to get along with or were more tractable (Gunn 1953). These sentiments and peripheral beliefs should not obscure the fact that these were exchange transactions for material goods that were necessary for the survival of the group.

Girls in these cases might be transferred from Du village at the age of seven to ten years, before they were sexually mature and eligible for marriage. While the treatment of these young girls varied greatly, it is widely held by some people that they will be forced to work as servants and to do the more unpleasant household tasks. Although a girl may have contact with her natal home from time to time, neither her father nor her brothers would be allowed to interfere, as they have transferred these rights to another kin group. If a girl is badly treated and manages to escape and find her way home, as apparently some do, her kinsmen will not attempt to compel her to return as they would in a proper marriage, nor would they endeavor to return the goods received for her. These are not considered bridewealth. How common it was that girls returned home under such circumstances will probably never be known. In some cases, the Pyomo groups voluntarily returned girls for various reasons. In one case, the Birom youth to whom the girl had been betrothed before her family fell on hard times was able to collect substantial wealth and go and retrieve her before she became mature.

Once a Pyomo transaction has been made, the Birom family from which the girl comes has no further moral or legal obligation to the Pyomo family, nor does it have further rights in the girl. The Pyomo family still owes economic obligations to the Birom family in that it must provide them with meat each year until the girl is married. They are also morally bound to treat the girl well and to allow her to return for a visit from time to time with her family. There is wide variation in actual practice, however. In some cases, contact between the two families is maintained so that friendship develops. When the girl is married, she and her children may return occasionally to Du village for visits. Some of the Pyomo settlers in Du are offspring of girls married at Pyomo many generations ago. However, in other cases, contact between the two families in Du and Pyomo eventually ceases, and after a generation or so, no one in the Du family will have any knowledge of the girl, to whom she was married, or the children she may have borne. The Birom, especially the women, see this situation of complete loss of contact with their loved ones as a sad and tragic one: This is why they will go to great lengths to conceal a girl who has run away. There is increasing opposition to these exchanges, particularly among Christians, and the British colonial government and the postcolonial administration have proclaimed this custom a form of slavery, which is illegal.

In neither of these transactions, Njem or Pyomo, is there a domestic unit created by the association between male and female partners. And there is no sharing of economic tasks in the same manner as in a regular marriage. More important, formal kinship ties are not established that can be perpetuated by and through the offspring of their union. These are fundamental differences between these exchange transactions and that of marriage.

The exchange concept in true marriage posits at once notions of both a simple exchange, value for value, and an elaborate process of interchange of gifts and services between the kin groups concerned. It is by means of this second feature, accompanied by extensive social interaction, that the economic elements in marriage are articulated with newly created social relationships. It is indeed the creation of new relationships and the establishment of new sets of rights and obligations between kin groups that constitute the focus of marriage. As Gluckman (1965b) noted, "Some form of transfer of property in simple societies is essential to create any rights and obligations" (183).

Traditional brideprice was one horse and six goats; today, this is always translated into money; £10 for the horse and £1 each for the goats or a minimum total of £16. The horse, as we will see, is essential to the transaction; it is not merely incidental that the Birom word for horse, *dwa*, is also the word for brideprice. But few men actually acquire brides on the payment of brideprice alone. When a young man is betrothed to a girl, both in precolonial times and today, the occasion calls for the brewing of a large amount of beer to entertain the prospective bride's family. From then on, the youth is expected to farm for his future father-in-law every year. In precolonial times, a man might be engaged for ten or more years, more normally five to seven, but young men today prefer to shorten this period to two or three years. In addition, at the time of marriage, the groom must pay *goro* (bridle money, to "lead the horse home") to the bride's father, normally ranging from £3 to £5. There are many additional gifts expected by both the bride-to-be and her parents, such as blankets for her mother and father and tobacco for the older people. Calabashes, oil, pomade, cloth, scarves, and jewelry are presented by young men, depending on their social positions, to the various relatives of the bride and friends who act as intermediaries.

The gifts and services are important to the transaction because they help establish good relationships with the future in-laws. But the critical payment that legalizes the marriage is the *dwa*, the bridewealth itself. This is considered a payment, not a gift, and when rendered in full it transfers to the groom rights to the girl's sexuality, rights to her economic labor and to her services within the domestic unit (in uxorem), and legal and moral rights to be pater (and genitor) to any children she may bear (in genetricem).[3]

Rights in genetricem are determined by the specific payment of the horse or today its monetary equivalent. It is a fundamental rule of customary law that the pater (social father) of a child is the man whose kin group has provided the full bridewealth. As among the Nuer, "the pater is the husband to the mother. His legal fatherhood is defined by his status to the mother of the children and not by his physiological functions" (Evans-Pritchard 1945, 18). A man could obtain rights in uxorem (sexual and domestic rights) over a woman by a special payment to her father that usually consisted of four or five goats along with gifts of beer, beniseed, salt, and oil. A man could then take the woman to his own residence and establish a domestic unit. The resulting arrangement was not considered a true marriage, although such a domestic unit functioned in much the same manner as other households. The major difference was that the "husband" could not be pater to any of the children born of the union. Such children belonged to the agnatic kin group in which their mother was born and would eventually be claimed by her father or brothers. However, a special payment could be made by the genitor and a special ritual performed that would establish paternity. The positions of individuals in such situations are the same as in the "simple natural family" of the Nuer (Evans-Pritchard 1945). Today, such unions are rarely found; any payment made by a man that has the purpose of establishing rights in uxorem is interpreted by all parties concerned as the down payment or initial payment of a full brideprice. If a man dies before completing the payment, his kin group must discharge the obligation if it wishes to keep children born of the union.

The right of paternity also includes the right to repudiate a child born to the wife. In the case of Honghei cited in the final section of this chapter, the legal husband refused to perform the naming ceremony for her child (which generally takes place a month after the birth of a child) and thus refused it paternity. Some informants said that a child in this situation would have no kin group (*lo*) and that in the past it might have been killed or that, if the mother were kind, she could give it to her own natal kin group. However, the Birom greatly desire children, so it is very rare for a man to repudiate a child born to his wife regardless of its genitor. Jural rights to any child born to a woman properly married ultimately reside in the kin group of her husband. Thus, if a man dies and his widow is not subsequently given in marriage to a man of another kin group, all children born to her after her husband's death belong to his kin group, and the dead husband is legally their pater (see Bohannan 1963; Evans-Pritchard 1945; Fallers 1957). Thus, the Birom have the true levirate but do not have ghost marriage.

In brief, the Birom have specific ideas as to what values in women are exchangeable under certain stated conditions. In the Njem custom, it is the sexuality of the married woman, at least initially, that is exchanged, but the ramifications of this relationship can be much more complex (see chapter 10). In the Pyomo transactions, the girl's labor, her future sexuality, and rights both in uxorem and in genetricem are transferred. Proper marriage within the Birom community transfers all rights in uxorem and in genetricem to a man and his kin group. However, a girl never loses membership in her natal *lo* (old women often say they are "always girls" of their father's kin group). A woman's natal kin group always retains what we might call "residual rights" in her person, a fact that may well be best symbolized by the mother's–brother/sister's–son relationship—the avunculate (compare Goody 1959)—as well as by the perpetual concern that a woman's natal kin group has for her welfare.

The cost of getting a bride today is high. Most men spend well over £25 in the process of getting married. With estimated earnings for the average young man of about £1 per week, bridewealth and gifts represented in 1960 half a year's income. But women are of great value, and the Birom themselves recognize this partly in the frequent analogies made between horses and women. Such analogies also reflect the ways in which a man's deepest emotions were vested in women and horses in the traditional culture. Men say that women are, like horses, fickle and without good common sense. They not know what they want or in which direction to go; they are temperamentally alike and equally difficult to please. Women and horses are expensive to keep; men must work hard to feed them. Women and horses give pleasure to a man, but they also tire a man. Still, a man's sense of virility focuses on the possession of women and horses. The sexual associations are expressed in metaphors that include not only the use of the term *dwa* for both horse and bridewealth but also a special payment, the bridle, given to the bride's father at the end of a marriage ceremony "to lead the horse home." Sexual intercourse is referred to as "riding the horse," and it is taboo to have intercourse in the same hut where the bridle and harness are stored. There are other taboos and mystical associations between the two.

Today, the large amount of money necessary for marriage and the difficulties acquiring it are expressed in much haggling over the monetary value of the woman at the time of marriage arrangements and particularly at the time of divorce. Despite the official standard brideprice, there are frequent and often bitter disputes over the actual amounts of additional prestations that must exchange hands. Fathers always attempt to increase the *goro* and *hono* money, demanding a great deal more if the girl has gone to school for several years. Divorce occasions even greater quarreling; the majority of such disputes center on the amount of money to be repaid and not the grounds for divorce. Normally, by the time a case reaches the district court, if there is bride wealth money available, the divorce will be granted. One such court case described next clearly illustrates the significance to the Birom of the exchange value of women.

Da Jang, the headman of the kin group, had betrothed a daughter (Bang) of his brother Jik Pam to one Nyam Lo Zeng. On Bang's maturity, Da Jang received an amount of money, estimated to be about £16, from Nyam. However, as the case revealed later, it was not clear to whom the money went, what it represented, or precisely how much changed hands. Jik Pam claimed later that it was £14, representing the *dwa* and part of the *hono* but not the *goro*. He subsequently changed his mind and admitted that he and Jang received £5 initial payment and £12 somewhat later from Nyam. This represented, according to Nyam, £16 for the *dwa* and £1 for the collar (*goro*, or bridle). In the meantime, Bang resisted marrying Nyam, a man of about forty-five, and took up with an Igbo man, Akawo. In the summer of 1960, Akawo paid £10 to Jang that he assumed represented payment for the transference of the girl to him. Jang and his kinsmen, in the meantime, consumed all the payments.

By the time the case was brought to court, what actually transpired throughout these negotiations was difficult to ascertain. It seems that Jang did indeed take Bang to Nyam prior to receiving money from Akawo. But after five days in Nyam's house, Akawo came and took her. Nyam tried to get the girl or his money returned, and as a result the case came to court. During the first two sessions in court, after much haggling, it was determined that Jang should repay Nyam his *dwa*. But Jang did not have the money and insisted that Akawo should pay £16 to Nyam because Jang himself had not taken her from Nyam.

In a later session in court, the chief asked Jang to return Nyam's "dowry," and Jang replied that Akawo owed him £5 for the goats that Akawo had not given him. At this session, Akawo was in the court for the first time, and he angrily replied that Jang had deceived him; he had paid £10 for the girl and refused to pay more. If such were the case, Jang could have his daughter back. Again, no final decision was taken, but it was decided that Akamo should bring the girl the following week in order to complete the case.

In the next session, Jang was ill and did not appear. However, after another long discussion about the amounts of money to be paid and queries about who was unjustly treated, the elders of the court admonished Akawo that if he wanted to keep the girl, he should arrange with Jang to pay *hono* and *goro*, and if he did not want her, the court would make other arrangements. During the long discussion, the chief of Shen village turned to the girl and asked her if she loved Akawo or Nyam, and she replied, "Akawo."

Before the final session, Akawo wrote a letter to the Dagwom Du (district chief) to say that he would try to obtain the rest of the money, £11 for *hono* and *goro*, if the court would allow him two months. At the final session, Jik Pam indicated his relief that the girl was to be kept and added that Akawo should pay the money to the former husband, Nyam, and that instead of £11 he should pay £16. Nyam was insisting that the full amount be returned to him, but Jang had continuously maintained that 1) he did not have the money and that 2) as Nyam had had the girl and "known" her and he, Jang, was not responsible for her being with an Igbo man, he should not have to repay all the £16. This issue of the case was not settled, and Akawo was given three weeks to raise the money that he owed.

Although the case in its many facts did not come to court again during the remainder of the time that I was in the village, it is obvious that it is not settled. Like many disputes, it may very well turn into a long-drawn-out affair with hard feelings and bitterness on all sides. But the major point seems clear: Women have a value, measurable today in terms of money. The question is, What is the value of the girl, Bang, to each of the men who could claim some rights over her? Nyam wanted her as a second wife. She was the daughter of an agnatic kin group that had not prospered in recent decades. Nyam had originally offered Jik Pam £9 for her, and her real father, a complacent person, was willing to accept the offer. But Jang, the Da Lo, held out for the full bridewealth, considering that at the time of the offer she was prenubile and a virgin. In later years, Bang showed some fickleness and got the reputation of being somewhat difficult. She went off to work in the mines for a few weeks, and it was thought that she had become "spoiled" by her widened experience. In any case, in the confusion of events that followed her marriage, Jang must have felt relieved to get rid of her to an Ibo man for £10. That he had already consumed the bridewealth from Nyam did not bother him. Although legally and morally he was obliged to repay Nyam, he did not have the money and was not likely to obtain that much. Nyam had to suffer the consequences, with Jang claiming only with a shrug of shoulders that Nyam was a "rich" man who had worked in the mines a long time. In other words, he could afford it. Jang and Jik Pam could feel that they got perhaps more than Bang's full value out of these transactions.

Akawo, on the other hand, who had apparently taken up with the girl in a clandestine affair, was willing to pay, but not that much. He well knew that bridewealth and associated payments was commonly over the £16 limit, but he was not willing to pay £10 plus another £16 to her first husband and *goro* and *hono* to her fathers as well. It may be that he loves the girl and with a little pressure will pay more cash. His altering his first decision and agreeing to pay additional *goro* and *hono* was evidence of this. But Birom girls who take up with foreigners such as he are thought throughout the plateau to be somewhat "loose." Should he risk paying a large sum for her and then have her abscond with someone else?

The tenor and mood of all the court transactions, whether the question is over bridewealth, divorce, and so forth, is one in which the monetary consideration with regard to the woman is dominant. Women sometimes bring a suit for divorce, only to be told that they must go back to their husbands because there are no means of making restitution. In such cases, women will often find their own potential husbands who will pay the bridewealth. Many arguments center on how much repayment of bridewealth should be made when there are children. Although there is an established general standard of £11 with one child and £9 with two or more, the variable factors are so many that I never saw the standard operate. There is always much bargaining and bitter haggling that is alleviated only in those cases where the woman can be remarried easily, that is, if there is another potential husband willing to take her and provide a brideprice. And, of course, women have learned to manipulate men in bargaining for their rights.

The difficulties attending this exchange system are a strong deterrent to breaking up marriages and thus the domestic unit. It is not easy for a man to collect enough money to refund the brideprice of his daughter or sister. His close agnatic kinsmen, who are responsible for helping him, are often reluctant to do so. Though today the men of a *lo* group will join together in a dispute with a husband of one of their women, they will not usually desire to see the marriage broken. I recorded several cases of quarrels of this sort in which the agnatic kinsmen of a woman retreated in an argument with her husband when the latter threatened to sue for the return of bridewealth. There were no instances to my knowledge in which a kin group collected among themselves the money to refund a girl's bride-price.

There is also a moral tenet that operates against a woman's leaving her conjugal home and returning to live in her natal compound. The Birom believe that it is not proper for a sexually mature girl, especially one who has been married, to sleep in the same compound with an unmarried brother who is also past puberty. Such a situation is even more heinous if neither of their parents is living. In one instance that I knew of, a brother left his compound after a heated argument with his sister who had returned home and flatly refused to go back to her husband. The brother slept in the fields the first night and later went to the home of an Igbo acquaintance in a nearby mining camp. The women of his compound, along with neighborhood women and various relatives, finally used pressure through much talk about her shameful behavior to prompt his sister to return to her husband's house.

A final point about the high exchange value of women as brides is the effect that it had traditionally as a stimulant to economic productivity (Kaberry 1952). Predatory activities such as raiding were once significant features in the economies of many societies, especially those that depend on the replacement of or increase in the number of animals (Sweet 1965a, 1965b). In precolonial times, it was primarily through raiding activities off the plateau and in other villages that more horses were acquired by the Birom, although some breeding may have been done. Older informants remembered very well when young men used to take part in raiding parties. Only the strongest and bravest men did so. If they were successful, the village prospered, many young men were able to get married, and their wives were fertile. Thus, the supply of horses, through their function as marriage payments, was related to the general prosperity and survival of the village people.

Young men began to seek jobs during the latter decades of the colonial period in order to get enough money to marry. This appears to be a major motivation for young men today, particularly those who are not in school and do not expect to gain a lifelong skill. In this connection, it is interesting to note the correspondence in time between the decline and disappearance of horses in the village and the entry of Birom men into the labor force. Both occurred chiefly during the decades of the late 1920s and early 1940s, while at the same time bridewealth was legally transformed into cash. Many older men explained to me that they took jobs specifically to raise bridewealth money, after which most of them went back to farming only or to farming and casual labor in the mines.

The Gender Division of Labor

In the introductory section to this chapter, I emphasized the complementary nature of gender roles. A strict division of labor by sex within the domestic situation has an important effect on marriage, as has been frequently shown for other preindustrial peoples (Colson 1958; Kaberry 1952; Richards 1939). Here and in the next chapter, I will explore the significance of this custom and point out its relationship to other features of the domestic unit, particularly to the social relationships within it.

The traditional specialized activities of men and women have caused them to be highly dependent on each other within the domestic situation. Yet one consequence of the conditions of their work situation is a high degree of separation of men and women both physically and socially. Important to the relationship is the fact that strict proscriptions on one sex against invading the province of the other are expressed in taboos that carry heavy supernatural sanctions. For example, women are forbidden to touch or have any association with the hunting weapons of men, and if they should hear the playing of the sacred instruments (*Jut*) of hunting ceremonies, they must run and hide. A man, on the other hand, may not cook for himself (except roasting yams on ritual occasions, a custom that emphasizes and thus strengthens the separateness and the interdependence of sex roles), and he must not ordinarily handle the utensils of women for fear of the ridicule and displeasure of dead ancestors. He may not even enter the compound of a woman who is cooking beer if he has recently had sexual intercourse.

The separate spheres of women and men are so ritualized and rigid that there have developed certain linguistic differences. Men frequently say that they do not understand women's language, and indeed there are many different terms for the same objects as well as a vocabulary and pronunciation that can be considered peculiarly feminine. In contradistinction, women always know what is going on in the world of men, even in some cases involving ritual secrets that are theoretically prohibited to them.

The observably different economic tasks of women and men are many. The men lay out the compounds and build the houses. They thatch the roofs and make all repairs to existing structures. They make twine and weave baskets, mats, and rain garments (*gobwa*). Some men smelt iron and make tools, implements, and pipes. Older boys and men cut grass and take care of any animals of the household and hunt wild game. Women prepare the food and keep the household clean. They must obtain the water for cooking and washing, gather fuel and make fires, gather wild vegetables, feed and tend to the children, make and mend pots, and carry goods.

Farming activities are divided according to the type of farm and the heaviness of the work. Men always hoe the ground and plant all the grain crops. Men build the larger yam ridges, and of the five main types of yam, the most important ones (*bikit riang* and *bikit din*) are usually planted by men with the reasoning that there is a technique to it that women cannot know. Women and girls do all the weeding in garden farms and the digging of yams at harvest. Women plant and grow virtually all the secondary vegetable crops, particularly those that are interplanted, such as beans, okra, and cowpeas. Women plant beniseed (*diara*) and do the transplanting of millet, while men always prepare the seed beds and nursery beds. Harvesting of yams and grain crops can be done by both men and women, with women usually transporting the crops except for some types of *acha* that men bring from the bush fields.

Children are conditioned at a very early age to follow the separate patterns. Little boys of two, three, or four years old who try to imitate women and girls are harshly rebuffed by the women. Although children are very rarely struck, I once saw a little boy who was trying to carry a pan on his head like his sisters smacked soundly by his mother after she repeatedly told him that head pans were only for girls. On another occasion, a four-year-old lad was severely chastised for stubbornly insisting on trying to pound guinea corn with a mortar and pestle. Through these strong sanctions, intense emotional significance is welded to beliefs about the duties of men as distinctive from women. Young boys soon learn that specific household chores are forbidden to them, and they do very little work until they are old enough to farm. Likewise, girls from toddler age on are prepared in both the techniques and the psychology of women's roles.

Now there is an inherent discrepancy in these patterns of work and the sentiments associated with them that serves as an underlying element in those cases of disruption of the domestic unit under modern conditions. At the outset, the sexual division of labor is a division of unequals, and the traditional ritualization of roles supports and maintains this inequality. No man may prepare his own food and thus is always dependent on some woman. But the reverse is not true, as we will see, despite the predominantly traditional Birom value that holds that a woman is always dependent on some man. The balance thus appears to the advantage of women. From the point of view of men in Birom society, this dependence poses a dilemma. The importance of this point was revealed to me in an interview with a sixty-eight-year-old man, Dung Gyang. While relating the story of his life to me, he became quite agitated at one point. He was remembering with vivid detail the circumstances surrounding the death of his mother. At the time, he was in his teens, one of many sons of a father who had five wives. Dung's own mother had borne five children of which Dung was the eldest. In his own words,

> When my mother died, I was already farming but I ran away because no one would feed me. When my father went to the bush, he usually stayed two or three days and that was the time when we would be left alone and not fed. When I went to the other wives of my father for food, they would only beat me. So, I took the baby son of my mother who was in his second year and ran to my Lo Gwasa [mother's agnatic kin group]. Before, I took Chundung to her Lo Gwei, to the house where one of my mother's sisters was married. Combo who was next to me stayed with the third wife of my father because she [Combo] took care of her small children, so they fed her. The other one died. I do not know why the other wives did not feed us. Our women are like that sometimes.
>
> When my father looked around and did not see me, he asked his wives where I was and started to fight with them. Then he came and took Pwajok and me back. When I came back, my father arranged for an early marriage for me in order that we could get food.

In the definition and characterization of the domestic unit, I stressed the fact that women are the core of such units. Dung's story conveys the full significance of this fact. The most essential function of the domestic unit is the provision and preparation of food, and the traditional division of labor allocates this function exclusively to women. Without a woman, no domestic unit can function and perpetuate itself from two standpoints: the provision of food and the reproduction of its members. Dung's story suggests another point about Birom domestic life. The awareness of this dependency on a woman to cook for men obtrudes itself at certain critical points or events. The death of a mother is a crucial point. Not only does it disrupt the functioning of the domestic unit in terms of its organized patterns of divided labor, but it also deprives those who depend on her for food of her vital services. Some means must be provided in the society for taking care of the dependents or mediating the effect of the rigidity of this dependency. Thus, in earlier times it was not an uncommon Birom custom to bury an unweaned infant with its mother if no other women volunteered to care for it. We note from Dung Gyang's statement his opinion that cowives and other women of the agnatic kin group will not usually care for orphaned youngsters. Most other Birom, both men and women, contradict this view. The Birom depend heavily on the ties of affection that exist with the female kin of the dead mother.

Older children usually are distributed among related women who would care for them. Girls are particularly useful because they help care for the young children of married relatives and frequently live in the households of married female kin for some portion of their girlhood. Later, of course, girls would be a source of bridewealth to their fathers. Boys commonly remain with their fathers, particularly if the latter has other wives. While cowives of the deceased woman are expected to feed the boys, some informants suggested that this often was not done. Such boys, however, could obtain food at the homestead of their mother's kin group, but their fathers always oppose this and in the past did everything possible to avoid driving their sons under the influence of their maternal kin. Therefore, Dung Gyang's father, being relatively wealthy, soon found a wife for his son as the only feasible option.

In the past, another alternative was to exchange the children of a deceased mother if they could not otherwise be cared for. A man would seek out among his own kinsmen those who were well off enough to rear his children, or he would send them to another, unrelated villager. With the accumulated wealth from these exchanges, he would invariably obtain another wife and thus reestablish his domestic unit. A man would still live and sleep in his own *lalla*, together with those of his children who remained with him. If he had no other wife or daughter old enough to cook, he would depend for his food on the gifts of kinswomen, particularly his own mother if she were alive, and on purchases of cooked food from other Birom. If he were farming, he would continue his activities, but he would take the grain to his mother or the wife of a brother to be cooked for him. In addition, at the funeral of his wife, relatives would have brought food, especially meat, and the supply would usually last for some time, provided there was a woman to prepare it for him. But he could not rely on these makeshift means indefinitely and would be expected to marry a wife as soon as possible. Today, however, a man has another option. If he has a few or no children, he might leave the village for work in one of the labor camps or in town at least temporarily. Small children could be left with their grandmothers, on either side, who would be given small amounts of cash and/or grain intermittently for their care. The death of a mother, then, is doubly tragic in terms of the loss to the child, for she is not only the fountain of love and comfort but also the immediate source of sustenance.

As an old man, Dung Gyang was well aware of another critical situation that is potentially disastrous for the Birom. We noted in an earlier chapter that when food is in short supply, old people are rarely or irregularly fed. One of the great fears of women and especially men is that they will not have children to feed them in their old age. This particularly applies to the lack of sons or to the failure of sons to marry, for the daughter-in-law is required by custom to cook for and feed her husband's elderly parents. Normally, when food is plentiful, she will have enough to go around. But when food is scarce, she will make sure that her children and her husband eat first, and whatever is left will be given to his parents. In lean years when food must be thinly spread, a wife and daughter-in-law may prefer to give extra food to her own parents or to her sisters and other close cognatic kin. Thus it is that daughters are frequently better insurance in one's old age than sons, particularly if they are not married too far away. One can depend to some extent on ties of close kinship and affection; however, there are limits to the generosity of daughters that depend in part on the personality and resources of the son-in-law, and this is somewhat more risky. It is important to have many persons to rely on for food in one's old age not only because of the scarcity of food but also because no single individual or category of persons is a good guarantee against going hungry for long periods.

The problem of nourishment in old age is not nearly as great for women as for men. Let us consider the situation within the domestic unit when a man and a woman become old. The man's chief tasks in the traditional division of labor (the heavy farming and hunting) terminate early. They decline naturally with his strength and agility and sometimes long before he dies. Outside of a few minor tasks, such as repairing the houses, helping with the gathering of thatching grass and tying it in bundles, weaving, or repairing occasional items for household use, an elderly man is economically useless, particularly in the production of food. There was a time when his wisdom and knowledge of the land was probably a valuable asset, but he can give very little practical advice in the modern world. Most old men today sit around the household occasionally playing with and watching toddlers but mostly waiting to die. Those who are still active enough to walk a short distance busy themselves at the courthouse during its sessions, listening to the cases and commenting on the nature of the values and morality of this new day. Because one of the basic Birom principles is respect for those who are senior to oneself, these old men are treated with a great deal of deference and politeness. It is only in the matter of sharing food that the traditional respect for the aged breaks down or at least is not fully expressed. Nor do old men expect to be fed at the expense of the young, although I have heard some old men complain that they are never fed at home and must go out to beg.

The age of retirement for men seems to vary with the individual. In my survey of male occupations, there were forty-seven men between the ages of forty-six and fifty-five and fifty men who were estimated to be fifty-six years of age and older. Within the younger category there were five who were doing no outside work and were no longer able to farm. Of these five, only one had no wife (he was a widower). In the older age-group, over fifty-five years of age, there were thirty-five men who were no longer farming or doing any other sort of work. Six made a meager living selling sylvan products, garden vegetables, cactus, and so forth, and nine were still farming. Of twelve widowers, one sold garden vegetables and other products and was being fed by his daughter-in-law, and another was still able to farm and produce his own food. He was being fed by his mistress in the Njem relationship. The rest were entirely dependent on kinsmen and women for food.

An older woman, on the other hand, unless she is ill and too feeble to move (in which case she would soon die anyway), can always feed herself; she can still maintain her active role as the central figure in the domestic unit. She can and usually does continue to grow small amounts of vegetables in her own domestic gardens and to cook meals both for herself and for those who are fed by her, unless, of course, she is fortunate enough to have daughters-in-law who do this for her. In such a case, the old woman is freed from most of the work and usually participates in the domestic economy of her own volition. On the other hand, if she lives alone and has no daughter-in-law available, she may not be considered blessed with good fortune, but she will still be able to handle her own needs. If she cannot grow enough yams, grain, and other vegetables to feed herself, she can always beg a little foodstuffs from relative, lovers, and friends.

Aside from their availability to continue their domestic contributions throughout old age, women long past child bearing are still useful for looking after young children, another role that they continue to perform throughout their lives, except in extreme illness. Grandmothers are always available to their grandchildren and have particularly close and affectionate relationships with them. I knew of one old woman who walked fifteen miles to help nurse a very sick grandchild who unfortunately died of pneumonia within a week after her arrival.

In many cases involving widows, however, the choice of the levirate ensures that they will not be obliged to bear the responsibilities of caring for themselves and their children alone. The levirate, while considered an important Birom custom, is but one option, as women have alternatives, some of which they usually prefer. This fact—the availability of several choices to a woman who has become a widow—suggests far more independence of action for women than Birom stated beliefs allow.

It seems, then, that the traditional division of labor, while serving satisfactorily the functions of the domestic unit through most if its existence, also harbors a conflict between the values and beliefs contained within it and the practicalities of its operation. It becomes a serious problem of social mechanics to deal with unproductive old men in a subsistence economy where food is frequently in short supply, where choices have to be made as to who gets what foods, and where individual adults who are nonproducers must be fed by those who can produce barely enough for themselves and their children. Concern about a man's welfare in the event of the death or incapacity of a wife is probably often expressed in preindustrial societies with fixed division of labor and subsistence economies. Thus, David Tait (1956) reported that a Konkomba wife once asked her husband when he was going to get his second wife. "What," she asked, "would happen to him if she fell ill (or died) before he did so?" (221). Polygyny would seem to provide some solution to the problem, and it may very well have developed partly as a product of such foresight. Elizabeth Colson (1958, 121) tells us that among the matrineal Tonga, women frequently abandon their husbands and go to live with their married children after they have passed the age of child bearing, leaving their husbands to care for themselves. Men anticipate this by striving to acquire a second wife before they are too old.

The underlying motivation for polygynous unions revealed in these instances also operated among the Birom. Men recognize and often express two reasons for their desire to contract plural marriages. One is that of gaining higher prestige and status via traditional avenues. In societies where there are no or few luxury goods and where the accumulation of wealth per se is meaningless because there are few forms of wealth for conspicuous consumption and no investment opportunities, one's personal standing and esteem revolve around other people. As I have already shown, Birom men competed and still compete with one another for wives, mistresses, and "horses." Two or more wives make it possible that a man may have larger numbers of children to survive, to enhance his kin group and following, and to found a *lo* in his name. In the precolonial era, half the children born to a woman died before they were three years old, and today there are many older women who have only one or two living adult children out of a total of eight or ten births. A man is best assured of posterity with polygynous marriages; a man without legitimate sons is a failure and becomes in time a social nonentity.

The second reason has a more pragmatic basis that relates to the de facto domestic dependence of men. Despite their verbal statements about the weakness, the incapacities, and the inferiority of women, Birom men are well aware that they must have some woman to feed them and give them personal care. Mothers perform these functions until their sons are married. Thereafter, it is the duty of a wife. In a monogamous situation, should a man's marriage be broken or interrupted by the absence of a wife, he and his children (if there are any) may be fed by other female kinsmen. Whether or not this can be sustained depends on the women. A man derives greater benefits if his own mother is still alive, is able-bodied, and resides (as would normally be the case) in his compound or close by.

Yet this is still a situation of hardship, as is the death of a wife. As a man gets older, his mother is likely to be dead, his brother's wives have no jural obligation toward him (though some women felt that they would be morally compelled to help out), and his daughters, if he had any, would be married away and caring for their own husbands. A second or younger wife is the best insurance against having to cope with this type of hardship and a better insurance in his old age that he will have someone to care for him.

There are, of course, other factors that either foster polygyny directly or provide the conditions under which polygyny is made possible and viewed as advantageous. We will see some of these later in this chapter. Although only 25 percent of married men in Du village had two or more wives in 1960, the actual number of men who have several wives throughout their lifetimes is much greater. Most of the men with plural wives marry their second and third wives many years after the first marriage, so a more accurate statement about the extent and nature of polygyny can be derived from a count of the marriages of older men. Late in 1960, I interviewed 156 men over approximately forty-five years of age. Eighty-one of these men had had only one wife, and some of these "wives" had come to them through the levirate. (A few of these men had had two or more wives but not, to my knowledge, simultaneously.)

The remaining seventy-five men had had true polygynous marriages, with two or more wives living in the compound simultaneously, although some of the wives had died at the time of the study. Both legal marriage with the bridewealth and leveratic marriages were included in the count of polygynous marriages. Furthermore, some older men with single wives (as well as some younger men not in this sample) undoubtedly will claim more wives through the levirate as older brothers die. This would increase the number of men, now constituting 48 percent of the men over forty-five years of age, who have had plural unions. My guess is that the increase would not be very great because many women now prefer to remain widows, to take lovers, or, if they are still young, to remarry. There is only moderate pressure brought to bear on widows to enter into leviratic unions, and much depends on the circumstances of the kin group and how well the widow has gotten along with her cowives and other wives within the group.

In this connection, it is of interest to note the small number of widowers compared with that of widows in the six inner wards of the village. There were twelve widowers out of a total of 312 men in the work history survey. One of these was a man of about fifty years of age, and the other eleven were all very old men with no chance of ever marrying again. By contrast, there were sixty-eight women out of 385 whose husbands had died and who had not subsequently remarried. Their distribution by age was: twenty-five widows over fifty-five years old, twenty-five widows between fifty-six and fifty-five, and one widow between thirty-six and forty-five.

These data indicate another important fact about Birom marriages, namely, the great discrepancy in age between marital partners. Traditionally, Birom men marry quite late, the usual age being about thirty for a man taking his first wife. Women, on the other hand, marry as young girls of about fifteen, and it is rare that a girl reaches her eighteenth birthday unmarried.

Max Gluckman pointed out that "with a probable sex ratio of 1:1, polygyny is only possible if men marry later than women and each woman marries more than one man during her life. This give a substantial total of more married years for all women than married years for men, and these extra years can be divided around among the men, so that some men have more than one wife at a time, the wives being passed on in levirate or new marriage."[4] Thus, wide differences in age between married partners makes possible polygynous unions; such a custom also makes available some young girls for the Pyomo transactions discussed earlier in this chapter and may counterbalance the attrition of young men who become "wanderers."

For the approximately 50 percent of Birom men who never have more than one wife at a time, the difference in age between them and their wives becomes a basic mechanism for mitigating the exigencies of old age. Women in all societies tend to outlive men, and a wife substantially younger than her husband has a greater chance of surviving through a husband's old age than a wife who is closer in chronological age.

During the colonial period, some Birom men began to acquiesce in the view that polygyny has a negative relationship to the prosperity of the domestic unit. Additional wives, they suggested, may add to a man's social prestige, but they are not necessarily an economic gain. More wives and children inevitably mean that a man must clear more land, particularly for grain, and have more garden farms for his wives for building more yam ridges. This is the work of a strong man. Wealthy men may also be considered to be strong men, and there is a high correlation between the notions of strength and virility and having many wives and wealth. However, many men today are considered wealthy because their land is good and there are many people in their kin group and not necessarily because they have many wives. One man who served as an informant on many occasions had four wives, but in terms of the food that they ate and the income of his household, he was a poor man. This suggests not only changing economic circumstances but also changing values with regard to the benefits of polygyny.

Women see the addition of a second wife in positive terms of her role as another worker. A first wife is always overwhelmed with work, particularly if she has small children. Thus, most women welcome the second wife, and jealousy is not a common characteristic of their relationship, especially after the first few years. Missionaries have not had much influence on this custom, although a few Christian wives seek to preserve monogamy for moral reasons.

This brings us to a final point in the analysis of some of the complex factors associated with marriage. It was the Birom custom to betroth their daughters while the girls are still quite young. Although in precolonial times girls were betrothed at three or four years of age, in recent times this practice has gradually changed so that today girls are normally about ten years old when they are betrothed. Because bride service is part of the contract by which a young man is bound to a girl's father and kin group, men with betrothed daughters derive important benefits from the annual labor and gifts required of their future sons-in-law. A young boy could hardly do the work of a man in the fields, so the betrothal of a daughter to a strong young man is highly desirable; indeed, it is virtually prescribed. As men always want their brides fairly soon after the girls reach puberty and are capable of childbearing, it is advantageous to a father to contract a betrothal for his daughter many years before the expected onset of menstruation. This practice contributes to widen the differences in the ages of men and women at marriage.

Most everyone is aware that not all men and women today observe the taboos or maintain the standards and values that once dictated their separate activities. Adjustment to the changing economic circumstances has meant a certain blurring of the activities of men and women. The few women whose menfolk are away working in the mines or in a Public Works Department camp or in the army now do many of the farming tasks that would have been done in the past by men. More important, the one occupation that would unquestionably be forever closed to women and that gave men status and power unrivaled by any other activity—hunting—has now virtually ceased. Eventually, mining gave a further blow to the separateness of sexual spheres. By hiring women, albeit at lower wages and not for identical jobs, the mines further helped reduce the traditional division between men and women. Mining laid the foundation for increasing the economic and social independence of women and brought into focus the dependency of men. By releasing the rigidity of sexual dichotomy in work patterns, mining has helped bring about a fundamental alteration in the character of the domestic unit.

The modifications that were taking place at the end of the colonial era are most manifest in the relationship between husbands and wives who were in their forties and younger. Older people were far more traditional and conservative in their behavior and seem to escape the penetrating effect of some of these external influences. In the next chapter, which deals with the personal and social relationships within the domestic unit, I will consider some of the problem areas of the relationship between husbands and wives in modern times.

The Creation of Kinship

For the Birom, there is no mechanism for building appropriate circles of kinsmen outside marriage: It may even be argued that the most important social purpose of marriage is to create kinship. Birom speak of specific types of kinsmen and kinship groups as if they were a necessary and normal part of life. An unmarried man, for example, is an anomaly, a "wanderer" who is socially incomplete. An unmarried woman is to be pitied, for she belongs to no one and is not even at home in her natal kin group. The latter is such a rare phenomenon that the majority of people had never known of a spinster, while several elderly informants knew of only one such case, that of a mad woman. There is indeed no term for "spinster" in the Birom language.

To speak of the "creation of kinship" through marriage is conceptually not a simple matter. Any approach to the study of Birom kinship must take into consideration that there are two arenas of kinship, each comprised of the same actors in their multiple roles. But actors and actions are viewed from dual perspectives (compare Fortes in his analyses of clanship [1945] and kinship [1949]). Every individual has personal kinsfolk, specific people who stand to him or her in certain defined relationships and with whom he or she has constant or frequent interaction. These people are normally cognates of both mother and father and later his or her own affines. They may be older, younger, or of the same generation or age level, and they include both males and females. The nature of the interaction, the closeness or distance of the varying degrees of relationship, the content of affection or lack of it, and the satisfaction to each individual of the relationship are dependent in large part on their personalities. From this perspective, personal kinship is open, largely unstructured, and idiosyncratic. But the behavior component—the actual kinship interaction—is almost always limited, physically, to kinsfolk of some degree of geographical propinquity.

The other arena consists of what may be called "structural kin"—culturally structured relationships between specific types of personal kin. These are the same people as personal kinsmen just described, but they are viewed from the standpoint of the institutionalized modes of interaction that are required within the culture. The relationships of persons at this conceptual level have theoretically nothing to do with individual personalities or proclivities. These are status positions whose roles are "fixed." Thus, everyone has a male parental figure or figures occupying a role that is factored about the qualities of group affiliation, jural responsibilities, superior (and often rigid) authority, guidance, support, and control. This role may be played by one's own father and/or by any man or men of the older generation of one's own descent group. It is this "structured kinship" that is the concern of this section, for this is the arena the Birom refer to when they describe the importance of kinship relationships for every individual. It is the creation of structured positions of kinship regardless of the content or quality of the personal interaction. Certain standardized, or normative, interaction patterns are posited, however, and the Birom anticipate that individuals will strive to attain the ideals.

Each Birom man normally has three basic fields of structured kin. They are 1) the members of his own agnatic kin group, which he calls *lo-hong* (literally, "my house"); 2) the kin group from which his mother comes, called *lo gwasa*; and 3) the affinal group created by his marriage, called *lo guna*. Women do not use this latter term for their affinal kin group, as they simply call the kin group into which they are married *lo-hong* or *lo rwas-hong* ("my husband's house") if there is a need to distinguish this kin group from their natal house, which is also called *lo-hong*. This points up an important difference between men and women. For the women, it is not usually necessary to make this distinction between natal home and affinal home with the exception of the comparatively rare events of funeral ceremonies, visiting back and forth, or possible hostilities between the two groups. These women, or course, have residence in both groups at different periods of their lives. It is for this reason (and others, as will be seen from the following discussion and in subsequent chapters) that these three structured kin groups have completely different meanings for men and women. There are other groups to which men and women can relate but not in a formal or structured manner, such as father's mother's kin group (*lo gwasa da mo*) or mother's mother's kin group (*lo gwasa ngwo*).

Structured kinship represents a closed system. Each unit is mutually exclusive; no man can be a member of more than one agnatic kin group, nor can he have more than one *lo gwasa* group. He can have more than one *lo guna*, but each is a separate group. The membership or genealogical limits of these groups are known (see the earlier discussion of *lo* structure), although there may be some confusion at that delicate period when *lo* groups are splitting. Within each circle of kinsmen there are prescribed limits on the type of behavior expected as well as standards of proper behavior that must be maintained. Each of these three groups of kinsfolk is important in its own separate sphere for certain types of relationships that are embodied in it. Father and son, brother and brother, are the crucial relationships in one's own house. *Gwasa* (mother's father, mother's brother) and the reciprocal *gwal* are the important link with the *lo gwasa*. And, as will be explored more intensively in chapter 10, the crucial relationship with *lo guna* is that of mother-in-law (*guna*) and son-in-law, who may variably be called *so* (son-in-law), *sa* (friend), or, more rarely, *hwei* (child).

Structured kinship is also institutionalized. It carries a body of values, principles, and mores, and structural alignments that persist from one generation to another, although the content of the relationships and/or the ideology may fluctuate from time to time. Moreover, the pattern of these interactions is set. Every man must have these structured kin because this is the nature of the universe. Animal species are "fathers" and "sons" to each other, and they have bi-*gwasa* (plural) and bi-*gwal*. This is particularly noticeable in the folktales, most of which concern personified animal forms. The mythical creature Gwasatong, however, is neither animal nor man but seems to represent a concatenation of the fears of most Birom men that the men of his wife's kinspeople will have more influence over and command more affection and loyalty from his son than will he, the father. Rituals, supernatural beings, and even villages are "fathers" and "sons" and bi-*gwal* and bi-*gwal* to one another. Men who have the important medicines (*bwal*) for the performance of the great ceremonies are positioned vis-à-vis one another as "father/son," or *gwasa/gwal*. The office of the Da Gwom Du (district chief) is *gwasa* to the offices of the chiefs of Zawang and Shen, and these men are called by the former his *gwal*, although there is no actual personal kinship between these men. Riyom is frequently called the "father" (*da*) to other Birom villages. Du is a "brother" to Forum, and so forth. And, as one old man once exasperatedly told me when I did not understand something, "Does not the moon have a *gwasa*?"—a statement that reveals the ultimate profundity of the relationship of structured kin.

The operation of these structural fields of kinship vis-à-vis one another constitutes a system. There is a patterned mode of interaction between the kin groups so that together they may be viewed as forming an organic whole. The constituent parts have a complementarity and interdependence such that the Birom deem all three fields necessary both for every individual and for the functioning of the society. A man or woman cannot have the full complement of kinsfolk, whether seen from a personal or structured point of view, without marriage. Although proper marriage does serve the function of legalizing children, legitimate status per se is not as important as having the full complement of kinspeople. But the two are inextricably intertwined. Social identity, a universal fact of life in human groups, depends on the recognition of the "jural" self within a systematized and ordered body of other jural identities.

The position of (and to some extent the attitudes toward) illegitimate children pinpoints this fact. Honghei, a girl who had left her husband and returned to her natal house with her two-year-old girl child, became pregnant again soon thereafter. This child, another girl, was not begotten by her legal husband, as he had acquired a new wife and moved to another village. I had often seen this second child being cared for as an infant and toddler by young girls in the area. When I inquired about her, one young man replied, "She has no *gwasa*." It was later explained that Honghei's legal husband refused to acknowledge the child in the special naming ceremony performed thirty days after birth. This meant that the girl belonged to her mother's father's kin group and would have no *lo gwasa* kin group. It was in this manner that Honghei's husband bestowed on this girl illegitimate status. Later, I came upon a young man, Apam, who I was told also had no *gwasa*. In light of the fact that all men of one's mother's kin group in the older generations are bi-*gwasa* and in the event of the death of such *gwasa* men of a related *lo* would perform the functions of this role, it seemed curious that this terminology should be used to designate illegitimate status. But there is an accuracy in this statement that is inescapable when one considers what happens, structurally, to illegitimate children.

Such a child is not treated differently from other children, at least overtly. It is fondled, loved, and fed from existing resources as are other children. The mother's father, in the event that the mother fails to marry, will take it as a child of his own. Thus, if one's mother's kin group replaces one's father's kin group, there is no separate mother's kin, that is, no *gwasa*. If the child is a boy, he will inherit property from his maternal grandfather or mother's brothers and in time will be identified as a true agnatic member of his mother's lineage. Future researchers would not be able to distinguish him genealogically from other agnatic kin. A girl would be married off as a "daughter" of her mother's kin group. Thus, there is no taint to the circumstances of illegitimacy. But there is a glaring and painful incompatibility in illegitimate status, and this is the fact that the illegal child's "father" (pater) is, under these circumstances, also his *gwasa*. These two structured kin positions are diametrically opposed to each other and so profoundly incompatible that there is no possible social mechanism for fusing them. One cannot be both "father" and *gwasa*, so the child who cannot acquire a legal status or legal paternal kin through the marriage of his mother is left without a *gwasa*; this is the real tragedy of illegitimacy.

This situation is so anomalous and so much of a threat to the social system that it is rare to find an illegitimate child among the Birom or one who remains illegitimate for long. The obvious simple device for terminating the condition is the marriage of the mother. Traditionally, a girl who became pregnant would be very quickly married. There was little stigma attached to such occurrences, and some men, although preferring a virgin for their first wife, were not reluctant to marry a girl who was pregnant by or had a child by some other man. I was told, however, that it was usually the child's father (genitor) who married the girl. In the case of Honghei, it is expected that she will soon marry again, and her new husband, by virtue of his proffer of bridewealth, will be enabled to claim legal paternity over her second child. Since both of her children are girls, the matter is not as pressing as it would be for boys. Much of the discussion concerning this second child centered on speculation as to whether the genitor would take Honghei as his second wife (he already has a Christian wife) or whether someone else would marry her.

What, then, was so unusual about the status of Apam was the fact that his real mother had died before she was married. In precontact times, Apam might have been put to death, sold, or traded elsewhere, but apparently the wife of his mother's brother had taken a liking to him, and as a result he grew up in his mother's natal house. It is of interest to note that it is only by innuendo that one learns of his status, for he has an attachment to an older man in another ward that might be called a fictional gwasa-gwal relationship, except that there is no recognized social device for bringing this about. This man, whom Apam calls gwasa, is a "vosun," a diviner and healer, who has learned his skills from a distant relative on his mother's side. He has no wife although it was said that he had once had one, and he lives in the compound of a "brother." There is no relationship between his kin group and that of Apam. It is likely that many people in the village do not know of Apam's status or that his Vosun friend is not his real *gwasa*. The situation directs attention to the indispensability of the structured role of *gwasa*.

The use of cash for bridewealth has become the catalyst for a very important social revolution, namely, the transference of the authority and power to establish marriages from the older to the younger generations. A man need no longer depend on his father, father's brothers, or mother's brothers for a bridewealth. Nearly all younger men are able to obtain the required amounts through the selling of their labor or some small-scale entrepreneurial activity, and it is becoming a common practice for fathers, in their search for husbands for their daughters, to consider a man with a steady job in far more favorable light than one who is merely a casual laborer or completely unemployed. Young men now seek their own brides and consult the older men and women about their choice only out of respect or in order to stay outside the boundaries of incest prohibitions.

This brings us back to the essential point of this section. Marriage creates kinship. All marriages establish affinity, and this is a statement that is universal, but some Birom marriages can and do take relationships that were once consanguine and based on agnation and transform them into relationships of affinity.

At all times, the nature of the marital relationship must be seen within the total context of the kinship system. Marriage is the foundation for the emergence of new sets of structured kin, and in many ways the stability and regularization of kinship behavior are maintained by the stability of marriage. No one single factor accounts for the stability of Birom marriages after allowances are made for the early years of adjustment during which divorce might occur. The several features discussed thus far tend to promote both domestic and jural stability.

Men rarely initiate action for a divorce, which ultimately means that both the jural and the domestic stability of marriage depend heavily on women. Since the economy rests on the maintenance of stable domestic units, it is clear that the more stable the marriage (the less cause a woman might have for leaving the husband), the more stable will be the domestic unit. Consequently, the Birom have developed extremely important incentives for a woman to stay in a marriage. As a negative sanction, there is the fact that generally no alternative residence in her natal kin group is available to a woman, that is, no role for the unmarried sister (compare E. Goody 1962). So a woman virtually always remains in a husband's household during widowhood and for the rest of her life. More important, a young widow will choose to remain in her husband's home if he is the pater of her children in order to protect her sons' rights to inheritance. The Birom do not have a "house property complex," and thus there is no institutional means of ensuring the inheritance of rights to farms for a woman's sons. Competition between brothers within the *lo* for the property of their fathers works to the disadvantage of a son whose own father is dead and who has no mother in residence to help preserve his rights. A mother's presence means that continued use of some farms will be ensured for her son(s).

Perhaps the most important factor is that a married woman is permitted a wide latitude for alternative relationships that provide her personal, social, and sexual satisfaction outside the bounds of marriage. Moreover, these relationships, or some of them, can be manipulated by her to her own advantage and to the advantage of the domestic unit of which she is the center. The existence of these options, not only in terms of social relationships but also in terms of a woman's command over and control of material goods (including especially food), provides the context for critical areas of decision making. These are available only to women, again underscoring the fundamental differences between the traditional roles of men and women. We take a closer look at this in the next chapters.

Attitudes toward Marriage

Before her marriage, the Birom bride-to-be is a girl (*hwong*) of her father's house. She maintains her membership by birth in her father's kin group throughout her life and is always referred to in this context as a "girl" of the paternal *lo* group. After her marriage, she is a wife (*hwa*) of her husband's agnatic kin group. (The Birom term for woman and wife are the same, and no distinction is ever made conceptually between the two, as the roles are not separated in Birom thinking.

Every girl grows up to be a woman and a wife.) As an unmarried girl, she is expected to be happy and fun-loving. She plays, sings, and dances with the other children at nightfall. During the day, she wanders the roads and footpaths of nearby areas with her playmates and is free to come and go with few restrictions. Although a girl is carefully instructed in the tasks of womanhood, she is expected to do only a minimum of work. Mothers frequently shoo daughters of tender age away from the domestic hearth during the day, admonishing them to go play (*sa jogo*) "while there is still time" or "while you are still a girl." Although she is under the nominal authority of some male or males throughout her life, a girl is unencumbered for the first twelve or thirteen years of her life. She is expected to obey her elders and generally to behave with deference toward her fathers and older brothers. In fact, however, men exercise very little control over daughters, whose instruction and directions are the province of their mothers and grandmothers.

After her marriage, a woman must work hard and accept confinement and a subservient position in her husband's house. She is expected to remain in or near the compound to attend her numerous duties. Because of childbirth, women have a common bond of suffering, but the reason seems not to lie so much in the pain or discomfort of bearing a child as in their common experience of losing their little ones. Late in my stay in Du village, I conducted a survey of marriages and childbirth among several wards of the village. The common reaction to my questions about pregnancy, childbirth, age at death, and so forth was sadness. Women told me that the memory was making them suffer in a manner in which they thought only women could suffer. Many women wept, in some cases turning to one another's arms for comfort.

It is little wonder then that girls look forward to marriage with ambivalence. It is the natural thing, part of the ongoing social order that marriage occurs if one lives to grow up, and every Birom girl, unless she is badly deformed (in which case she might have been killed at birth in the past), is married. But the time of marriage is considered one of sadness and great anticipation. Girls reluctantly accept the fact that once the initial steps have been taken, marriage ensues. They also accept and like the gifts that come to them from the groom-to-be. The engagement period can often be very pleasant as the future husband may make attempts to attract the girl to him. Although sexual license is prohibited by custom, an engaged girl can use her wiles to elicit many services and material gifts from her young man. Today, some girls expect their partners to take them to Jos, to the markets, and to local festive occasions, such as the dances, parties, and ceremonies held by church groups. Still, girls are expected to engage in the traditional ritual of resisting marriage and attempting to run away at the time of their wedding.

The customs surrounding the actual marriage ceremonies are indicative of the ambivalent feelings associated with marriage. A girl does not want to leave the security and familiarity of her natal home to go to a strange compound where she will have an inferior status. Thus, custom dictates a fairly long period of marriage ceremonies in which traditional practices allow an easing of the abruptness of the transfer of the girl from one house to another. When the elders fix a day for the wedding, a number of visits back and forth between the two houses, timed at specific intervals, are initiated. The girl is taken by the male relatives of the groom on an appointed night in a fictitious act of "capturing" the bride. The girl cries, and there is a "battle" between the friends and relatives of the groom and those of the bride, who attempt to prevent her capture. The bride spends a few days at the groom's house, usually five, and returns to her natal house. The groom comes the next night literally to bribe his father-in-law with a chicken to relinquish the girl. He will not get her again for two more nights, at which time the bride is escorted to the house of the groom by her relatives. After some intervening rituals during the next three days, the bride will again return to her natal home to sleep alone one night, and early the next evening she will be brought back to her husband's house by young unmarried girls who before their departure share her last meal in her father's house. From this point on, she enters fully into her married life.

While girls have some negative feelings about marriage, young men look on marriage with a more positive attitude. Every young man wants and looks forward to marriage, to having a wife and begetting children. It also means a certain amount of freedom from the authority of his father. He will have his own land-holdings within the kin group's estate, and eventually he will be master of his own domestic unit. But while young men want to get married, there are pressures from the social milieu that resist and prevent early marriages. There is the problem of accumulating the necessary bridewealth and gifts. In addition, some men do not like their sons to marry early because this ultimately prevents them from helping their fathers with their farming. Finally, the marriage of a son also frequently conflicted, in the past, with a father's desire to acquire more wives for himself. He might feel that the bridewealth allocated for the son could be better used to ensure himself a young new wife who, in fact, would be of better service to him in his old age than a son. Several old men told me that in earlier times some fathers made little effort to provide for the marriage of a son, and frequently only one or two of several sons would obtain the bridewealth from their fathers. All other sons either raided other villages for horses or remained bachelors and wanderers. Much depended on the wealth of the kin group.

Thus it was (and still is to a certain extent) with these values and attitudes that young girls and men entered into a marital contract and established domestic units. In the next chapter, I analyze the interpersonal relationships that come into play in the marriage of two young people.

Notes

1. Readers should refer to some of the more important early literature on the topic of marriage, especially Barnes (1959), Cohen (1961), Colson (1958), Evans-Pritchard (1951), Fallers (1957), Gluckman (1950, 1953, 1963), E. Goody (1962), Leach (1959), and Schneider (1953).

2. This, of course, is not an assessment of rate of divorce, as some of the younger women will undoubtedly be divorced in the future, something that is not true for older women.

3. Malinowski (1927, 1930) was among the first to recognize and articulate what he called the "principle of legitimacy." See also a classic paper by Gough (1959), in which she discusses the function of legitimizing children as the basis for a definition of marriage.

4. Personal communication from Gluckman.

Internal Relationships within the Domestic Unit

9

THE FUNCTIONING, the composition, the mode of operation, and the whole complexion of the domestic unit are affected by the nature of the social and personal relationships of the individuals of which it is composed. In addition to its minimal member—the focal woman maintaining her own hearth—most domestic units will have at least one male adult and a number of minor or unmarried children. In a large number of cases, there may also be another adult female. These persons will be related to the focal woman in a variety of ways, and they are all bound together essentially because she feeds them, although ties of love and affection also exist. In this chapter, I attempt to deal primarily with the most crucial dyadic relationships—husband/wife and daughter-in-law/mother-in-law—that exist at some stage in the development of virtually every domestic unit. I also analyze other relationships, such as daughter-in-law/father-in-law, parent/child, cowives, wife/husband's siblings, and so forth, involving cross-generational, cross-sex, and affinal interaction. But I consider these to be of secondary significance in the household for reasons that are revealed in the text.

The Life Cycle of a Marriage: Husband and Wife

In all human societies, a good wife is a valuable and highly desired asset to a man. But what constitutes a "good wife" or, for that matter, a "good husband" may certainly differ from one society to another, although I suspect there are common elements associated with what are thought to be the different functions of spouses. The basic Birom ideal is essentially that a husband is always dominant and a wife always submissive to him. All other factors and all types of nonmarital behavior are evaluated in terms of this ideal. A wife obeys her husband and looks after his needs first of all. A good wife is pleasant and cheerful to her husband, to his kinsmen, and to his friends. A good wife does not complain, nor does she carry out actions or effect a demeanor that are antagonistic to her husband. A good wife, above all, works hard and is never remiss in her duties. And a good wife is faithful and chaste in the ideals of Birom womanhood.

A good husband, on the other hand, is one who looks after his wife, providing her with enough food and an adequate dwelling. He labors hard in the fields to supply food for his wife and children and does not waste the products of his labor. He does not beat his wife too much, but if punishment is required, he strikes her with a proper stick, not his fist or a metal implement. When he has a mistress (*hwa-njem*), he does not give her so much that his wife becomes jealous. If he has more than one wife, he treats them both equally, favoring no one above the other(s). He does not fight with his wife unnecessarily, and in quarrels between his wife and his mother, he does not automatically or consistently support his mother against his wife. (But an obedient and loving son makes a good husband.) He is generous to his wife's kinfolk and helpful with their farming and other chores.

As in all societies, there are some set and predictable patterns in the relationships between married partners that do still accord with custom. Throughout the life cycle of a marriage that follows traditional norms, the roles of spouses vis-à-vis each other undergo certain very specific changes that are correlated with modifications of the position of the wife within the household. In the beginning of the marriage as a new, young bride, her lowly status is best expressed by the state or condition known as *njiik* in the Birom language. Like so many terms that deal with nuances of feeling and subtle emotional or psychological states, *njiik* is difficult to translate into English. A girl enters a state of *njiik* when she is "captured" and taken to her husband's home. There, she will not look at or talk to anyone. On the one hand she is bashful and shy, and on the other she is full of remorse and sadness. As the wedding events proceed, there is the symbolic performance of certain tasks—fetching water, the cooking of special foods, sweeping the *lalla* yard, and so forth. During this time, certain chores are done for the new bride; her mother-in-law, for example, cooks a special meal for her (which she is supposed to refuse). While this takes place, the new bride must stand away—aloof, diffident and demure, and feigning strong loathing for doing these adult female jobs. This is also *njiik*. The bride is always indifferent, sorrowful, and listless, spurning all around her; especially those women of her new husband's house who attempt to care for her needs. At the end of the ceremonies when she takes up her new place in the house, she will be expected to maintain *njiik* in that she remains shy, silent, and obedient.

It is only after the birth of a child that the new bride becomes established in her home and is no longer required to do *njiik*. Now she has some recognizable status; she is free to talk to her mother-in-law and to converse more freely with or even complain to her husband. She is still a junior female in the compound in terms of her chronological age and maintains this vis-à-vis all older women. But her status is strengthened by the birth of children and more particularly if the marriage of another man in the compound brings in an even more junior woman.

As her children grow up, a woman takes on a status of greater equality with the other women of the household, with cowives, and with the wives of her husband's brothers occupying other households in the compound. As petty jealousies, competition, and arguments among the children may erupt, a woman comes more and more to the defense of her own children. During the time when her children are young, her position will also be strengthened by the establishment of her own cooking area and a separate set of buildings for cooking, storing, sleeping, and so forth. Moreover, at this time it is commonly the case that a woman will have one of her own young female kinsmen living in her *lalla* and helping to care for her children. Usually this is a sister, real or classificatory, who has not yet reached the age of marriage, but it may also be someone from the wife's *lo gwasa* or even cognates of the husband. By this time, the not-so-new wife should have become well adjusted into the new extended family setting, and mechanisms for settling quarrels that flare up from time to time will have evolved. She will have acquired a moderate amount of personal property in the household, such as cooking pots, utensils, and cleaning equipment, and all this, along with her strong attachment to her children, will have brought about the permanent rooting of her life in her husband's home.

By the time a woman becomes elderly and is no longer capable of bearing children, she has spent the greater part of her life in her husband's house, away from her natal home, even if she has had several husbands. Home is where her children are, where they were born and grew up. Her own natal primary family has probably ceased to exist; her father is likely dead, and even if her mother is still living, the reins of authority are now in the hands of her brothers, men who have wives and children of their own. At this time, her relationship with her husband will have lost its intensity. If he is alive, both will have reached a comfortable arrangement in which they perform their domestic functions as routine.

After menopause, husbands cease to exert strong control over their wives, and, as an old woman, a wife has very nearly complete freedom. In fact, a postmenopausal woman has liberties that cannot be exercised by men. She may go and come as she pleases and is no longer required to remain in or near the compound as are women who are still of childbearing age. If she has a son who is married, a woman is further freed from the work of the household because her daughter-in-law will be required to cook and care for the old people, just as she did when she was a new bride. Her relationship with her husband becomes that of an equal in many respects, although she may still cater for his needs out of habit, and long-established patterns of deference to him will still be observed.

In large part because of the age differences in marriage, most women in the village become widows, and, as noted earlier, the traditional preferred method of taking care of this situation is the levirate. But Birom custom allows a woman a number of alternative arrangements, some of which can be established in combination to give her the greatest possible range of security for herself and her children. If she goes to a brother of her husband, she may still keep her lover (*rwas-njem*). The variations are many and depend on the age and personality of the woman, the number of her children and their sexes, and how well she gets along with her affines.

A woman without children will generally seek to marry again, but a woman with sons will make an effort to stay in her dead husband's compound for the sake of those children. The Birom do not have the "house property complex" found in some East African societies that guarantees productive property for their sons (compare Oboler 1985). In addition, if a woman has only one child or only daughters, she is more apt to remarry and thus leave her husband's home than if she has several children, particularly sons. Women know that they can best protect the rights of their sons if they remain in the paternal home. Such a woman will go to a husband's brother in the levirate, or she will remain in her husband's compound and *lalla*, working his lands with the help of her *rwas-njem* (lover). Many women in this position prefer an attachment only to a lover. The levirate, which is not a new marriage even though a widow will be called a *hwa* (wife) of the "brother," is considered a "suffering" (*yom*) relationship. Some women say that they will never be treated well by a man of the husband's house, and so they prefer lovers who will always treat them well. From the point of view of a man, the levirate is a burden with few benefits unless he already has a wife. The lover must care for a woman who can never be his legal wife, nor will the children that he may beget by her ever belong to him. Such children are always considered as belonging to the deceased legal husband of the wife. In many cases where a man's holdings are small and there is little cash income, he can never hope to gain enough property to acquire and maintain a wife for himself.

In cases where a man already has a wife, the responsibility of another woman and possibly several children has the practical consequences of increasing the amount of work that he has to do and of widening the divisions of already short supplies of food. Unless a man is fairly well off and can hope to gain from attaching his brother's wife and children to him, he may prefer to look about for another husband for his brother's widow.

The case of Choji and his "wife" Pwachom, already mentioned, illustrates the hardship caused by the levirate. Choji was a classificatory brother to Gyang (their fathers were "real" brothers), who was the husband of Pwachom and had died only a few years before. Three children, all girls, were born of the marriage. On several occasions, Choji was known to have beaten Pwachom, and because she lived so close, she ran each time to her brother's compound. On one occasion, the argument was taken to the chief, who merely warned Choji about his excesses. According to those who took Pwachom's side, Choji had never taken care of Pwachom and her children properly. He had taken food crops that had been grown by her in her husband's fields and sold them for money. He was also accused of taking money from Pwachom for himself, and no one knows what he did with it. Pwachom and her children were left with no food except gifts from her brothers' families. During one argument that I witnessed, Choji yelled at Pwachom that she was no good, that she would not take care of him, cook for him, or give him the money she had made from the sale of beer. Davou Lo Matta, brother to Pwachom, shouted back at him that he, Choji, was not the person to whom she really belonged and that is why he beat her and ill-treated her so often.

In several cases that I know of, the widow stayed in her deceased husband's *lalla* for the simple reason that she had a close attachment to the mother-in-law. The close association between these women is extremely important for the maintenance of the domestic unit and often influences the manner in which the domestic unit of a *lo* group are dispersed. Indeed, one of the major factors in all marriages is the establishing of ties between women. If a woman "loves" her mother-in-law, she would not mind being married at a distance or moving away from the environs of her natal home. I knew of one woman who threatened to leave her husband after some twelve years because she did not want to leave her mother-in-law and her husband wanted to move to a "bush" ward. Many men undoubtedly find the combined influence of two determined women somewhat formidable, and while they may be pleased that the two women get along so well, they grudgingly give in to their wishes. The relationship of a wife to her female affinal kin deeply affects the relationship of husband and wife and ultimately the stability of a marriage.

One very important aspect of the traditional sexual division of labor is that it places men and boys, as against women and girls, in separate places during most of the day. In doing so, it has a profound effect on the nature of the personal relationship of husbands and wives in marriage. In the rainy season and at other periods of the farming cycle, such as the period in mid-October and November when yam ridges are built, the men are up and on their farms at the first sign of dawn and remain there until just before nightfall. During the dry season, from November to March, men of all ages, if they are not working in the mines, cluster with their friends and acquaintances in the village center and spend the day in the company of their own sex. Even those who work in the mines tend to return home only for the evening meal and later gather with their friends at a common village meeting spot or at a neighboring compound where beer is being served. Within the compound area itself, men have little to do except to tend their stores of grain, make repairs to the compound buildings from time to time, and weave baskets and mats once or twice a year. They do not spend their time in light conversation with their wives; conjugal companionship per se is not valued in Birom culture. Conversation when the men are home normally is not compatible with women's work, and most conversation during the day takes place between persons of the same sex and age or between women and children.

Rarely do members of a nuclear family partake of a meal together (I have seen this only among a few Christian families); men and youths are fed first and women and younger children later. It is only coincidental that several members of a family are seen eating at the same time and usually not in the same place. Women almost never eat in the presence of their husbands, just as they never call their husbands by their personal names, as this would be a sign of disrespect. Thus, the division of labor and associated taboos and prescriptions about the proper behavior of women and men to each other serve to prevent husbands and wives from seeing much of each other or having any form of social intercourse during the day. What is valued in the daily relationship of people in marriage is that both spouses do their tasks and do them well. Each knows his or her own job and expects of the other only that he or she perform the tasks required of their respective roles in the domestic unit. Whenever disagreements occur, they are virtually always concerned with the manner, efficiency, or degree of satisfaction with which one spouse is performing his or her role with respect to the other. Men punish their wives for not tending to their material needs, such as providing drinking water (very important in the dry season) and/or food; for being lazy about household work; or for wandering out of the compound to be sociable with others and not caring for the children. Women complain to their brothers and father when their husbands beat them too much, are niggardly in their provisions of grain and other foods, or fail to provide them with money for the proper wares necessary for running the household.

Thus, the traditional concept of a "good marriage" or a "good husband" or a "good wife" has little to do with compatibility of personalities, the presence or absence of physical attraction, or any number of features pertinent to marriage in the Western world. This does not mean that these factors are not important in the personal lives of individuals, only that they are not part of the norms and ideals of marriage. Emphasis here is on the cooperative features that are involved in the maintenance of the domestic unit formed through the association by marriage. In fact, the cooperative element of marriage may be strengthened by the separateness of daily activities for the simple reason that separation precludes disagreements or quarrels.

The Causes of Divorce

In precolonial days, a man and woman married to establish a domestic unit, and a couple "broke" the marriage (*gas wining*) only when one or both of the spouses failed to carry out his or her functions within the domestic unit. Divorce was not common, nor was it easily obtained. Men tried to prevent their daughters and sisters from leaving their husbands and always returned them after a traditional cooling-off period of three days when they ran away. Women say that most women leave their husbands at some time and return to their natal home, but they always return, especially if they have children, as they do not wish to leave them. Such temporary separations do not amount to an actual breakup of marriage, but they do cause some strain in the domestic unit because of the absence of the woman's services. Women who run away in such cases take their small children with them, but after the birth of several children, it is uncommon for a woman to leave again. Thus, nearly all separations, including those that became permanent, took place when the wife was still quite young and early in the marriage.

Traditionally, the only way in which a marriage could be formally dissolved was by the return of the *dwa* or some portion of it according to the number of children born of the marriage. Men whose daughters or sisters flatly refused to remain with their husbands must seek another husband for the girl in order to terminate the first marriage. And it was and is a not uncommon practice for a woman who wished to divorce her husband to initiate a new marriage herself by finding a potential husband able to repay the bridewealth. It was even less common for a husband to seek a divorce than for a wife. As long as the wife continued to tend his minimal needs, it was much easier, were he dissatisfied with her for some other reason, to ignore trivial faults. Men are aware of the difficulties of getting bridewealth and gifts returned.

Women list as the major causes of divorce (1) the failure of the husband to provide food, (2) the inability to conceive, (3) the deaths of children, (4) excessive or ignominious behavior on the part of the husband, and (5) an inability to get along or conflicts with in-laws. Lack of food was most frequently cited as a common cause of divorce, but this was often associated with beatings and inability to get along with the in-laws. One very old woman told me that she was divorced because her fathers had married her to a man at Zawang, and this was too far away. She had run home six times before her father relented and arranged a marriage for her with a man from Lo Gwom, nearer home. A small number of divorces are occasioned by accusations of witchcraft or the feeling that one is a victim of witchcraft. The deaths of many children are presented as evidence of witchcraft; so also is inordinate illness. A few girls were divorced because their kinsmen had too frequent quarrels with their husbands and finally persuaded their daughters and sisters to accept marriage elsewhere.

Marriage was not taken lightly. It was planned with great consideration and forethought for the consequences of particular unions. Nor was the termination of a marriage based on capricious grounds or arbitrary decisions made by the partners to the marriage. The breakup of a domestic unit affected many persons. It was largely for this reason that the vast majority of divorces took place before the birth of children.

In the colonial period, the setting in which divorce occurs is different, and it reflects the changing significance of marriage to a woman. Divorce at the end of the colonial period is still relatively rare, and it is still occasioned by the failure of spouses to perform the basic gender-linked functions within the domestic unit. The most common complaint that women advance in seeking a divorce, aside from their failure to conceive, is that their husbands beat them for no reason. Some people claim that the incident of physical abuse has increased since the Europeans came. It is also claimed that today women will fight their husbands in return, angering the husband and increasing the frequency and seriousness of the situation. In the old days, when a woman ran to her fathers and brothers after a beating, the latter would ask her, "What did you do to deserve a beating?" If the wife were physically injured by the husband, that is, if her skin were broken, the father would take her to the chief, who could impose a fine of a goat on the husband for drawing his wife's blood. In a special ceremony, the goat would be killed to purify the husband and wash away his evil deed. Then the wife would be returned to him, with admonitions to both to behave properly. In recent years, however, it is said that the wife's natal kinsmen will be more likely to want to fight with the husband without trying to determine who was the guilty party. Many do not attempt to force their daughters and sisters to return to the husband, as was the common practice in the past.

Women leave their husbands for a wider variety of reasons than those given in the past. Some say that their husbands no longer love them and that their husbands drink too much and stay away until late in the night. Three women left their husbands because they wanted to be Christians, something their husbands did not want. Some women left because they were quarreling all the time with other women of the compound, either cowives or in-laws, most often over profits from selling beer or foods. Some simply do not like their husbands and want to be rid of them. Others claim they love another man, prompting one elder in the court to burst out with, "What is this 'love' thing? Does it feed you or put children in your belly?" (By this he apparently meant, give you a proper legitimate child of whom you can be proud.)

The reasons for the breakup of modern marriages in a majority of cases are interpreted as direct consequences of influences from the external world and the newly recognized options and independence that women have. As the district chief once explained to me,

> It has now become the habit of some of our women to be going to places to drink which is against the wishes of their husbands. Husbands try to stop them. But the women do not like the idea of stopping, and this will all the time lead to divorce. Wives don't want to stay at home all the time now but to go out and taste of the new freedom and life in the *barki* [barracks in mining and labor camps].

Girls of marriageable age today still look for and want men who will provide them with the material necessities and symbols of a good life. Young women say they want men who are "rich," not just adequate providers. This is especially true of girls who have gone to school; the young men who assisted me claim that this applies to all the few girls in secondary school. As I was once told, "Women love men not because of their appearance or because of true love but according to their riches." Girls accept men as husbands today for their property and the possibilities of having good jobs in the future. And the stubbornness of women, along with their obvious preference, has led in recent years to an increasing number of Birom girls, especially around Du and Gyel, running off with strangers (Ibo, Yoruba, Hausa, Sierra Leonean, and so forth). Girls believe that by marrying strangers they will avoid the harsh life of the "bush" peoples and obtain a level of material security unavailable to their sisters in the village. These girls do not marry non-Birom who are not well off. Older Birom believe that marriages of this sort are brittle.

Kangyang Pwol was first married some years ago to a young Birom man named Pam but did not stay long with him. After leaving him, she married Dung Choji, taking with her from her first husband's house two body cloths and a box of trinkets and other personal belongings. Dung had agreed that she should have these things. However, Kangyang was a "modern" woman, greatly concerned with material things, such as her dress and adornments, and in time Dung, after quarreling with her about her neglect of his needs, took away her clothes. Kangyang ran from Dung to her father's house; subsequently, Dung came after her, and she promised to return in a few days. In the meantime, Kangyang met and ran away with a Beri-Beri man who had a good job in Kaduna. After a while, this man left her, and she returned to her father Pwol.

Dung Choji wants his bridewealth back and brought a case in court against Pwol. What he paid for the marriage was £6.10, which was the regulation payment at that time for a married woman. Shortly afterward, the official bridewealth was raised to £11, which was the payment in 1960. The chief in his decision said that Pwol should bring this £11 to give to Dung, and he gave Pwol four weeks to get the money, expecting that in that time he should marry his daughter to someone else to obtain the brideprice. If after four weeks he has not done so, Pwol should bring his daughter back to the court, and the chief would decide whether to give him another four weeks or to force Kangyang to follow her husband Dung. Dung actually wanted her back, but she said, "No! A man who made her naked among the people—to follow him again? Not me!"

Although a woman who is a good homemaker is highly valued in the traditional setting, young men today look for other, somewhat more ephemeral qualities. There is emphasis today on "good looks" and sexual skill. An attractive girl is one who has smooth skin, preferably of a reddish brown cast, and who swings her hips when she walks and behaves coquettishly. Some young women today do not cast down their eyes and become shy in the presence of a man as was thought proper in precolonial times but look men boldly in the eyes. Many young men say they are captivated by this sort of slightly defiant behavior, especially if it is accompanied with coyness and flirtation. Physical attraction, some education, and sophistication are important criteria in the choice of brides today. This accompanies the fact that many marriages are no longer arranged completely by a young man's father(s). Marriage is often initiated by a young man himself who is in a better position to be able to earn his own bridewealth. Such a young man will still consult his fathers and other kinspeople about the propriety of his choice and leave it to the older people to arrange for the interchange of gifts and the final ceremony.

At the same time, men still expect their wives to be subordinate to them and to perform their household and domestic tasks in traditional ways. But a young man is also more willing to renounce a wife if she should be displeasing to him personally, flirt with other men, argue unnecessarily with him, or annoy him in any way. Some young men today also state that they like an industrious wife who is willing to work for pay, as in the mines or selling beer, in order to help them. It is only when these women take up with other men, keep their own money, and demand too much independence that husbands complain.

Gender and Property

Men are the "owners" of the land, but, as in most of Africa, "ownership" is subject to a variety of claims and rights that others hold with respect to farmland. By customary law, women are excluded from the formal inheritance and holding of land and other property. And while this may appear to represent a disability, and no doubt it does in some cases, there are other customs that tend to nullify the restrictions and even convert them to an advantage. Phyllis Kaberry (1952) observed that although women's rights vary from one group to another, among some of the people of the Cameroons, men own the land, but women own the crops. This can be said to be true of many societies in Africa, whether it is formally recognized or not. Because women transform the raw crops, regardless of who grew them and on what fields, into edible form, they exert greater control over the distribution and consumption of foodstuffs than do men.

Because the garden farms are primarily the work of women and most of their products are "women's crops," a woman is usually allocated farms early in the marriage. This can be done by the headman of her husband's compound or by her husband. Such an allocation is almost always done by the birth of one or two children, but if the *lo* group has sufficient garden farms, it will be done much earlier. Thereafter, a young wife will work these small farms (which are prepared by her husband) with the occasional aid of relatives from her natal house, from other members of her husband's compound, from a lover, or from a female friend or neighbor. Except for yams and a few other tubers left in the ground, the bulk of the products of *bwi* farms will go into the husband's or father-in-law's storerooms. In some cases (and this is the ideal), a new storeroom may be built just for the products of these farms.

If the compound membership remains fairly stable and no new reassessment or rearrangement of farm plots among the men is necessitated, a woman continues to use these same farms. In time, she becomes closely associated with them so that they are spoken of as her farms in the intimate terms in the household and compound. Her rights to the use of them increase, and despite the fact that the kin group, through its headman, can theoretically resume control over the farms, by the time she has held and used them for several decades, no one would conceive of attempting to dislodge her. This kind of undisputed tenancy was quite evident among nearly all older women whom I knew. They held de facto control over their farms, exercising acknowledged priority of rights as long as they remain married in the kin group and in residence in the compound. Widows seemed to have the greatest independence in the holding of such garden farms, especially if they have young sons. Any attempt on the part of their husband's agnates to evict them would be tantamount to the worst form of kinship behavior: taking food from the mouths of children. It is so evil that it would anger the ancestors and bring death and destruction to the *lo*. Some men, however, do try to persuade these widows to give up some of their farms if they have many of them and there is not enough for other members of a growing kin group. But the rights of such widows are greatly respected.

Younger wives have less security in their cultivation of garden farms and are subject to greater controls from their husbands and mothers-in-law in the use of these farms. Two of my older informants told me that when women are young and first married, they do not know very much about farming. Therefore, their husbands have to tell them what to do. In the ensuing conversation, I reminded them that girls start helping their mothers with the garden farms quite early, long before they are married, and that their mothers have taught them a great deal by the time of their marriage. One of the women then suggested that men like to exert their control over the new brides and that such young wives must obey their husbands and consult them about the crops to be planted—when and where. They agreed that once a woman has farmed these areas for many years, her husband need no longer interfere. Both the women admitted that they seldom consulted their husbands about the planting of garden farms but made most decisions themselves.

These women, who seemed quite independent in other ways, may have been atypical, but I think not. Men on the whole appear to be quite reluctant to enter into the sphere of women's lives. As long as the wives are tending their crops and not deviating from established standards of responsibility, there is no reason to intervene. The older a woman gets and the more children she has, the greater the respect accorded her by men, including her husband. Men joke about incurring the anger of these older women. Their way of avoiding conflict with them is to shrug their shoulders and say, "These are women's affairs." Men will argue with other men over rights to garden farms but rarely with women. This, I believe, is because the rights that women enjoy are very different from those of men.

Once when I was visiting the home of a man who had invited me to meet his family on the other side of the village, I learned of an event that amply demonstrates this point. Chuang Zi, a man from a related *lo* group, was angrily relating a story of his continuous argument with a neighboring kin group over a *bwi*. Each of the protagonists claimed that the land had originally belonged to their kin group, and the dispute had been going on for many years, with sporadic threats from one side or another to take the matter to court. During this time, they claimed that neither kin group would send their men out to work the land; as they said, fighting would have occurred. The men said that no one was working the *bwi*. But I later discovered that an old woman from Chuang Zi's house continued to grow yams, beans, and some tomatoes in the garden with the help of her *rwas-njem* and a son-in-law, two men who were exempt from the disputes of the two hostile groups. She did so apparently undisturbed. Men explain these apparent contradictions by shrugging their shoulders and saying, "These are women's things."

The various crops that a woman cultivates on her husband's land belong to him. Of this, women voice no overt objection. A woman may not officially give, sell, or otherwise dispose of these crops without her husband's knowledge and permission. But though a woman accepts the legal right of the husband, in practice women have greater control over these foodstuffs than their husbands, and, as I have shown with regard to the *bwi* themselves, in general this control increases with age. It diminishes only when a woman voluntarily relinquishes some of these garden farms to a new bride. There is also individual variation among women in the exercise of control over the harvested crops. Men almost always say that they control the storerooms, but some women have managed to gain such a high degree of autonomy in food matters that their husbands' opinions are either not expressed or simply ignored.

Birom women are all well aware that there is power in the cooking pots. Even the most subservient young wife has many methods of extracting more daily rations from her husband. She may argue and bicker and claim that it is not enough. She may threaten to complain to her agnates or to leave altogether. She may stoically prepare the meal and serve only small and very inadequate portions to her husband (as I have seen), then face him with the simple logic that it is the husband's fault. On several occasions, I heard a wife remind her husband, quite calmly, that she was only a mere woman and could cook only what he gave her. By virtue of their control of the cooking pots, women, if need be, can make their husbands' lives quite miserable. When a man chooses to maintain complete control over the daily food supply, he must expect sooner or later to have to cope with this instrument of women's power, sometimes in incessant form. It is little wonder that many, perhaps most, men choose to abandon the role and leave the de facto responsibility of handling food supplies to their wives (see Kaberry 1952, chap. 6).

There is yet another custom that adds to the security of a woman with respect to her rights to some farmland and ensures her a greater degree of independence of action. Women have traditional rights to certain small plots called "Lo Bwi" and "Gakap Chop." Lo Bwi are small strips of fertile land given to women and cannot be alienated from them as long as they are alive. They are usually located adjacent to the compound and may be cut from a regular *bwi*. Here women grow any crops that they so choose, generally condiments and small vegetable plants such as turnips, onions, peppers, okra, runner beans, tomatoes, and so forth. Since by custom the choice is exclusively the women's, men have nothing to do with these areas. Gakap Chop are strips of relatively fertile land that can even be located in intermediate farms. Like the Lo Bwi, they are given to a woman by some man, with the consent of his *lo* agnates, but they need not originate from a woman's husband's kin group. One old woman, for example, told me that when she was a girl, her father gave her a Gakap Chop that she was accustomed to working. When she married, she continued to farm this portion of land, as her brothers did not need it. Now, she said, she was too old and tired to farm it but would give it to her married daughter.

The exclusive rights that women have to these two types of farms are thus predicated on their relationship to some man or men, mostly those of their husband's kin group or their own natal group (brothers and fathers). Moreover, these rights persist throughout a woman's lifetime and are not subject to other demands or limitations. Finally, some women seem to be able to dispose of or alienate these farms at will during her lifetimes, although they would not have the right to sell them. Thus, women lend and borrow such farms among themselves with some ease. As in the case of the woman who gave her farm to her daughter when she retired, such farms can be passed down a generation to an offspring, to a daughter-in-law, to a sister's daughter, to a lover's daughter, and so forth. However, a transfer of this type is not considered an inheritance, as the rights of the recipient are seen as temporary and terminate theoretically on the death of the original holder. Thus, a woman's daughter should surrender these rights on the death of her mother. On the other hand, a daughter may receive back these same plots from a donor brother or father if her father's kin group is the actual owner. Hence it is that some farms are in effect passed on by women even though legally they are debarred from owning, inheriting, or developing them. Often when a man claimed he did not know who was working some *bwi* that was owned by his *lo*, the cultivator turned out to be a woman.

Perhaps even more important than the concrete identity of some *bwi* as women's farms is the fact that women can and do borrow the use of a farm, whether a *bwi* or a *chuel*, with greater ease than can a man and from men to whom they are variously related. A woman may "beg" a farm from her fathers and brothers, from her mother's brothers, from lovers, from sons-in-law, and even from neighbors and friends. It is not unusual to find older women, particularly widows, handling such transactions independently of their men, and it is common for a man who finds it difficult to borrow or rent a farm himself to persuade his wife to borrow one for him.

It was not easy to get quantitative information on whether an event of borrowing was initiated by a man or a woman. Nearly half the economic survey was completed before I discovered that some men would say they borrowed (or rented) a farm when in fact it was their wives who did so. Men tend to see these transactions in terms of male ownership of land and ultimately responsibility for all matters involving land. The Birom do not think it unusual for a woman to act as the vehicle through which transfers of land are executed.

There are no reliable statistics on the amount of farmlands that can be classified as women's farms or the degree to which these farms add to the food supply. Women informants told me that it was difficult to know how much of the daily foods come from these farms; they never measure the products. Some women said that they used vegetables and seasonings from these farms in the porridge every day and dug up the yams only as needed. There were very few women who reported having no Lo Bwi or Gakap Chop, and all these were very young wives who in the normal course of events would expect to receive such farms in the future.

Today, women also engage in such practices as renting, pawning, buying, and selling farms; the distinction between such transactions, as I have already shown, is not always clear. These are transactions that are very different from borrowing and lending, as they all involve some return consideration. They represent contractual relationships that implicate the entire kin group as a corporate unit and thus would traditionally be outside the sphere of women's competence. Yet of the thirty-one women in he economic survey who maintained themselves alone or with minor dependents in a household, several gave information on their direct involvement in such transactions. One woman pawned a farm for £2, and three others rented farms for amounts that ranged from 9s. to £1. One man admitted actually selling a farm to a woman for £2, but she refused to confirm it, saying only that this was a thing for men to do. She was a recent widow; both her husband and her husband's father had died within a few months of each other. After these deaths, she was "afraid" in the house and moved to the compound of one of her *rwas-njem*. These examples reflect the fact that economic exigencies often necessitate that widows particularly act in the role of household head, with an independence that may not necessarily be accorded a woman with a living husband. Of the thirty-one women householders, only two had living husbands, and these men were working away from the village. Married women prefer to borrow farms, which represents an act of amity rather than a commercial transaction as in the case of pawning, renting, and purchasing.

From the foregoing discussion, it is clear that in any household the focal woman may have access to the use of more garden farms and from a variety of sources than her husband's kin group actually owns. In reality, of course, this does not obtain for every woman at all times because there simply are not enough garden farms today to satisfy every household's needs simultaneously. But the major point should be clear. This is that traditionally women exercise quite different sets of rights, privileges, and powers with respect to farmlands than do their men. In effect, we can argue that women have a system of land use that must be seen as separate from the formal system of land tenure in which their husbands and other men are involved. In the separate formulation of a unique system under which land use by women is regulated, within the broader structure, there are engendered areas of both conflict and cooperation. But the conflict is not fundamentally between husband and wife; indeed, much disputation is obviated by the existence of alternatives to which the wife can repair, and the cooperation results in reducing the risks that any household faces and increasing the sources of sustenance available to a woman and her children.

There are other forms of property, such as fruit- and nut-bearing trees and small livestock, that are not so crucial to the livelihood of the household. They are contained for the most part within the kin group, although increasing emphasis on individual ownership among younger men sometimes upsets the ideal. This may generate conflict between men of different generations in the kin group but not often between men and women. From time to time, some women will sell chicken, thorn bush, or euphorbia (the Birom term is translated as "cactus") as fuel from the household supply. Unless they are widows, this will commonly be with their husbands' knowledge. Men do not object to their wives raising chickens, pigs, or rabbits to earn some cash in the market, and virtually all older women on occasion sell cactus for a few shillings. Such undertakings are now widely becoming accepted as signs of an industrious woman. At the same time, these activities may generate a degree of ambivalence among the men because it means that the women will be going more frequently to the market and thus be exposed to strange men and the trappings of a more glamorous and affluent world (see the discussion later in this chapter). Some women are quite sensitive, however, to their husbands' concerns and go out of their way to avoid situations that might kindle or intensify their anger. Once when the women of our compound were sitting around during a rest period, we began discussing Bukuru market. All the women expressed an excitement and a love of going to market. They talked of the things they could buy there, of the unfamiliar people and sights that they saw, and especially of the foreign people and their behavior. Unexpectedly, two men of the compound arrived home, and I was surprised to see a sudden shift in the direction of the conversation to the extent that two of the women began condemning the market as an evil place.

This raises a final point of this section: The one form of property above all else in the colonial world that has affected the relationship of husbands and wives is money. I noted in an earlier chapter the large number of Birom women who have at some time in their lives earned money, albeit in small amounts. A woman working for cash wages in the mining paddocks or selling beer, cactus, or food for cash engages in an area of activity outside her husband's immediate jurisdiction and control. Not only that, but away from her husband she may encounter temptations that may have at worst a potentially explosive effect on her values and her regard for the woman's position in Birom society. In addition, her absence from the compound, whether it is to go to work in the mines, to trade in the market, or to sell goods in the village center, has a disquieting effect on the extended family. It can and does disrupt family life and the regular activities of the domestic unit and is thus a potential threat to the domestic unit.

Perhaps a greater effect on the domestic unit, however, is caused by the new sense of power and independence that some women have acquired because of their ability to earn money and thus gain a living in the modern setting quite independently of their attachments to men. This development was very slow in appearing among the Birom, and it still is not widely recognized as a threat to domestic life. What may have prevented its early emergence was the absence of a pattern of migratory labor and the reluctance of the plateau peoples to engage themselves as laborers in the mines away from their home territories. It is still a rare occurrence for a man to leave his wife and family in the village permanently and go away to work. Migrant labor is now more prevalent than two decades ago, but the vast majority of men take their wives with them. Thus, even if a woman did work for a time for cash earnings in the mines, she remained still under the protective authority of her husband.

Within the last two decades of the colonial presence, the pattern of growing independence seems to have been set by widows, women usually over thirty-five or forty years of age, who chose not to remarry or enter into a leviratic relationship with a man of their husband's houses. They chose rather the alternative of maintaining the custom of Njem and staying in their husband's home. But almost all of them also had some cash earnings throughout the year from their own efforts. In my economic survey for 1960, there was only one exception: a very old woman. The more conservative elements in the village comment on this kind of behavior as being not only different from the ways of the past but also somehow morally wrong.

This development has spread its influence to the young married women and to some who are not so young. Its effect on existing marriages has been variable, but in every incident that came to my attention, there was an underlying element of growing tension over basic values. The case cited in the following section is typical in its demonstration of the areas of antagonism between men and women as they try to reconcile older Birom values with elements of the new setting that would contradict and subvert these values.

Dispute between Pam and His Wife, Combo

Combo and Pam had been married for some twenty-two years and had five living children when I met them. The oldest girl, Katchollom, was married to a young Du man who lived and worked in Jos. The next child, a boy named Gyang, lived in Bukuru, where he was apprenticed to a Hausa man who was instructing him in tailoring. Kaneng, the next child, was almost mature and lived at home except for some occasions when she stayed with Katchollom in Jos. The two younger children were at home. Early in 1960, Combo, who is still of childbearing age, began to sell meat and other foods to earn some cash. Like some of the other village women, it was her custom to buy cow heads from butchers in Bukuru at the cost of from three to fifteen shillings a head. The meat was boiled off the heads, cut into pieces, and sold on Sundays wherever people were drinking beer. On Saturdays, meat would be sold at the "Bauda" area, a place frequented by both Birom and non-Birom men who were working in the mines. On Mondays, Combo and other women sold foods near the courthouse to litigants, members of the court (the elders), and hangers-on. Women who regularly sold foods in the village in this manner are always represented as having the permission of their husbands. But the activities of some women evoke frequent quarrels with their husbands and can become catalysts for divorce actions.

In April, just before the rains started, Combo began to complain to the chief and to Davou Matta (the Da Manjei of Rugut ward, where she resided) that Pam was abusing her. He beat her without provocation, and, she said, he took the money that she has earned and went off to spend it on himself. The chief referred the matter to the Da Manjei to resolve it. Pam, called on to answer to the charge by the Da Manjei, did not deny it. Yes, he admitted, he beat her, but the reason he did so was that she left home early in the morning and did not return all day until dark. She failed to cook anything for the children or for him. The children were home and crying all day. Pam claimed that he had been telling his wife repeatedly that she must not stay out until night but must come home and care for her children. Combo, he said, does not listen to him, so he beats her. (He beat her with his hand, which is not good. A man should beat his wife with a stick and not strike her with his hands or fists.) In any case, Pam had a good argument against his wife, although unsubstantiated. The Birom consider it a dreadful and heinous crime against nature that a woman who has food will not feed her children.

Combo continued to sell meat, and the two continued to have their quarrels, coming occasionally to talk over their troubles and get warnings from the Da Manjei. Matters came to a head on a Sunday night, when Combo was off selling meat. She had been gone all day, and when she did not return in the night, Pam went looking for her. He found her in Lo Gyang, the compound of her parents; she was drinking beer (and not, apparently, selling meat). She was drinking with some men. Pam was upset when he found her and asked angrily, "Is it day or is it night? What are you doing here? Where are your children? Have they been fed?" Combo had been drinking a lot of beer and did not answer her husband but merely looked at him.

Pam then told her to carry the remaining meat home and said she could go off and sell it the next morning. Combo then said, "No," she didn't agree. She told her husband that she was selling meat here and some people were still eating, so she would stay and finish her selling. This made Pam very angry, and Combo, now quite inebriated, started to laugh at him. Pam shouted to her to be quiet, and when she did not, he hit her. Thus, a fight started between them. A number of people immediately came to separate them. (Whenever a man and wife are fighting each other, the women hold the wife and the men will hold the husband. It is Birom custom to intervene and attempt to end all fights between spouses.)

Combo began calling her husband abusive names, shrieking that he was a mean and irresponsible husband. Exhausted by the fighting and the beer, she finally broke away and ran from her parents' compound to that of the ward head, Davou, Lo Matta. Although it was already fairly late and Davou had retired, she came crying hysterically that her husband had punished her and was going to kill her. Davou tried to calm her and made her come into the compound and rest.

In the meantime, Pam had collected all the money that Combo had made and left at Lo Gyang in her flight. He, too, then came over to see Davou to relate what had happened, apparently unaware that Combo was in the compound with the other women resting. Davou brought Combo out in the open *lalla*, saying, "Here she is," and he proceeded to listen to both of their accounts of what had happened that night.

Davou upbraided them both, saying that they should be ashamed of themselves. He said that they were too old for such foolishness and that they were setting a bad example for their son Gyang, who was about to take a wife home. He warned Pam and Combo that their son would imitate them, thinking that such behavior was proper. Here they had been married these many years, and it was a very bad thing to start this fighting now. Let them go home and say nothing more about it and live in peace.

But Combo would not agree; she claimed that she did not want to go home with Pam, that she did not love him any more because of his beating her, and that she wanted a divorce. Somewhat exasperated, Davou finally told them to go home and come back tomorrow morning, and he would listen to their case. During the discussion, Pam had returned the money to Combo (it was about eleven shillings), and she in turn gave it to Davou for safe-keeping because, she said, if she gave it to her husband, she would not see it again. Then they both left. But the next morning, the couple did not show up. In fact, they were not seen for six days, and it was surmised that maybe somehow things had been patched up between them.

On the following Saturday afternoon, it was clear that things had not gone well. Both Pam and Combo arrived separately at Lo Matta compound during the lull in the afternoon when the women and the children were sitting out in the front courtyard of the compound resting. Davou Matta was sitting on one side of the broad pathway passing the time of day with several neighbors. Pam Lo Kin Kan had arrived and was shaving the hair of a man of Lo Pam Mo. All these men, with the exception of Davou and Pam, left shortly afterward. The women were sitting together on the opposite side of the path when Combo began her complaints to Davou.

"Tell me, why doesn't he love me any more? If he doesn't want me, let him say so. If he does, tell him not to beat me. He says he beats me because I come home late from selling, but no matter when I come home, early or late, he beats me. Every week. Is that the way to behave?"

Combo was sitting directly in front of Davou on the women's side with her legs spread in front of her. She was not crying or shouting, simply explaining, but with a little whimper in her voice. While she was talking, Davou sat counting some small change that had been taken from a string bag. Pam said nothing but quietly listened to her harangue while Davou grunted occasionally to show that he was listening. Both Combo and then Pam went through the same arguments, but with newer flourishes and tales of fresh incidents to bolster their positions.

While this scene was taking place, the observers—some twenty or more people from Lo Matta and neighboring compounds who had gathered from the beginning—were watching intently and listening to everything. Even the little children, particularly the girls, were keenly interested in the matter. The women were making comments among themselves, including a great many disapproving clucks of the tongue. From time to time, they made joking comments among themselves, much as middle-class matrons in small towns in the West would make derisive remarks about one of their members caught in a sordid divorce case. During the proceedings, the women's attitude of strong disapproval was expressed to all around. The unmarried girls who were close to maturity had the least to say but undoubtedly had the most to learn from the expressed and implied values communicated during the afternoon.

Davou Matta finally stood up and leaned against a large rock near the edge of the path. After fixing his pipe, he began to talk quietly to the couple. He again exhorted them to stop fighting and go home and live in peace together. He said that such fighting was not the way of the Birom. He reminded Combo that she was the "arm" of her husband and that bad times would befall the people if their women behaved thus. Both Pam and Combo listened and seemed to agree. Pam did not want Combo to stop selling meat but agreed to stop beating her, and she in turn consented to come home early in the day. Ruffled feelings appeared to be smoothed, and Pam finally told Davou to give the money to his wife. Davou did so, and Combo took it and counted it, then turned and gave it to her husband, who also counted it and said it was right. Pam then said that he was going to take a shilling to go and enjoy himself drinking beer. This immediately angered Combo, who exclaimed "Wei, wei!" (No, no) and ran over to grab the little bag away from him. She cried that Pam was not to take anything out of it, not even a penny.

At this, there were loud murmurs and clucks of disapproval from the adult bystanders, Davou Matta angrily shouted that she was wrong to object to her husband's taking the money. Even if he took four or five shillings for himself, was he not her husband? Did he not have the right? And Honghei, Davou's first wife and most senior woman in the gathering, told Combo to hush and take the reminder, that she should not refuse her husband because was he not her care-taker? What sort of a woman was she anyway? But Combo stubbornly stuck to her position. There was no dispute over whether Pam had rights to her money—at least she did not argue this, whether she had the audacity to think such a thought or not. She simply maintained that she would not accept any of it, if not all of it; not a penny was to be taken out by him.

With everyone getting excited and several people talking all at once, Combo's reaction to this disapproval was suddenly to throw the whole lot of coins on the ground at her husband. This brought gasps of shock and surprise from the onlookers. Pam, after watching his wife fling the money to the ground, without so much as a flicker of an eyelash stooped and gathered up the coins, turned, and started off to the road home. Davou Matta suddenly shouted at Combo to go home, too, and started back into his compound. At this point, Chundung, Davou's second wife, came out of the compound. She was grinning and playful as usual, and after perceiving what had happened, she glided up to where Combo was standing and told her to go and get the money from Pam. Even though he takes a shilling out of it, she told her, it was better that Combo get the rest of it, or he would spend it all. Davou bristled at Chundung's interference and told her sharply to get back inside the house.

During this scene, everyone became very quiet; the murmuring of the women stopped, and everyone watched expectantly as if awaiting the consequences of Combo's unexpected outburst. The latter, who seemed taken aback by her own brashness, stood looking for a moment bewildered at her husband and then turned toward Davou. The silence was indicative of the high tension of the moment. Everyone expected that Pam would strike Combo for this behavior, and she, too, clearly expected it. (I was later told that my own reaction was correct. Had they not been in the Da Manjei's compound, Pam would have done so. But not only is it not good, decent, or proper to fight in the Da Manjei's house, there is also the complication that it may give the Da Manjei a reputation for not settling fights but causing them.) At that particular moment, it was a very serious matter, indeed. Davou used harsh tones with Chundung primarily because he did not want the situation to escalate into a physical fight. If she or anyone else had continued speaking, Pam's anger might have come to a head, and he would have turned back and beaten his wife before everyone present. Moreover, he would undoubtedly have had the approval of everyone because, in their view, Combo's behavior was obviously reprehensible.

In the silence that followed, Pam continued on his way home across the road and field. Combo stayed behind, as if partly afraid to follow him home immediately because of his righteous anger and partly to justify her own actions. All the other men had left. Davou told her several times to go home and then went into his compound. Chundung, who had retired rather subdued, later came out and joined the other women saying nothing. Combo replied that she was going home but would not receive the money with a shilling missing. She went on to explain that she wanted it all because she had borrowed the money to buy the meat and wanted to pay it back. Honghei then told her that she would simply be beaten again. It was her duty to receive whatever Pam wanted her to have of the money so that they could settle their differences. She further warned Combo that she must have patience with her man and reminded her that it was she, Combo, who was at fault.

Combo then explained that she had borrowed £2 from someone the previous year to pay taxes for her husband so that he would not be put in jail, as he had no money himself. This year, she got the money back from selling meats. But Pam would not allow her to repay the loan. He wanted to keep it for himself. However, she had taken the money when Pam was not around and repaid it. It was for this that he had beaten her. As she was telling of this incident, Combo was slowly ambling off in the direction toward home. She finally walked off to the road, looking it up and down as if she has not decided whether to go home. In the end, she adjusted her blanket and walked off determinedly toward her compound.

The bickering and quarrels between Pam and Combo continued sporadically, although for the next few months Combo was much more reserved and restrained in her behavior. When I left the village some months later, they were still together, and there was no indication that a divorce was in the offing. Pam did not beat his wife during this period.

The immediate surface issue in this case raises the question, What rights does a Birom woman have with respect to the control and/or handling of the money that she has earned by her own efforts? The Birom have yet to develop a consistent set of values or practices in this regard. Combo's attitude about her money, taken out of the context of her personal relationship with her husband, is for the most part neither unusual nor unexpected in the modern situation. It is undoubtedly the most common cause of disputes between husbands and wives of all ages and conditions of material well-being. And there are many precedents for this position. As noted earlier, widows were some of the first women to start earning cash wages, and those who did not or were not remarried were not obligated to turn such earnings over to men. But perhaps of greater influence for the Birom women is the widespread custom among other West African peoples that husbands and fathers do not have absolute rights to the earnings of their women. Some Birom women are well aware of the practices of southern (Ibo and Yoruba) market women and their rights to control and invest their own money (Sudarkasa 1974). In fact, it was in large part the desire to emulate these women, as the Birom perceive them, that stimulated the trading activities of Birom women. Many women say that money is not property, at least not in the same sense as other valued goods. They see it as enabling them to better the economic conditions of their households, for which they bear the major responsibility. Men use money for quite different purposes—for drinking beer or for acquiring material possessions such as clothing, shoes, and bicycles—that benefit only the men in their relations with the larger, dominant world. Thus, in the dispute between Combo and Pam, Combo argues the justification of her more pragmatic concerns, whether or not these were the actual considerations behind her behavior.

The traditionalists take the position, consistent with Birom beliefs, that women should not or cannot own property, at least economically valuable property, which money, because of its command over goods, is. This position is revealed in the comments and arguments of Davou, his wife Honghei, and the other older women who adjudged Combo wrong in denying the money to her husband. But this position is not inflexible, as can be seen by the assumption on the part of some that Combo had the right to keep the remainder after Pam had taken what he wanted. There is the vague belief even among older people whose comments I solicited that Combo has some rights to the money. What was disquieting in this situation, as in others, was the lack of clarity and definition as to what her rights were.

There were in this case other factors that indicated the breaching of even broader principles. In every dispute of this sort that came to my notice, the most powerful forces for resolution were those of compromise. It is not within the character of Birom culture to approach a problem seeking absolutes. Matters must be discussed and cases litigated in such a way as to restore social tranquility if not social equilibrium. The Birom "talk out" matters not as if there were some objective standard of social justice or personal and social morality but in order to find solutions that will bring harmony and enable people to get back to the business of making a living. Thus, Combo's behavior was all the more shocking because of her obstinate refusal to compromise on the matter of sharing some money with her husband. This is antithetical to Birom ways.

Combo's behavior laid bare, in a palpably public manner, the underlying conflict that faces Birom women and their men. This was the growing social and economic independence of women as against the traditional ideals of semiseclusion, subordination, and obedience. Her position with regard to the money as well as her behavior in other contexts posed, perhaps inadvertently, a naked challenge to these ideals, and the challenge was not lost on the adults watching the proceedings. It would have been better had she equivocated and couched her behavior in less abrasive and more traditional terms of conflict or clouded the issues in peripheral matters. As it was, she angered and alienated even those who would have supported her. Human societies everywhere take umbrage against those who would flagrantly reveal the painfully festering and insoluble contradictions that are so disturbing when consciously faced that they are normally kept suppressed. I found that Birom men and women were loath to discuss conflicts between the sexes in an abstract manner. They do not perceive the world in terms of the rights of women vis-à-vis the rights of men and were immune to the divisiveness inherent in this element of Western cosmology.

The issues in this case were complicated by other factors in the personal relationship between Pam and Combo: the beatings, the failure of Combo to perform her domestic duties, and "love." Combo had a surreptitious lover who was not a real *rwas-njem*, for he had not paid the traditional goat for his privileges. The affair was begun long before she started selling meat that year. Pam's feelings about Combo's neglect of him and the children were undoubtedly aggravated by his own anger over this affair. Thus, Combo's involvement in the cash economy enabled her to flaunt other customs with such a high degree of self-interest that her traditional role was being eroded.

This case indicates not only how money brings complications where there are other problems but also how its existence becomes a problem in itself between husbands and wives. The Birom are quite aware of this situation, and some men try to avoid the problem by forbidding their women to work in the mines or to sell foodstuffs or other goods. Another method by which many Birom handle the problem is to use the age of the woman as a criterion for the rights that she may exercise with regard to money. Both Honghei and Chundung, Davou Matta's wives, brewed beer for sale from time to time. Honghei, who was past childbearing age, was allowed to keep most of her money, and having collected fifteen shillings during the dry season, she went to the market and bought herself a blanket. Chundung, however, was required to turn all her earnings over to her husband. She was still of childbearing age (that is, he still went to her at night), and therefore he exercised stricter control over her behavior. This was also the common practice in several other households with which I was acquainted.

Money is an element so powerful in its influences, and these have so many ramifications, that it virtually threatens the underlying factors that make up the traditional domestic unit with its interdependence and exclusiveness of roles. Money strengthens the position of women with respect to property holding to the extent of threatening the whole system of property relationships. There were several women in the village whose incomes were high enough that they were able to hire men outside their natal *lo* or their husband's kin group to do farming for them. Many widows were enabled to act as heads of their own domestic units (and they are so described in my economic survey) because they had independent cash income (often in the form of money from employed sons and/or lovers) and thus did not have to rely for food supplies on the produce of their farms. As women become more educated and sophisticated in the ways of the modern world, they will undoubtedly seek greater control over farmland, either through purchase or through claiming inheritance rights in the absence of male heirs.

Even without the added aggravation that money often brings to the relationships between Birom husbands and wives, it is important to note that women are very much aware of the unique dependence of men on women. They know that a household cannot function long without a woman, and they use this knowledge to their advantage. In a tape-recorded interview with one of my elderly informants, one line stands out as a significant summary of a discussion about the nature of men. She said, "If a man is doing wrong, you speak to him and tell him that you will leave (go away), and he will not do the bad things." To "speak to" the husband accords with Birom values about correcting disharmony in social intercourse. Although a woman may not "correct" her husband in the sense that an individual of higher social standing can chastise a subordinate, she can "speak to" him and utilize the threat of leaving in a retributive or punitive manner. With few exceptions, women whom I knew were quite circumspect in the handling of disputes with their husbands. At no time have I ever heard a woman spell out in detail the nature and extent of her husband's dependence or any man's ultimate dependence on women.

Women do not see themselves as in any way engaged in active competition with men, nor do they sustain perpetual antagonism toward men on account of their superior positions. If anything, the majority attitude toward men is supportive and conciliatory. Such conservatism in attitude does not prevent women from recognizing and adjusting to external economic changes. By attempting to identify and establish for themselves a sphere in which they exercise control over cash, it is women who are largely inspiring changes in the social and economic system.

Cowives and Affines

The traditional husband/wife relationship in Birom polygynous marriages carries many of the vexations, as well as the benefits, found in all societies with polygyny. There is not only sexual jealously but also disagreements and quarrels over food and personal items, over rights to certain household properties, over children, and so forth. But this is compensated by such features as the sharing of work and mutual aid. It is recognized that women's work is hard in Biromland, and the Birom set great value on cooperation among cowives. The ideal situation is for each wife to have a separate cooking place, separate sleeping rooms, storage rooms—in other words, a separate *lalla*. But there were a few rare cases (less than 5 percent of polygamous marriages) in which such separateness of physical accommodations was not maintained. In these cases, the domestic unit was a kind of consolidated arrangement in which cowives shared everything except sleeping rooms. They either cooked and cleaned together or took turns at the various tasks.

One example of unusual cooperation and division of labor among wives is that of Da Jang, a neighbor who had three wives. Each of these women cooperated in tasks that, in traditional times, they would have been expected to undertake separately. Bi, his third wife, was blind and of necessity remained home or close to the compound. She was able to do much of the sweeping, cleaning and cooking, and other household tasks. She pounded most, if not all, of the grain for the nine persons in the household. The two other wives farmed the three large intermediate farms as well as six garden farms together, growing vegetables, various yams, cassava, *acha*, and a small amount of millet. Whenever Jang had extra money, he gave it to these wives to purchase grain for cooking beer. They bought guinea corn in the market and together earned four to six shillings each week from selling beer at the Bauda on Saturdays. While Jang's wives have separate huts, only one cooking area was in operation throughout most of the year, and whenever I visited them, I found all the wives tending pots and preparing their meals together. Because of Jang's precarious economic situation, particularly the necessity to rely on an irregular cash income, this domestic unit had to invent, as it were, expedient measures that consolidated the activities of what were once separate producing and consuming units.

Such unified operation could not have been effected without the voluntary cooperation of all of Jang's wives and an unusually high degree of esprit de corps among them. This attests to the early and successful conditioning of girls and women for self-constraint, cooperation, responsibility, self-discipline, and concerted action.

The maintenance of satisfactory economic and connubial relationships with her husband and good relationships with her cowives is not the only important area of interaction of a wife in the domestic unit. At some time during the life of a domestic unit, a woman commonly has siblings-in-law and/or parents-in-law present either within the *lalla* or in a nearby part of the compound. Less critical in its effect on the domestic unit is a woman's relationship with her father-in-law. Custom dictated that a fairly strict avoidance pattern be established between them. All matters even remotely related to sex are taboo between them. A woman goes out of her way to avoid contact with these older men and should never be alone in the compound with them. They take pains to avoid sitting on the same mat together or near to each other. Where contact and communication occur, respect and subservience are demanded of the younger woman, particularly if she is newly married. Even the most modern younger women today still observe the appropriate conventions. As the young wife grows older, however, the formalities become more relaxed. She appears increasingly more comfortable in the presence of her father-in-law. He in turn becomes increasingly more dependent on the daughter-in-law for food, as his wife may have turned over the cooking duties to her. As he retires from active farming, depending on his health, he may stay about the compound, and she may call on him to do minor repair jobs for her or to tend the younger children while she is away or some other form of aid. He may become her friend and counselor, and though her real power in the household has expanded, she maintains her respect for him.

More informal and approaching a true joking relationship is the mutual attitude of wife and husband's younger male siblings who are unmarried. These young men and boys must treat her with respect because of her status as a wife (and the respect grows with the birth of children), but they also are expected to laugh at and with her and to tease her, as long as it is not too risqué. She is in many respects like a sister to them, while at the same time there is the possibility that she may one day go to one of them in the levirate as a wife. With young female affines, such as husband's sisters, all of whom will generally be younger than the new bride, there is frequently established a relationship of conviviality. I know of many cases where sisters-in-law have become quite good friends and maintained this friendship even after the marriage of the younger girls. A new young bride has a distinct advantage in attracting the help and companionship of these girls. Of all the individuals in the household, she feels the most free with her husband's younger sisters. She plays with them in her leisure time and may even connive with them in various sorts of activities that may net her some benefits. There is, however, the danger that if she forgets her new wifely role and spends too much time joking and playing with them, she will encounter the censure of her husband, her mother-in-law, and other older members of the compound. All in all, where there are such younger sisters, they can make a new wife's lot less onerous and more pleasant and provide her with services such as baby tending and household help.

However, the most crucial and delicate of all relationships is that between a young wife and her mother-in-law. Here is the arena of greatest tension, potential and actual, within the social relationships of the domestic unit. Theoretically, these two women are each the hub of what will be separate domestic units, representing potentially different branches of the wider agnatic kin group. Their functions are distinct only in time. Yet, even though each represents a separate core of relationships, at some time (generally twice) in nearly every woman's life, her existence is juxtaposed intimately with that of another woman, a woman who has a very different status and value within the household and the wider community. At these times, the points of social contact between these women span the entire day. It is literally the case that a woman may spend a greater part of her lifetime in the company of her mother-in-law than her own mother.

The relationship of the one woman to the other, be she senior or junior, may be fraught with ambivalence, envy, and jealousy and the kind of discord that leads to open strife. At this phase in any woman's life, cooperation is essential, for strife with a mother-in-law or daughter-in-law is or may be a heavy contributor to the breakup of a marriage and consequently of the domestic unit.

As in all close relationships, there are norms, values, customs, and traditions pertaining to the mutual behavior of daughter-in-law and mother-in-law. In the case of the younger woman, compliance, obedience, and a kind of gracious deference is expected. The older woman is required to be tolerant and accepting of her daughter-in-law, to give guidance and good counsel in teaching her new "daughter" the ways of the household, and to give advice about the proper behavior of a wife. Older women look forward to when their sons will bring home wives, for then they can relinquish the drudgery of household work and gain a measure of freedom. Thus, the relationship begins at marriage and undergoes a major change only when and if the younger woman acquires separate physical facilities of her own. Custom requires that at least one son remain in the *lalla* with the aged parents, so that in most cases there will always be a daughter-in-law who can expect to remain with her mother-in-law. The relationship is then terminated only at the death of one of the women.

Throughout the period of its existence, the relationship alters in often small but significant ways that more or less correspond to the various socially recognized stages in the life cycle of the younger woman within the household. We have already noted some of the aspects of *njiik*, a state or condition that is assumed early in the marriage. A new bride does not speak directly to her mother-in-law until the birth of her child. At the time when she feels her first labor pains, she cries out her mother-in-law's name and calls her for the first time *ngwo* (mother). With each new child, her life becomes further entrenched in her new home, and she takes on higher status and greater privileges. It is during this period of adjustment that a new bride's life is most closely intertwined with that of her mother-in-law, for she is closely watched by her mothers-in-law and other women.

Disputes and misunderstandings between the two women are often expressed in small, seemingly insignificant events. One major area of dispute is over grain and grain allotments; other areas include such matters as the use of certain household implements, the timing of meals, the amount of food cooked for the older people, the manner of cooking, farming, gifts from the working husband/son, and so forth. Sometimes the arguments are extremely petty. Once I saw an argument flare up when a young mother put a yam in the fire to roast for her three-year-old, and her mother-in-law insisted that she wait until the latter had completed stirring the pot. On another occasion, a few birds' eggs became a matter of dispute. Women may argue over certain pestles, as they vary in weight and effectiveness; although a bride brings some cooking utensils with her, it is common to rely on the husband's house for the heavy items. On one occasion, a quarrel arose when a mother-in-law's goat trampled a tomato plant that a daughter-in-law had planted. In this case, the women were pacified by the men of the house.

A mother-in-law may complain of trivial matters. From the beginning, she seems to be watching to see that the bride does things properly. All the older women seem sensitive to the bride's behavior, and some are quite ready to accuse her of not showing proper respect. They watch to see if she scours the pots and pans with sand properly. Is she lazy and forgetful about gathering enough fuel? Is she argumentative or too bold? And, of course, does she treat her husband properly? However, there is a check to any mother-in-law's fastidiousness. She does not want to alienate her new daughter-in-law completely, and especially she does not (usually) desire to break up the marriage. Her own daughters are or will be undergoing the same situation, and it would be a bad reflection on her should they not be well trained. An older woman is especially grateful when her new daughter-in-law renders her extra services and shows a desire to get along well.

When there are cowives or other wives of husband's brothers, the mother-in-law has a rather pivotal position. When the younger women have arguments, she frequently serves as a kind of arbiter and peacemaker. On other occasions, she may be accused of favoritism as daughters-in-law bicker over small favors, such as a favorite winnowing pan, promised to one but delivered to another. Arguments between any women who are the focal point of separate domestic units within a single compound threaten the cooperation that must be established.

Since the possible situations for dispute are so many and the intimacy of the relationship is so prolonged and intense, it is perhaps not at all fortuitous that the Birom have developed some formalized customs that serve to mitigate or ameliorate conflict. One such custom is that of *kyeng*, in which the different *lallas* of a compound or a closely related compound nearby go through a daily ceremonial exchange of cooked food. A small amount of whatever is cooked in each household is taken by the women to the other bi-*lalla*. In a formal manner, *kyeng* is explained by the Birom, especially the women, as if it were a part of the principle of the unity of agnatically related domestic units. They will say, "We do this because we are one." Overtly, it would appear to help strengthen the bonds of male siblings and fathers and sons who now have divided lives, devoting much of their time and energy to wives and children. It might be satisfactorily explained if left at this point. But I noticed both in my own compound and in others that I visited that, strangely enough, the men were not around when the exchange took place and that they were unconcerned about the exchange. Indeed, one man, in describing *kyeng*, said, "It is a matter for women."

What in fact does happen is quite interesting. *Kyeng* provides the occasion, usually in the afternoon, for visiting back and forth between bi-*lalla* by the women, for asking about the health of particular people, and for chatting and pleasantries. Even women who had recently heated disagreements would appear mollified and engage in the *kyeng* as if there had been no dispute. All arguments that might have erupted were curtailed at this time; I do not recall ever seeing or hearing one occur. Partaking of any food or other nourishment together is a sign of amity and affection among the Birom. It is a common standardized custom for two men who are friends to drink from the same calabash together, for lovers to drink together, and for older people of either sex who are members of the same neighborhood and have shared a lifetime together to "raise" the same calabash. Although this is particularly true with beer (the food of all rituals), it also holds for such mundane items as roast yams or porridge. Thus, the occasion of the *kyeng* signifies not only the unity of the *lo* at its most elementary level but also the cohesion and cooperation of the women, the individuals most important for maintaining the *lo*. It seems to me that it functions essentially because of its contrast to the ordinary bickering and pettiness that may be found in the daylong relationships of the women of the house.

There is another device that helps prevent the occurrence of disputes between women in close domestic contact. In the literature on preindustrial societies, it has been frequently noted that the status and social personality of a woman changes when she has reached menopause and is no longer capable of bearing children. The custom has already been described for the Birom. Its basic characteristic is a lifting of the usual types of restrictions placed on younger women in the society. If they have daughters-in-law and are too old to do much farming, they will not be bound by chores but spend their time quite idly except for looking after grandchildren (a task that is not required but expected). They joke as equals with men and are notorious for semiflirtatious behavior with younger men and telling off-color jokes. This behavior is sharply in contrast with that of younger women, who are expected to be demure, shy, and morally proper.

All old women are addressed as *ngwo* (mother) whether or not they have borne children and are accorded the respect due to mothers. As they wander throughout the village, they often make demands on young people to give them small change so they can go and drink beer or to fetch things for them. They appear to have the complete freedom of the village and surrounding areas, and if they are able, a few old women will walk five or six miles to the town of Bukuru to purchase small items. They may ignore the needs or desires of their husbands, particularly if there is a younger cowife or daughter-in-law to cook for them. Moreover, they are the only persons in the community who are allowed to make sexual jokes in public. Such joking behaviors are most often aimed at young men; old women may deride or question their sexual prowess and sometimes teasingly invite young men to come visit them. Young men and teenage boys sometimes say that they are embarrassed by the behavior of these old women. Yet no one dares to object, nor can anyone criticize them; it would be disrespectful and in bad taste.

There may be a number of contributing factors that together account for this custom. One of the more important of these factors must be the effect that this freedom for the older women has on a domestic situation that includes a number of other adult women. By permitting the older women the freedom to remove themselves from the domestic unit and from competition with the other women, this custom stems the tide of disruptive quarreling between persons who have varying and sometimes conflicting interests. It is not suggested here that the development of this custom was purposely designed to bring this effect, but its consequential benefits in reducing the possibility of friction undoubtedly determine its perpetuation.

Cooperation among women, whether or not they occupy the same compound, is essential in Birom life, if for no other reason than the fact that food is never abundant and always unevenly distributed. We have already seen that women have many other means of obtaining food, and they exercise a high degree of informal authority over how it is to be divided. As women are cooks, providing the food in its final edible form, the large amount of sharing found in the community is at this level.

Thus it is that informal cooperation among sisters, sisters-in-law, kinswomen of different generations, age-mates, and even wives and their husbands' mistresses exists to a high degree. Women help one another with farming chores, food preparation, gathering materials for fuel, preparing beer for sale, obtaining water, and so forth. While this aid seems generally sporadic and unpredictable, it is so widespread that no woman ever goes without the possible cooperation and assistance of another. The strength of the bonds with which some women may be tied together through this cooperation can be very enduring. The first funeral I observed in the village was that of Funong, an old woman who died three years after her cowife. Because these women had loved each other so much in life, they were buried together in the same grave. Informants reported that when the first wife died, the people had to restrain Funong from following her in death. She mourned over the implements of her cowife and refused to let anyone else touch them. These women were old and had lived together for many years, long after the death of their common husband. At another funeral, I saw a grief-stricken surviving wife pound her shoulders and breast with her fists and throw herself on the ground despite the efforts of her children to console her. All the while, she cried out, "Oh, why did you leave me? You have left me alone! Why did you not take me with you?" Her relatives explained her grief very simply: She had loved her cowife.

Social Networks: Webs of Kinship and Friendship

10

D OMESTIC UNITS CAN BE SEEN as hubs in a vast network of social relationships that link together diverse individuals and kin groups within and beyond the village. On the one hand, they are structural components of the more inclusive corporate kin group. On the other hand, households have a wide range of interconnections based on principles that are not those of agnation. In this chapter, I describe and analyze the various forms of mutual interaction with other domestic units, emphasizing those beyond the immediate compound. The most important links among domestic units are essentially personal ties that connect two (or more) persons of different household situations together. The most critical of these are those involving women.

I have argued that men and women within the same unit are the embodiment of two separate processes, the one sociostructural and political and the other basically grounded in the production, distribution, and consumption of food and other goods. A household gains its material welfare from the relationships and activities that center on its focal woman. It is from the perspective dictated by these latter processes that I am viewing the domestic unit.

The arena of all social interaction is what I have called "structured kinship." In Birom society, the fields of kin relationships do not have the same meaning for women as for men. Women have different positions and roles within the kinship complex, and the meanings of kinship are not as formalized with women. There is a degree or quality of flux in the rules and regulations of kinship behavior that renders kinship connections extremely malleable for women. One very soon gets the impression that the operation of values and beliefs about kinship tend to be highly personal and subjective for women. The relationships among men are more deeply embedded in structural principles and characterized by a good deal more rigidity and adherence to strict conventions. This becomes much clearer as we examine the three basic fields of structured kinship: agnatic, maternal, and affinal.

Fields of Kinship: Agnation

In earlier chapters, I stressed that structured agnatic relationships are basically property and power relationships among men. The key to agnation lies in the various aspects of property holding: rights to the use, control, dispensation, and inheritance of property in land and other strategic resources; rights to the services of other men regarding the use of property; and responsibility and obligations predicated on such ties. Since all economically or ritually valuable property is theoretically owned, controlled, transferred, and supervised only by men, the significant overt dimensions of agnatic relationships pertain exclusively to a male domain. Thus, from a male point of view, a woman may be given a farm plot for her own use by a father, brother, husband, or lover, and theoretically she cannot further dispose of it. Should she discontinue cultivating it or die, the farm reverts back to the original holder/owner's agnatic group. Women often borrow farms temporarily from men: kinsmen, lovers, and even neighbors. Men, however, tend to see these features of landholding and land use by women as negligible. It does not interfere with or alter the fundamental relationships of men to one another and to the land. Under any circumstance, men see the rights transferred to a woman as simple rights of use derived from her personal relationship with the male donor.

At one level, such rights as a woman may enjoy may seem somewhat intangible in that, while they may be implicit in custom and habit, there is no socially sanctioned traditional law or regulation that governs and protects her rights such as exists in the relationships among men. Any woman's ability to obtain and maintain special farms for herself depends on her personal relationships with men, for she has, in the traditional agnatic system, no jural rights.

A man's use of farms is based on structural principles that stabilize and provide some degree of rigidity and permanence to individual, group, and property relationships. Each agnatic kin group is a self-regulating body with the power to punish and reward its members as well as the responsibilities of sharing and cooperation. There are broad sentiments about the cooperation and loyalty of agnates to one another. The morality that underscores their solidarity is that of love, respect, duty, and obedience. Such sentiments strengthen already existing ties based on property rights, but, as we have seen, they cannot delay or prevent the processes of segmentation that are fundamental to (indeed, necessary components of) the ongoing life of kin groups. The social structural process should be understood as distinct from the actual sentiments that male agnates may have for one another. But the structural elements may often shape the sentiments that men develop for one another over time.

The amount, availability, and fertility of land unquestionably affects the size of the population exploiting it (that is, the number of mouths to be fed). At times of population expansion, the protected garden lands would be utilized to their maximum potential, and intrusion onto unprotected bushlands might well take place. During times of warfare, an expanding kin group could well be under stress as it retracted its farming activities to the more protected areas, those closest to the village. The boundaries of protected areas were fluctuating ones, dependent on the size of the village, the intensity of hostilities, the topography of the land, and the strategies that each village devised to protect itself. Any retraction to better-protected areas meant a reduction of foods produced. However, there were certain social mechanisms developed for reducing or adjusting the population to a size that could be supported within the protected areas. One was the phenomenon of the "wanderer," as we have seen, whereby some young men failed to marry in the village and eventually left. In the words of the Birom, these young men left because either they had no garden farms (*vide be*) or no bridewealth (*dwa*, or horse). The sloughing off, as it were, of these young men before they could marry and reproduce was an obvious social mechanism for relating the *lo* group size to the temporary limitations of its natural resources.

The long-term mechanism for adjusting kin groups to farmland was and still is the process of segmentation resulting in cycles of new corporate units every four to seven generations. Segmentation ultimately means the reformulation and redefinition of male relationships and the redistribution of lands among them. Property that is conceived as being held in perpetuity is reshuffled in divergent patterns, and the most fundamental kinship relationships among men are redefined. A man, if he lives long enough, may be aware of the process of segmentation only once in his lifetime. But all men are aware that impending divisions present a trauma to agnatic ideals. Men thus have to be prepared for it socially and psychologically.

These facts pinpoint something about agnatic relationships that no observer could ignore. Although the personal relationships of particular fathers, sons, and brothers may appear close and reflect solidarity, there was inherent in the structural aspects of agnation potential strife, competition, and eventual divergence of interests and personal goals. Men who are "brothers" are in competition with one another for wives and the highly valued garden farms of the "fathers." "Fathers" are in competition with their "sons" for wives. These facts pre-date the colonial period and continue up into the present, albeit such circumstances are diminishing in the modern world. Where there are several sons, competition among them presents obstacles to their continued solidarity as a *lo* unit. In precolonial times, the Birom say, fathers sometimes had to choose for which sons to provide bridewealth and land, and the others would of necessity become wanderers. To a much more limited extent and not for all kin groups, the same sort of choices must be made today.

Not only is potential conflict inherent among male agnates for certain types of property, but quarrels among these men occur as a crucial step in the process by which new *lo* units are born from the lines of cleavage in older ones. Many of the disputes among close agnates attest to the indigenous sources of strife as an important facet of the total social process. Among several families whom I knew intimately, I was aware of mounting tension between certain sets of brothers. In one case that reflected a common problem, each of two brothers hoped to benefit from the incoming bridewealth payments for their younger sister. One son hoped to marry a wife with the *dwa*, and the other desired the money, a total of £21, to pay for his training as a carpenter and to buy tools. Before colonialism, this second alternative would not have existed. Still, only one of the brothers would have been able to get the horse, presumably to be replaced with a wife, and the choice would have been made by the fathers or the headman of the kin group. Most likely, the elder son would have obtained the horse, as normally he would have been expected to marry first. But this was not invariably true, as men sometimes said that they preferred to marry their "best" son first (a fact that was and is both a cause and a consequence of fraternal competition). In this case, the younger son, who sought the training and skills of the modern world, was preferred. Their father's choice created immense bitterness in the older son (who, incidentally, had been married previously, but the girl had run away with an Igbo man). Although the elder son was working in a construction gang, he drank a great deal and threw away his money. He claimed that his father had promised him the *dwa* and that it was rightfully his because none of his fathers had helped raise the bridewealth for his first wife. But his father thought it best to invest in the younger, more obedient son, who also had the greater potential for success in the modern world. The rift between the two brothers was looked on as a bad thing but also as something that happens in the natural course of events.

In another case, Pwol was a younger classificatory brother of a well-established man with two wives and many children. On his return from a brief period in the army, Pwol requested of his older brother, Toma, his share of their father's land. Later, Pwol claimed that Toma would not give him any land but argued that since Pwol had no wife, he did not need it. During several months, the brothers were known to have engaged in many arguments, mostly over petty things. Toma publicly accused the younger brother of being a ne'er-do-well and of living in his (Toma's) house, eating the food prepared by his wives, and contributing nothing to the common good of the family. He claimed that Pwol now thought that farming was beneath him, as he had been to school, and that if he, Toma, should relinquish some of the family land to him, Pwol would simply squander it away. Pwol, on the other hand, argued that Toma wanted to keep all the land for himself for his sons and that his brother really wanted him to leave the village for good. "Am I to become a wanderer?" Pwol queried. Eventually, there was a terrible argument over a trivial matter, and Pwol, in a state of anger, beat one of Toma's wives. When Toma returned from farming and heard of it, he threw all of Pwol's belongings out of his sleeping hut and barred the doorway. It was several weeks before the argument was patched up sufficiently so that Pwol could return to his home. But this was not the end. Other petty incidents followed, and in a few months Pwol left to seek a job in Zaria.

Within the same generation, disagreements between "brothers" who are parallel cousins are more frequent than those between full brothers. There is a tendency for full brothers to fuse together against the wider circle of agnates, including half siblings. Informants often assert that in the old days, real brothers never argued or fought, but today all agnatic kinsmen show the strain of conflicts. Many observers claim that kinship of this sort is breaking down and that men are going their separate ways, ignoring the moral values that once held kinsmen together. It is easy to make the mistake of assuming that there were in fact better days when the ideals of agnatic closeness did operate in reality. But a close scrutiny of the nature of these relationships, particularly those between fathers and sons, reveals a high degree of tenuousness, ambivalence, and often insecurity in the relationships. These qualities have deep roots in the traditional structuring of these positions and particularly in the inherent competitiveness of men in agnatic relationships (compare Skinner 1961).

The content of the relationship between fathers and sons, involving men of adjacent generations, is characterized by an emphasis on differences of power, authority, and rank. The most common basis of authority is through differences in age and generation. The proper behavior of sons is that of obedience, respect, receptivity, and loyalty. Sons fear the power of their fathers (and all ancestors), and out of this fear, as well as love, they obey. Fathers have the role of stern disciplinarian, instructor, adjudicator, and leader—all positions of dominance. Until a son is about eight or nine years old, his world is that of the women of the household. It is they who care for him, chastise and correct him, provide what training is necessary for his successful incorporation into the household and kin group, and look after his security and health. He soon learns, however, that he occupies a position of dominance vis-à-vis his sisters of whatever age, a fact that is associated with a growing social identity with the other males of the household or compound. Eventually, he realizes that he is subordinate only to the fathers and older brothers. While his relationships with the women may remain warm, casual, and affectionate, those with his fathers take on more formal aspects, with obedience strictly demanded.

One feature of this formality is a concentrated attention on testing, an institutionalized custom by which fathers gauge the obedience and honesty of their sons. It is an experience that virtually every boy is thought to undergo at some stage in his life. In the father/son relationship, the worst offenses that a son can commit are stealing, telling lies, and refusing to do something that he has been instructed to do. Since stealing is the most heinous of all crimes, a father at some time will test his son by giving him an opportunity to steal something valuable that will not be easily detected. A common item used is meat because it is so highly valued. A father will, for example, tell his son to place a piece of meat in a storeroom and will leave it there for several days pretending to forget it. Only the father will have access to the storeroom, and only the son will know about the meat. The father will then watch it very carefully, and if small portions begin to disappear, he will know that his son is stealing from him.

At the first transgression, when a son is found to be a thief, Birom fathers say they only give the boy a warning. A man will explain the nature of his son's wrongdoing to him and demand that it not be repeated. If a boy commits a second offense, he may be beaten with a cane or a stick, depending on his age. Should a son continue in his behavior and become an inveterate thief, in precolonial times he would have been sold into slavery or put to death, but only with the agreement of all the agnatic group members. When a son pilfered from an outsider, the father was liable for restitution. Birom men say that a father would redeem a son only once or twice in the hope that the son would mend his ways. But if a man had several sons and were a stern father, he would soon refuse to make the repayments and would arrange, without the consultation of his brothers, to sell the son, and the produce of the sale would be used to repay the victims. A father or the headman of the kin group would also set traps for a son if there were reason to believe that the latter went out at night to steal. Some men used ingenious devices to ascertain whether anyone left the compound and who did so. Some of these devices were punitive. Two men whom I met (one from a distant village) had had broken legs as a result of their fathers' setting traps that caused heavy logs or stones to fall on them. It would be known that a man who carries such an injury around for the rest of his life was a son who disgraced his father so much that the latter no longer cared what happened to him.

Thus, in the structuring of the father–son relationship among the Birom, there are situations that militate against mutual goodwill, trust, and harmonious cooperation. Sons resent the extreme uses of authority by their fathers, leading to discord. Older men are required to exert their dominance in order to maintain the law and order that is so vital to the perpetuation of the social system. It is in the handling and control of property that friction between adjacent generations reaches its extreme, and the friction penetrates even to the youngest generations. In precolonial days, the older men controlled and dictated the use of land, horses, and other material goods owned by the kin group. They also controlled access to these essential resources and to wives. No son was ever completely assured of obtaining these goals. The scarcity of resources was always constant, and it was exacerbated during the first decades of European contact. Illness, especially prolonged, and ill luck (such as crop failure and accidental disaster) sometimes affected a man's competitive position vis-à-vis his other agnates. Consequently, some young men found themselves virtually disassociated from the land, though not completely ostracized from the kin group. In the old days, some of these young men would depart and become wanderers, seeking a new life in another village. Even today, there is sometimes much bitterness in the arguments between men over resources, though other, newer means for gaining wealth are now available.

In some kin groups, the causes of conflict increased during the colonial period. First there was the problem of landholding and the use and control of money that was derived from land. Numerous arguments occur over land transactions made by individual men without the consent of their headmen or other agnates. Sons are accused of selling or lending plots arbitrarily when they have need for cash. Brothers and fathers and sons argue over the use of particular plots, and these arguments rankle even though they usually achieve a satisfactory settlement. Inheritance is frequently disputed with the result that some men may be prevented from inheriting for such reasons as laziness. Most important, there are numerous disputes over the divisions of money obtained, particularly compensation for mining lands. This latter fact in itself has added a new source of friction to the relationships among men. Additionally, there are disputes over personal properties and over status. One often hears quarrels over clothing and jewelry, such as rings, tie clasps, writing implements, and watches. There is jealousy leading to dissension on account of disproportionate incomes and material possessions and the failure of some men to share. Some men express occasional envy of another person's more favored standing with the chief of the village area or district even though he may be a close agnate. Many of the disputes between men of different generations have to do with the disposal of bridewealth, whether girls may go to the local primary schools, when and whom certain sisters and daughters may marry, who is responsible for repaying damages (in cash today) to outsiders, and what are or should be the limits of agnates' responsibilities for and to one another. The Christian young and the non-Christian old dispute over matters of the morality of interpersonal behavior, especially among kinsmen, and on such practical manifestations of "right" observances as the drinking of beer, use of tobacco, attractions to town life, sexual practices not recognized by the church, and a host of other seemingly minor matters. Finally, there are disagreements involving household affairs, food supplies, storage rooms, sleeping quarters, animals, meat, personal implements, tools, and the services of other agnates.

The frequency of occasions of discord may indeed be greater among agnates today. However, this is not due entirely to the breakdown of an indigenous system of morality. The important facts discernible from the data are 1) that lines of cleavage and disjunction were aspects of the traditional social process, instituted out of ecological circumstance in which competition for scarce valuables was inherent, and 2) that property relationships that had developed in an older ecological setting have been and are being destroyed, and they are being replaced by new relationships of men to property and to one another. The morality that buffered and sustained the older system is still operative, but it is losing its force as traditional sanctions decline.

Young men are no longer entirely dependent on their fathers and membership within a corporate property-holding unit for their livelihood. The freedom that the modern situation gives a man is expressed partly in his willingness to argue with his kinsmen and partly in his ability to become mobile and yet remain within the setting of the village and kinship relationships. At the same time, young men express that they do not wish to be separated from kinspeople, especially their mothers. Even the rumor that a sister has been injured or that a young kinsperson is ill will prompt a young man to return to the village.

There is also the traditional institutionalized process of severing agnation at the fourth to seventh generation level, a mechanism that has allowed some units to maneuver themselves into and out of associations and ritual groups from time to time. After the government forced mining companies to pay land compensation in the late 1940s, the flexibility of kinship ties has provided the stratagem by which individuals and groups of agnates put claims on the relatively large sums of money paid out by the mining companies. Compensation, paid in cash and thus highly divisible, is the only shared property that can and does cut across the boundaries of emergent corporate kin groups.

Agnates are supposed to engage in cooperation and mutual aid for all sorts of activities. The height of cooperative activity occurs when two or more related men farm together and share the crops. This kind of activity entails sustained contact over the entire farming cycle from the first sowing to the harvesting, threshing, and storing of grain. Persons who farm together, whether or not they are of the same kin group, are always on the friendliest of terms. This is, indeed, a kind of test of mutual trust and friendship. Various individuals, both friends and kinsmen, may and do give one another personal help from time to time over and beyond their participation in work groups (*yat*). Persons who agree to farm together generally are known to have a long-standing, congenial relationship.

The Birom continually describe an "ideal" situation, namely, that "real" brothers and "real" fathers and sons always worked their lands and shared together. The reasons given stem from the notion of the great strength of ties between men of the same blood—"we are one." Yet a detailed study of the actual farming situations of the men of six wards in Du shows a surprising divergence from this ideal. One hundred sixty-eight persons in the economic survey were involved in farming-and-sharing relationships during the 1960 farming season. Of these, eighteen were women, living alone or with small children, and all of them farmed with men who were variously related to them. Of the remaining 150 men, only fifty-three farmed and shared with agnatic kin, and four of these were with women. There were sixteen separate partnerships of two men each with both partners living in the six surveyed wards and twenty men who farmed with agnates living elsewhere and not in the survey. The results are given in table 10.1.

Forty-eight of the fifty-three men designated in the table had primary male agnates available in the village with whom they might have farmed. Yet more than 80 percent of those with primary agnates chose to work with more remote lineal kinsmen or, as in the case of four, with female agnates. Two-thirds of these men neglected both primary and secondary kinsmen as farming partners. What accounts for this apparent discrepancy between an ideal formulated in terms of the closeness of agnatic ties and the "real" behavior with a definite preference for more remote agnatic kinsmen? It would seem that the application of an ideal-versus-real dichotomy here would be a simple but entirely erroneous perception and interpretation of social facts. The "ideal" in the case of the Birom system of

Table 10.1   Agnatic Relationships of Men to Their Farming Partners

	Relationship[a]				
	Primary agnate	Secondary agnate	Yere	Yere or chang (links unknown)	Total
Partnership	3	8	2	3	16 (29)[b]
Individuals[c]	3	10	4	5	22 (20)[b]

[a] Primary agnates are defined here as "real" fathers, sons, or brothers. Secondary agnates are any other members of the *lo*. *Yere* includes relationship between men of different *lo* groups whose previous connections are known, that is, groups formed by segmentation in the immediate past. The last category includes all relationships described as *yere* or *chang* where no genealogical links are known, but agnation is postulated as the basis for the connections.
[b] Three men had two partners, each with whom they worked separate farms.
[c] Two men had two partners, each with whom they worked separate farms.

agnation is a statement of structural principles that have to do with the organiza-tion of the total society in relation to its major resources. It is an accurate state-ment about relationships in which property is held in a state of relative permanence. The statement has intrinsic moral and jural implications that color the views that the Birom themselves hold about how land is worked as well as held.

Meanwhile, the "real" behavior operates in a completely different context, for what agnates actually do for and with one another in terms of mutual aid is a concern of the domestic unit. Hence, the choices and decisions made by individu-als in working situations must be understood not in terms of the degree to which their behavior approaches an ideal set in the context of corporate agnatic land-holding but rather in the context of all other economic affairs and relationships that may affect a particular domestic unit. One must take into consideration, for example, the amount of farmlands over which men of the *lo* unit hold rights, the extent of their dispersal, their varying fertility, the number of mouths to be fed, the number and sex of workers available, and what other possible alternative per-sons, relatives, and unrelated people can be called on for cooperative activities and/or donations of foods. Indeed, in most cases, it may not ever be economically feasible to confine one's cooperative production efforts to primary or secondary agnates (who are by definition members of one's own *lo* unit). Thus, the problems of real versus ideal behavior constitute a kind of false dichotomy when these are perceived as different types of social facts taking place in different contexts.

One has to view the Birom social system as operating on at least two levels. One is the level of larger-scale structure and involves principles that must effect stability and continuity in order to maintain the established relationships of social segments to one another and to basic resources. This is the level of ideal behavior, codified into a system of morality about unchanging relationships. The second is the pragmatic level of economic processes and involves those social devices and behaviors that maintain the material welfare and security of the household. At this second level, there must be room for flux, for alternative social and individual choice. This is the area of real behavior in which daily and seasonal decisions are taken to enable the household to survive. It is at this level that both cyclical and progressive changes can best be accommodated and observed, for it is here that the day-to-day flexibility and adaptability in the social process are made possible.

The key to understanding these different levels of the social process is pro-vided, as I have already argued, by the differentiation of the adult female role in the total system of agnation. Not only does agnation have different meanings for women and men, but women do not figure into the large-scale structure; that is, they are not involved in the property relationships that are the common denominator of agnation. As we have seen in previous chapters, a married woman is the focal point of the domestic unit, the sine qua non of the processes of preparation, distribution, and consumption of food. Women enter significantly into the agnatic system at the level of real behavior. They are able to make choices about the use of farms and the cultivation of land independently of the jural rules governing male agnates. In addition, the putative choices and alternative means of obtaining resources available to a woman are much broader and more diverse than those available to men. Finally, women can and do have de facto control of food and other materials because of the nature of their role in the domestic unit.

The two processes represented by the ideology and the reality of agnatic relationships are mutually interconnected. The ideology constrains, guides, and channels the areas in which choices are made by men. It is a cosmological codification of broad values and sentiments through which all experiences are sifted; that is, it provides the cipher through which experiences are interpreted and made meaningful. In this manner, it feeds back into the de facto patterns of economic cooperation and exploitation. Its influences are expressed in many ways, channeling behavior, providing models for the setting of goals, and generating cooperation and solidarity where necessary. Agnatic ideology is a dynamic phenomenon that, while functioning to maintain an enduring structure and systemic continuity, is also flexible and capable of absorbing contradictions, changes, and modifications. It affects and influences the behavior of women as well as men but in different ways.

One of the more curious and striking behaviors that I observed in the village was the frequent antagonism that women showed while I was collecting information about kin groups. Generally, both men and women were cooperative and polite. But when I inquired about relationships among men in earlier generations and asked how certain *lo* groups were related to one another and especially why a single group might use two names, it was the women who, sometimes quite sharply, retorted, "Why are you asking about that?" and "What do you want to know that for?" On several occasions when I apparently probed too deeply and touched on sensitive wounds, women yelled at me that I was trying to divide the house (*lo*). The feedback from the ideology, as these incidents demonstrate, is manifest in women's verbal support of the social structure and their hostility to any suggestion that threatens the image of agnatic solidarity. In point of fact, I found that women often appeared to know more about the membership and structure of the group and the disputes leading to eventual segmentation than did the men. That they also showed greater concern about preserving the unity of their husbands' kin groups and the agnatic principles on which such kinship is founded should not be attributed to the myth that women everywhere are more conservative than men. Women bear the sons who perpetuate the patrilineal group, and they are always vigilant about the rights of their children. It is also my contention, and I have already set out some of the reasons for this, that women derive advantages from patrilineal ideology despite and because of their exclusion from the formal system of property holding.

Women are the links through which men of discrete agnatic units are bound together. Through a mother, a man is tied to her agnates and especially to her brother in the avunculate relationship; through a sister he acquires an affinal unit, brothers-in-law (*mwali*) and later sister's sons (*gwal*); through a daughter, he obtains a son-in-law and a *gwal* (daughter's son); and so forth. Men are also bound to one another by the Njem custom through their common sexual and affective interests in particular women who are wives to some men and mistresses to others. None of these men will be members of the same agnatic kin group, but each man is tied to the others and they to him by their common interest in and affection for the same woman. Because a woman is also the ultimate source of food, regardless of the nature of her relationship with these various men, their obligations and responsibilities to her are always potentially and actually recipro-cal. Finally, it should be noted that, particularly in the precolonial era, the women of a man's agnatic group were the principal means by which a man acquired a brideprice for himself and his sons. Men without daughters were at a special dis-advantage and would have to obtain their *dwa* through raiding or the exchange of a son.

To a woman, male agnates represent security for herself and her children beyond that of her immediate marital household and husband's kin group. Women depend on their brothers and fathers for help and services of many types, from voluntary help with farming chores to the making of cash loans. Brothers and their households may be expected to provide food in emergencies, and later a woman's brothers and fathers are an important source of many goods and ser-vices for her children, especially her sons. Of equal or greater importance is the protection that men provide for their sisters and daughters and for the children of these women. Both men and women frequently say that they do not like the women of the *lo* to be married far away or to strangers, for then their women will have no one to protect them. In some cases, so great is the concern and fear that their daughters will marry strangers that men will not allow them to attend school or live with relatives in town. One man of Du whom I knew well was quite sad-dened when he told me how he had warned his daughter, one of the first girls in secondary school at Gindiri, not to marry a stranger. When she did marry an Igbo man, he sent word that should she ever return to Du village, he would kill them both. Men will go to great lengths to settle marriage disputes between their daughters and their husbands, but they will even go further in protecting their kinswomen from the excesses of their husbands. It is, indeed, the treatment of these women that is one of the major causes of disputes between male affines.

Brothers and sisters appear to be particularly close, a fact that is also expressed in common sayings and folktales. Although the taboo on incest prevents actual physical contact, meetings between these siblings are usually very joyful and pleasant. This ease of relationship between male and female siblings is possible because of a parallelism in their aims and interests. Brothers and sisters have few areas of conflict, for they do not compete with one another for the same (economic) goals. It is this absence of competition that is the essence of the differences between male and female agnates. With women, the tension and potential strife that exists in the relationships among men of the same kin group are completely obviated. This means, moreover, that there are no reasons structurally inherent within the social order for breaking agnatic kinship ties with women. The ties are not formal and structural as with men but essentially personal in their scope and content.

The Mother's Brother (or Father)

The structured role in the avunculate, or the mother's brother/sister's son relationship (*gwasa/gwal*), can be characterized in some ways as being both diametrically opposed to and complementary to that of the father. While the father–son relationship centers on the formal exercise and acceptance of authority and differences of rank and power, it is the almost complete lack of these features that is emphasized in the relationship of men (and women to some extent) to the men of their mother's natal *lo* group. The contrast even appears as an exaggerated one; young men behave toward their *gwasa* with little inhibition and almost complete freedom, knowing that in these situations they will not be corrected or punished. There are, of course, limits defined by custom to what a sister's son (*gwal*) may do with respect to his mother's brother. But specific to the *gwasa/gwal* relationship is a pattern of indulgence and permissiveness that is not found in any other relationship. The contrast in the two types of structured kin positions is best revealed in the following notes from a tape-recorded discussion with two older men (one in his early sixties) and two younger ones. (The statements are presented in the sequence in which they occurred. The individual speakers are not identified.)

"Boys receive many gifts from their *gwasa* [mother's brother]. *Gwasa* is expected to give his *gwal* everything he wants more or less. Everyone must visit their *gwasa* frequently, but how often depends on how far away the *gwasa* lives. Our fathers sometimes encourage their sons to visit the *gwasa*, but they will not like it if you visit the *gwasa* every day. The reason for this that some boys would run away and stay all the time at the *gwasa*'s house. There he has a better life. His *gwasa* gives him everything, and there is no father to punish him or chastise him for wrongdoing."

"But the boys will run away to the *gwasa* for other reasons. If the mother no longer loves the father very much but goes often to another man's house or if the mother runs away from the father to her own house, a boy may decide not to stay with his father. Some boys stay at the *gwasa*'s house because they never eat meat at the father's house. [Names of some young men who did this.] At the *gwasa*, a boy can have the best of everything. All the meat of his *gwasa* can be his, and the *gwasa* won't refuse it. Fathers refuse their own children meat but never refuse the *gwal*. Even when the father has meat, say at the time of a burial, boys won't get any because this meat is eaten at the burial feast only by certain people. Fathers are selfish with their sons even with beer. Fathers punish their sons, give them a hard life. The *gwasa* does everything for the boy and gives him a good and easy life."

"It is the father's responsibility to marry a wife for his son, but if the father isn't rich or if other circumstances intervene such as a big breach [break] between the two houses, the *gwasa* will give him the *dwa* if he is able."

"When a boy visits his *gwasa* he can always expect something, usually a hen. Not if he visits him every day, but after a decently long interval, so that the *gwasa* says, 'Kai, why have you not come to visit me sooner!' He always brings out the best food for the *gwal*. He can even kill a goat, madam! Nowadays, it is usually money that is given if the *gwasa* has some."

"Yes, boys and girls are taught by their mothers from the time they can walk that the home of the *gwasa* is like a 'paradise.' We go when we are infants on our mothers' backs. When the children are old enough they go to the *gwasa*'s by themselves."

"Girls are not so important as boys. They can go any time to the *gwasa*'s house, they can even stay and be raised there. The father won't care. Mothers usually take a young girl from her own house to look after her children."

"But, if a boy wants to go too frequently to his *gwasa*, the father will always try and stop him. He may beat him, or he may give him a lot of work to do and say, 'You are not a girl; why should you go to your *gwasa*?' A wise boy will report his father. The *gwasa* can make the father do anything because he is senior to him and his daughter's husband is as a child to him."

"If the man feels that his daughter and his *gwal* are badly treated by their husband and father, he would take steps of retribution." [In ancient times, some *gwasa* who were wealthy and powerful men were said to have destroyed the son-in-law's whole family by selling them off one by one. Not his *gwal*, or his daughter, though.]

"A long time ago, before the Europeans came, a boy could be sold into slavery by his father's house if they decided he was not worth keeping. But if the *gwasa* were fond of the boy, he might prevent it, or he might take vengeance on the sale of his *gwal* by grabbing someone from the father's house. Kai! He might take more than one."

"A father could kill his child in the ancient days. If a child disobeyed he might cut him in a fit of anger. Whenever such a dispute happened, the only recourse was to the *lo gwasa*. Even the chief could not intervene because it was a private matter of the families."

The full description of these relationships as given by these men reveals the strong emotional involvement that is invested in them. Although the perspective taken is most frequently that of the *gwal*, the relationship is much more than a unilateral one. The mother's brother or father can expect a *gwal* to perform many services for him. Men say that they always help the *gwasa* with farming and that the *gwasa* is kind to his *gwal* in order to obtain this help, which is thought to be completely voluntary. "Even when he does not ask me, I help him," said the old man. Gift giving is common and expected both from and to the *lo gwasa*.

The *gwasa/gwal* relationship is thought to be a very strong one, and there are mystical overtones elaborated in the institution. The *gwasa* sees in his *gwal* a continuation or extension of his own personality, not his social person, which is determined by father right, but his individuality as a human being. The Birom believe that the human personality can be reincarnated, reborn within a new child. Some of the traditional ritual associated with childbirth must be carried out by the child's *gwasa*. Thirty days after the birth of a boy, it is given a name in a ritual that requires the mother's brother, who is allowed to see the baby for the first time, to chant prayers and place a small gray spider on the child's forehead.

In many cases, some strange event or circumstance will reveal to the *gwasa* that his sister's child is himself. From then on, he will refuse to drink or eat from the same dish (calabash) as the boy and will observe many taboos, sometimes self-imposed, with regard to this particular *gwal*. The mystical relationship is transposed into myths and folk legends that serve to reinforce the benign quality and spirituality of the relationship.

The closeness of the *gwasa/gwal* tie is attested to by another custom among the Birom that again suggests a type of personal identification between mother's brother and sister's son. If a man has no male child or is unable to beget a child, he can give one of his young wives to his mature but unmarried *gwal* in order that the latter may beget a child for him. The number of children who are begotten in this manner is unknown, and the fact is unimportant legally, although, if known, it may further strengthen the emotional ties already existing between the two men. Consistent with this custom is an older tradition, probably more wide-spread, by which young, unmarried men may have easy sexual access to the young wives of men who are *gwasa*. In these instances, the woman need not belong to a "real" mother's brother, as any woman in this kinship category (*bwa gwasa*) is theoretically available to her husband's *gwal*. Young men say that their *gwasa* do not mind this extramarital playfulness and admit that it is one of the features of the relationship that helps attract and keep their attention and loyalty. Whether or not young men engage in these only slightly clandestine affairs with their *gwasa*'s wife or wives, the common term of reference for these young women is *bwa-bong* (my wife).

Although the *gwasa/gwal* relationship is restricted primarily to the men of the mother's house, it can be extended to the *lo gwasa* of the boy's father (that is, father's mother's house). But it is believed that *lo gwasa da-me* (father's gwasa) will not treat you as well as your own *gwasa*.

"They can refuse to give the boy things, and he cannot complain. Only a real *gwasa* can complain if he is refused. The son of *gwal* is nothing to '*lo gwasa da*.' But still some people take the son of *gwal* as important. If the *gwasa* is kind, he may give him anything he likes." On the other hand, it is difficult for a young man to know the *gwasa* of his mother, for such men have no structural importance. Many men do not even know the name of this kin group. Other informants said that, in the olden days, some men preferred to marry from this house ("to marry in a circle") as long as the couple were not related within four generations to a common ancestor.

The content of the relationship between *gwasa* and *gwal* is never uniform for all persons. Children tend to gravitate toward one maternal uncle, generally the one who treats them best. By the same token, maternal uncles have favorites among uterine nephews, although many men hesitate to admit it. What points up the structural and institutional features of the relationship is the manner in which such relationships may be used, particularly in modern times. One day when I was out surveying some fields with a young Birom man, Lawrence, from the government farm at Riyom village, an old man approached us, joining several others who stood around watching us work. He soon discovered the name of my assistant, to whom he was a compete stranger, went up to him and said, "Ya gwal, give me a shilling!" My assistant's first inclination was to refuse, but some brief discussion (along with a few questions on my part) brought out the fact that the old man was indeed from a *lo* that had stemmed from the same house from which my assistant's mother had come. Although the members now used separate names, the houses were *yere* to one another. The old man lived in a distant village, and my assistant had never known him. Even though Lawrence later complained that he did not have to give the old man anything as he was not a real *gwasa*, the outcome of the encounter was that the old man did indeed receive a shilling, to the nods and murmurs of approval of all around. It is probably unlikely that the old man would have asked for the money had he not believed that the appeal to kinship connections would have been effective. In circumstances of this sort, the *gwasa/gwal* relationship is one of the most effective types of kinship ties to have because of this quality of extendability of certain kinds of obligatory behavior contained within it.

A brother or father of one's mother can only be a *gwasa* if he is a man of the same agnatic kin group as is the mother. One case may be used to illustrate this point and the principles on which the relationship is established. Ojo Tok is a man in his forties and is a senior member of the group Lo Bi. In 1960, Ojo farmed and shared with Bot Laba, a man of Lo Go Zang, an unrelated house. Ojo referred to Bot Laba descriptively as his *gwa ngwo* (literally, brother of mother) but never called him *gwasa*. During interviews with Ojo, certain facts came to light. Ojo's maternal grandmother Pwa was married first to a man at Zawang village and there gave birth to Ojo's mother, Honghei. Then Pwa divorced the Zawang man and married Pwajok, Lo Go Zang, and gave birth to Bot Laba (Bot Pwajok). Since each marriage involved proper bridewealth payments, Pwa's children were legally of two different houses. Ojo properly calls *gwasa* only those men of his mother's natal *lo* at Zawang, not her brother Bot Laba "by the same womb." But Ojo obviously feels quite close to Bot, as they are frequently seen together and render many small services to each other. Yet there is no doubt that he is some-what discomforted by the problems presented in his situation. His *lo gwasa* is only a fifteen-minute or so walk from Lo Bi, yet his interaction with the men of the house is not so warm and frequent as it would be if there had been a "real" mother's brother or even half brother there. The three men of the category *gwasa* are remotely related: two second parallel cousins of his mother and an old man who is a classificatory "father" to his mother. Ojo states that he must help his *gwasa* and has given them farming services in the past, cut bamboo with them, and shared a *kumu* (firewood) tree with them. But despite his feelings of obligation to *gwasa*, his real affection is for Bot Laba, with whom he farms and drinks beer. Several times he has been placed in the position of having to make a choice. His *bigwasa* (plural) have not failed to note his disposition toward Bot, and when I was on a visit to them, they complained of it to me.

Ojo's case emphasizes a number of structural facts, not all of which can be discussed in this study. First, it demonstrates a principle that has been emphasized several times: Marriage, not birth or the actualities of biological connections, cre-ates kinship. Second, this case reveals that in this society, as in other kinship based societies, there exist two types of kinship ties: "structured" ties that are created by legitimate marriage contracts and personal kinship ties based on links by birth or, more succinctly, links through maternity. In most cases, personal kinship and structured kinship will coincide in the same individuals so that one need not conceptualize the distinction. Third, this case shows that divorce confuses the legitimacy of relationships, the structured kin positions established through marriage. A woman bearing legitimate children to two different men "divides her house." The question that Ojo faces, to whom is due his allegiance, love, loyalty, and services—his *gwasa* or the real brother of his mother—is one that, by the very asking, threatens the principles of patriliny. Needless to say, the question is rarely, perhaps never, stated in Birom society, for Ojo and everyone else unhesitatingly agree that the *gwasa* comes first. From the point of view of structured kinship, Bot Laba is not a kinsman to him at all.

Patriliny is not only a principle of group formation but also a method of structuring and controlling individual behavior both within the paternal group and to the maternal patrilineal group. Thus, claims to the specific kinds of services of a daughter's sons that are distinct from those of one's own sons or son's sons are part of the fundamental rights derived as part of patrilineal ideology. Patriliny operates by a process of exclusion based on the subordination of close ties of relationship through women to the ties with men. The *lo gwasa* cannot maintain its control over the sons of its daughters (a specific kind of control and interest) if the "closeness of the womb" (Bot Laba and Honghei) is going to take precedence over legal paternity (Honghei and her father's patriline) (for a discussion relating these differences to landholding and inheritance, see Goody, 1959).

The significance of the *gwasa/gwal* relationship in Birom social structure lies essentially in the way it connects male kin positions. The women of the mother's natal *lo* are not singled out terminologically, and young men may have very little interaction with them after they are married out. In the older generations, such women are simply called *ngwo* (mother), and in the same or younger generations, they are designated by the classificatory sibling term (*gwa*) and by the common term for all children, *hwei* (plural, *nei*). Children's relationships with these women, however, may often be very deep and intense, especially in the younger years, for these are the women who will quite often feed or keep a small child if its mother dies or some other disaster occurs. There appears to be no moral obligation here. Women say that they will take these children, sometimes even when their husbands object, because of love for their sisters and daughters. This lack of definitive obligations and the wide range of choices that can be and are made on the basis of purely personal factors give further evidence of the absence of the constraints of structured kinship among women and between women and their male consanguine kinsmen.

Made explicit in the taped conversations presented earlier is the relative insignificance of women as participants in the *gwasa/gwal* relationship. As *gwal* to their mother's brothers and fathers, young girls derive the benefits of the avunculate but without the disabilities. Young boys and men are often caught up in conflicting loyalties pulling them simultaneously toward diametrically opposed poles. Too much interaction with the *gwasa*, especially in the form of aid, provokes anger and resentment among the fathers in the boy's own kin group. Jealousy and deep, wrenching arguments can be the result. But a girl is at liberty to develop these relationships without feelings of rancor or fear of competition and jealousy. She can visit and even live with the *lo gwasa*, helping out the young wives of the household, and never incur strain or tension in relationships with her own natal kinsmen, for no one is vying for her loyalty and allegiance in a structural sense as they would be for her brother's. None of the men of her *lo gwasa* can even make a claim on the bridewealth paid for her, except in those rare instances where a *gwasa* provides the bridewealth for a sister's child and there is agreement to repay him through the incoming bridewealth of a girl of the *gwal*'s kin group. This lack of friction and strain with respect to girls and women operates to their advantage and is further evidence of the unstructured and highly personal nature of women's relationships with men.

Affinity: *Lo Guna*

When a young man marries, he enters into a third field of structured kinship, that of affinal affiliations with individuals who constitute a *lo* unit that is terminologically distinguished only for men. The kin group(s) from which his wife (wives) comes is referred to as *lo guna*. A woman never uses this term, nor does she ever come to stand in any corresponding relationships. Her affinal kinsmen become her "fathers," "mothers," "cowives," and "siblings," and she makes distinctions between her affines and consanguine kin when necessary only by using a kinship term plus a proper name for the former.

But for a man, a number of distinct terms are used for the various members of his wife's *lo* group, as they represent kinship positions that are structured for differing specific roles. There are, first of all, his father-in-law(s), whom he calls *tya*, and his mother-in-law, *guna*, both of whom use the reciprocal term *so*. These terms are also used for siblings of the parents-in-law, but as with all classificatory terms of this sort, behavioral expectations differ between the "real" or legal in-laws, their true siblings, and their patrilateral parallel and cross-cousins. Of similar or greater importance are the male siblings of a man's wife. Brothers-in-law are all called *mwali* (reciprocal, *mwali*), and their wives are called generally *hwa mwali* (wife of *mwali*). However, as I will describe later, the *hwa mwali* is a key person within the *lo guna*, the significance of her role being merely suggested here by the fact that she reciprocates with the term *rwas* (husband), although there are other terms that she can use, such as *rwas shin*. A man calls his wife's sister *shin*, a term that is used also by women for all in-laws, both male and female, of the same generation as themselves. All children of this generation are simply called "child" (*hwei*) or "my child," with a suffix when necessary to denote the sex of the child or his age vis-à-vis younger siblings.

One terminological peculiarity is observed here. While the terms for other kin groups are usually the same term as for the man of the unit who stands in a particular significant relationship to "Ego" (that is, *lo gwasa* and *lo damo*) in the case of the in-law group, the term used is not that of the father-in-law but that of the mother-in-law (*guna*). The mother-in-law is the crucial figure within this group, for, as we will see later in this chapter, her role is the pivot around which many other roles function. But perhaps the most important practical reason for her eminence lies in the traditional age structure of Birom marriage. Since men marry quite late (thirty years or so, as we have already seen), a girl's father was and still is generally in his late forties or older at the time of her marriage, while her mother would still be in her thirties. Considering the death rate and even the number of widows at the present time, it is quite likely that the father-in-law would live through only a few brief years, if those, of his daughters' marriages so that the main sustained interaction develops between the son-in-law and mother-in-law. This does not mean, of course, that the *guna* takes on the role and status of her husband vis-à-vis her son-in-law. The point is simply that for most or the whole of any man's marriage, the chances are that the real *tya* is already dead and thus could not function in a role of kinsman. Although this applies primarily to earlier times, it is still true for the present generations, with the modification that since World War II more men are marrying at younger ages.

I have already noted the obligations that a young man had, in former times, to his father-in-law in terms of both bridewealth and bride service. In the absence or death of his wife's father, the services and payments continue, with the obligations merely transferred to the brother(s) of the wife. My data record many marriages in which all the payments, arrangements, and services went to the brothers of the girl. Once the agreed-on obligations are completed, the son-in-law owes nothing further. He has obtained his wife "free and clear" as it were, and the contract between him and the men of his wife's natal house has been fulfilled. As long as he continues to observe the conditions of the marriage contract, in terms of his treatment of his wife, through the provision of food and shelter, a man theoretically need have no further contact with his wife's male agnates. This is what might be called his legal or jural position.

But such is not the case with his mother-in-law. This relationship of *guna* and *so* (son-in-law) is an interesting one because of the many facets that are enveloped in it. When evaluating and/or listing the strengths of the various obligations that he recognizes, a man invariably states that he must help his *lo guna* first because this *lo* gave a daughter to him. A man always helps his wife's mother either with farming, through direct gifts of food or cash, or today even by hiring help for her. A woman frequently calls on her sons-in-law for aid, particularly at harvest time, or to help her with some difficult task. Even when a man voluntarily helps a father-in-law or brother-in-law with farming chores, it is usually interpreted as aid to the *guna*, who benefits thereby. I can remember no case where a man voluntarily performed some service exclusively for a male affine, even when they got along well together, that was not also directly beneficial to the *guna* or done at her request. Of the twenty-nine widows who were recorded as heads of household in my economic survey, six farmed and shared with sons-in-law on their dead husbands' lands. (In these cases, the sons-in-law also benefited by the extra lands available to them for productive purposes.) Nine others received farm help from sons-in-law without formal sharing. Two women had four married daughters, each of whose husbands produced virtually all the food crops for their wives' mothers. Only three women with married daughters received no farming help from their sons-in-law, and two of these latter men and their families did not even live in the village. (One of these men brought two bags of grain and many other foods to his mother-in-law during the year.) Twenty-two of these twenty-nine women had sons who were considered their primary caretakers. Even so, they always received additional help of various sorts, especially from sons-in-law. It might be stated that, on the other side of the relationship, daughters encourage their husbands to give aid to their parents, particularly their mothers. Some women threaten to leave their husbands periodically unless they are more generous to their mothers.

This relationship between mother-in-law and son-in-law as against the strict mother-in-law avoidance characteristic of many patrilineal societies is a friendly, easy one. A man has great respect for his mother-in-law, and yet their meetings are generally permeated with much familiarity and congenial joking, albeit never on sexual matters. Many men appear overtly much more relaxed with the mother-in-law than with the wife's father. The taboos against intimacy are of the same nature as exist between any unrelated man and woman but not as strict as those between brothers and mature sisters.

One of the more notable features of a kinship-based society is the distinctiveness of the various roles that individuals play. Individuals have traditionally quite specific relationships with one another. There is normally no room for casual friendships between unrelated individuals of opposite sex and rarely a role for close or "bosom" friends. Yet in the Birom situation, the *guna/so* situation comes quite close to being basically this type of friendship. It will be recalled that up until the present generation, custom dictated that the vast majority of women were about fifteen (and more) years younger then their husbands. This means that mothers-in-law and sons-in-law were frequently quite close in age. Considering also that most marriages took place within a neighborhood or between contiguous ones, a woman and her potential sons-in-law probably grew up together, played together as young children, and may indeed have experimented with illicit and frowned on lovemaking as they became sexually mature. Once marriages have been effected and the *guna/so* relationship established, sexual unions between them would be strictly prohibited. But friendship, which might have been generated in their early playmate years, is possible. In fact, I would argue that the mother-in-law traditionally is the only possible female friend in the structure of Birom society. This conclusion is further strengthened by the fact that men often address their mothers-in-law somewhat affectionately as *ya, sa-hong* (my friend) (see the section "Institutionalized Friendship" later in this chapter).

The relationship is further characterized by an absence of the feature of rank differences (authority/subordination) that obtains in other male/female relationships. Although the son-in-law as a man has a dominant position in the society, his generational position is not equal to that of his mother-in-law regardless of their chronological ages. He is always of a younger generation and "as a child" to his wife's mother. Furthermore, the latter is not a dependent subordinate to her son-in-law as she is with her fathers, brothers, and husband. The cohesiveness of the relationship is represented in the common interest that they have in the wife/daughter. This interest differs quite radically from that which is shared with the father-in-law or brothers-in-law. In the former case, there is no legal threat from the mother-in-law if the daughter is not treated properly. On the contrary, a man is sometimes motivated by his friendly relationship with the mother-in-law to show much kindness to her daughter. In the latter case, there is always the threat of punitive action that can be taken by any man of his wife's natal house. Thus, potential if not actual conflict exists between male affines, and it is increased when children are born, for the attractions of the *lo gwasa* to a man's sons are well known. This undercurrent of competition and jealousy does not exist in relationships with women.

Perhaps because the mother-in-law is not in competition with her son-in-law and because of her age, she is able to exert considerable influence over the men who are involved in relationships through her: her husband and his male agnates, her fathers and brothers, her sons, and her sons-in-law. Women often serve as very informal mediators in disputes between their husbands and their sons-in-law. It is not uncommon for a young man to talk over certain problems with his mother-in-law, and he listens readily to her advice.

Men say that they like to go and work for the mother-in-law because she will treat them well. But there are other attractions in her house that reveal another facet of the relationship between mother-in-law and son-in-law. All men who are brothers (both real and patrilateral parallel cousins) of one's wife, as I have noted, are called *mwali*. Some of the women who are considered proper objects of a man's sexual advances in the Njem relationship are the young wives of *mwali*, provided that they are otherwise not related. One of these women may, in fact, become a man's Njem partner at some time (see the next section). It is considered proper behavior to make advances to the *mwali*'s wife and/or conduct an affair with her while the *mwali* is away. This requires some arrangements and specifically some means of indirect communication. Informants told me that it was the Birom custom to effect these liaisons through connivance with the mother-in-law, for such "old" women knew everything that went on in the compounds. Thus, frequently on the pretext of visiting the mother-in-law or under the guise of working for her, these men and their mistresses are enabled to arrange their assignations. As sexual intercourse in the fields or "bush" is taboo and fraught with supernatural dangers, the vast majority of such meetings take place in some compound hut, and the one person who knows about and facilitates the successful arrangement is the mother-in-law. A man sometimes uses the assistance of his wife's mother, rewarding her with small gifts, in arranging affairs that are not conducted with the *mwali*'s wife.

If, however, a man does have as a *bwa-njem* a wife of someone whom he calls *mwali*, by his farming services and gifts he may very well be "killing two birds with one stone." He is obliged in the Njem relationship to help his mistress who is undoubtedly receiving food crops from some of the same fields as their common mother-in-law. Thus, a man who helps work these fields is giving personal assistance to both his *guna* and his mistress at the same time. This is particularly felicitous if the *bwa-njem* is an actual wife of a real son of the mother-in-law, for, as we have seen, these young women are responsible for cooking food for their husbands' parents. The few arrangements of this sort that I observed appeared to encourage an all-around amiableness on the part of the individuals involved.

The Institution of Njem

This brings us now to a consideration of this major institution by which individuals of separate domestic units are connected together for the purposes of mutually beneficial aid and services. As there is no comparable feature or custom in the

English-speaking world, it is difficult to define or classify the phenomenon of Njem. C. K. Meek (1925, 1950), a trained anthropologist and colonial administrator who collected some of the earliest ethnographic materials on this area, identified the custom as a form of cicisbeism, and I will continue the use of this term. Features resembling this institution or related in some way to it are found among other peoples of this general geographic region. The several writers who have dealt with the topic have maintained distinctions between cicisbeism, concubinage, and secondary marriage (Gunn 1953; Muller 1969; Netting 1969; Sangree 1969, 1972; Smith 1953).

A cicisbeo is briefly defined as the recognized lover of a married woman, and as previously noted, I have translated the Birom terms of the actors as "lover" and "mistress." However, one should be aware that the connotations that these terms have in the English language do not apply to the Birom situation. I use the term "lover" partly because of the limitations of the English language and partly because it does denote a sexual expression and affection that are characteristic of this relationship. The relationship traditionally is a legitimate one in that it is recognized by the Birom as being good, appropriate, and even necessary, but it is not by any means considered marriage. It creates neither a domestic household nor kinship, even though sexual acts involved in the custom may occasionally lead to procreation.

It is not easy to obtain information about Njem, as many Birom have been exposed to the idea that westerners consider it immoral. They are aware that they have been accused of promiscuity on the basis of the limited knowledge of local tin miners and missionaries. Nearly all the data that I was able to collect apply to men and women of older generations and to some of the younger women. While young men, both Christian and non-Christian, may have illegal affairs on the side, most today do not enter into a traditional Njem relationship, with all the responsibilities and ramifications that characterize the circumstances of older persons. The set of conditions under which Njem operates may no longer apply to these young men. There is no doubt, however, that the Njem relationship was a universally recognized custom in precolonial times and second in importance, in terms of the relationships between the sexes, only to marriage. The principles and values on which it is based persist in an undiluted manner for nearly all persons in the older generations, and the custom itself is widely known even to young children, who were the first to introduce it to me.

The relationship comes about in this manner. After a young woman has been married, a man will present himself to her and ask to become her *rwas-njem*. If she agrees, the matter is then taken to her husband, and the initiator brings a goat to finalize the transaction. This is an important step, as the relationship is not considered proper and socially acceptable until the transfer of the goat. Some older women stated the female view that the prospective lover brought the goat to the husband to demonstrate his love for the wife.

Women have complete freedom in their choice of lovers. Among my informants, several old women recalled with delight and much laughter how many men vied for their affections and were made jealous when they finally made their choices. The relationship is maintained for as long as the parties concerned agree on it. A woman never moves out of her husband's household and never relinquishes her domestic duties while she has a lover. A woman may have more than one *rwas-njem* in her married life, although older women say that they preferred to settle on one who remains a lover for life. It is important to note that to have several in rapid succession or at the same time was considered not promiscuous but selfish and demanding. In any case, the Birom say that husbands would not allow many men to become lovers to their wives. If a woman took more than one lover, there would be fighting. A man, however, could have as many *bwa-njem* (mistresses) as he was able to support. A wealthy man would have many such relationships. The headman of my compound had three, one of whom was a very old woman, the widow of a man whose sister had married into his kin group several generations before. Poor men, on the other hand, would not be able to afford a Njem partner. As one old man told me, "I never had a *bwa-njem* because I was not strong and did not have much food. The girls would not look at me, and their husbands would not agree." There was one point on which all informants agreed: In precolonial times, every woman had a *rwas-njem*.

The most important feature of this relationship is the obligations that Njem partners have to provide each other with gifts and services. Both women and men are expected to help each other with farming. When I asked some women why they had *rwas-njem*, the answer always related to the material benefits. Most women replied, "Who will feed your children?" Others responded, "If no *rwas-njem*, who will bring you gifts?" They were surprised that I should ask the reasons for Njem relationships and even more surprised that women do not have this formal custom in my native land. After her marriage, a Birom woman does not expect gifts from her husband, only food, shelter, his farm labor, and perhaps personal favors. With the Njem relationship, she expects the lover to do a number of specific things throughout the duration of their relationship: 1) to kill a goat once a year and bring her the meat, 2) to provide her with food when she and her children are hungry, 3) to help her every year with farming, and 4) to provide her with things to adorn her body, such as oil and trinkets. During the great festivals of Bwuna and Mandyang, the *rwas-njem* is especially attentive, bringing all that the woman needs to decorate herself. Moreover, the *rwas-njem* may help provide the bridewealth for any of his *hwas-njem*'s children, and they in turn look to him as a kind of godfather.

The importance of the Njem relationship cannot be overestimated. When a man does not have enough farms or enough crops to feed his family, his wife will turn to her Njem partner to borrow a farm or to obtain food. This may occur even before she or her husband request aid from their consanguine or affinal kinsmen. One old man told me that the *rwas-njem* of his wife was expected to do even more than a brother. He argued that each man thinks more of his *rwas-njem*'s or *hwa-njem*'s family than of his brother's family and that people prefer even to live nearer to the Njem partner. Others who were listening in did not entirely agree. My data indicate that if a kin group has only a few men and they are relatively poor, it is more likely that the role of Njem partners of the women in the group will be greater. There was one *lo* that consisted of only one man who had a number of minor sons. He was a very poor man, rather old and unable to work because of illness, but he had four wives at one time, all of whom had Njem partners and who were being almost fully supported by them. One *rwas-njem* even paid tuition fees for the oldest son to attend the local primary school.

Some women say that they prefer to go to the *rwas-njem* first before asking aid of anyone else because they and their wives will not refuse you if they have food. The *rwas-njem*'s wife will even bring food to her husband's *hwa-njem* without being asked. And the *rwas-njem* is said to become as a friend (*sa*) to the husband through their mutual interest in and affection for the wife. A woman's lover tries to please her husband. He will bring gifts to him, such as tobacco and hens, if he has plenty, and at all times when beer is prepared in his house, he will bring some to the husband. Some women claim that if their husbands had mistresses, they will be friendly to them in the same manner. But they will love the wife of their *rwas-njem* more than the *hwa-njem* of their husbands and do many things to please the former. The affection that they have for these women is said to be second only to the affection that women have for their own sisters. The reason explicitly stated is these women will feed your children when they are hungry.

It should be noted that the *hwa-njem* of a man never comes from the same house as the *rwas-njem* of his wife, so that at least three kin groups are involved in this relationship of mutual obligation and help. If men follow the custom of taking as *hwa-njem* the young wives of men who are their brothers-in-law, there is the possibility that many domestic units in the village will be linked together by the two basic relationships of marriage and Njem.

An important feature of the Njem relationship is that it can be a long-lasting one; it may, indeed, cover more than just the lifetime of two individuals. One finds that an old widow almost always receives help from a *rwas-njem* even when she has many sons or a husbands' brother who are economically and socially responsible for her. Fifteen of the twenty-nine widows in my economic survey admitted to having *rwas-njem* (some even newly acquired) who helped them with farming, and six of these also farmed and shared with a *rwas-njem*. I am certain that there were others who did have *rwas-njem* but would not the divulge information. Many men farmed and shared with women who were their mistresses.

For some people in the village, the relationships established by Njem may be perpetuated into future generations. There were several men who farmed with a descendant of their mothers' or fathers' Njem partners. I met one young man who farmed with the son of his paternal grandmother's *rwas-njem* although both the old people were deceased. Friendship between the descendants of such partners is overtly and widely promoted. Such extension of mutual aid and support illustrates quite markedly the fundamental economic nature of the Njem relationship.

Njem has obvious economic advantages for the woman who is a mistress, for her children, and for her husband who is the recipient of goods and services that he himself has not expended effort to produce. From the perspective of the male partner, he shares, at the minimum, residual responsibilities for his *bwa-njem*'s welfare in return for sexual access rights shared with her husband. In traditional times, this custom was also an important concomitant to a man's status and prestige, an adjunct of political privilege, and a mechanism for the recruitment of loyal supporters. I have already noted that men who were successful in obtaining and keeping mistresses were regarded as wealthy, strong, and virile. The number of women who were in part dependent on him and serviced by him was symbolic of his status. Having women and taking care of them was and still is one of the most important goals in a Birom man's life.

A "big man" who held some of the major ritual offices and who could exercise informal power by virtue of his office, the size of his kin group, his health and wealth in land, and his wives and mistresses was also a man who might have many rivals. Such a man maintained his status partly on the basis of his personal characteristics of leadership and his effectiveness in the village polity. But because of competition within the kin group, there would arise factions and rival claims to power, so a prudent man was compelled to command a larger following from among people who were not kinsmen. From time to time, a challenge to his dominance might be posed, and he would be forced to take action to protect his status, his lands, and his resources (see the case of Da Jang Da Gwong Go in chapter 3). In these instances, a man who had many mistresses and who had established warm relationships with large numbers of kin groups through them could rely on the loyalty and support of his mistresses' husbands and possibly the latters' agnates.

An old ex-*gwom* (chief) told me that a man would depend on and trust the husband of a mistress more than his own brothers-in-law.

The composition of raiding parties at the turn of the twentieth century as remembered by older informants and of hunting parties then and at later times is pertinent here. A leader of such a sortie counted on the backing of his mistresses' husbands, his agnatic kinsmen, men from the *lo gwasa* or *lo gwal*, occasionally men with the status of *mwali*, and assorted neighbors and friends. The wife's lover and mistress's husbands were always mentioned and were the most common category of supporters, along with agnatic kinsmen. One individual, remembered for his great reputation as a leader of raiding parties and as a proficient hunter, was a man who had nine mistresses. The husbands of these women were regular members of his coalition. Such a man could command the loyalty of these men by virtue of his prestige as well as the links that he had with them through their wives. His prestige was in turn buttressed by their support and willingness to be followers. Some men, unable to attain leadership or high-status roles themselves, actively sought out "big men" to become Njem partners to their wives.[1]

Finally, since the children of a lover may be involved in the obligations stemming from the relationship, a man further insures his old age through this custom. Children of Njem partners are thought to be especially close, and it is traditional for them to call the partners of their parents by the same terms as those used for their parents. They are encouraged to play and work together, setting the stage for their later cooperative aid to one another. I have shown earlier that agnatic ties are such that an old man, in the event that he himself has no sons, may not be able to look to his brothers' sons and grandsons for support in his old age, although this is clearly the ideal. But he will have possibilities of at least three other types of ties that may serve as sources of sustenance when he is too old for farming: his mother's kin group (*lo gwasa*), quite possibly his sister's sons (*gwal*), and very probably the children of his Njem partner. The same is true for a woman, except that her own children would be first on the list, then her sons-in-law, and next her Njem partners' children.

It seems clear that the qualities of generosity, kindness, and friendship that have been woven into this institution serve to reduce the possibilities of jealousy and conflict and to stress cooperation. To this end, the Birom have prohibited legal marriage with a Njem partner. If a woman leaves her husband for any reason or if her husband should die, she may even go and live with her *rwas-njem*, especially if her natal kin group is small and poor. The *rwas-njem*, however, cannot offer bridewealth for her if her husband is still alive, for the latter would refuse to accept it. A marriage of this sort would be known as a "fighting" marriage. The husband will think that the *rwas-njem* broke up his marriage by luring his wife away. By custom, an offer to pay bridewealth is tantamount to initiating a duel. The husband would have the right to fight the *rwas-njem* and even to kill him. At the same time, if a young woman does leave her husband and returns to her father's house, she can bring no man into this house except her *rwas-njem*, who is permitted to see her at any time. If a husband loves his wife and wants her to return, he will go every night to try to entice her, and he will fight with any man except the *rwas-njem* who shows any interest in her. More important, if she refuses to see him or his entreaties are not effective, the husband will urge the *rwas-njem* to go to her and to try to win her back for him.

A *rwas-njem* may legally marry a woman after the death of her husband, but such an act might serve to upset already established friendly relationships among the kin groups and especially between his wife and the former *bwa-njem*. As cowives living in the same compound, there would be a greater possibility of the two women not getting along well together. For this reason, it is better to retain the social relationships intact, and most women prefer to remain in their husbands' homes, working their husbands' lands and sharing with *rwas-njem* who continue their obligations to them. Occasionally, a lover may even go and live with his widowed mistress in her husband's house (there were four such cases in my economic survey). In cases of this sort, the two lovers retain access to the lands and properties of their respective kin groups. A woman who has children, especially young ones, has a particular interest in remaining in her husband's home to help protect the rights of her children. A woman in her old age considers it better to have a lover than a husband, for she gets all the benefits of having a husband but has fewer responsibilities and virtually no quarrels with her lover.

This element of congeniality and friendship also affects the relationships of male affines who call one another *mwali*. If a man has as his *bwa-njem* a wife of his *mwali*, such a relationship in his affinal kin group will usually tend to counterbalance some of the potential conflict that is inherent in affinity. There are many ways in which this tendency operates, but the relationships and the processes of working out the multiple factors involved can be very complex. One relatively uncomplicated case will illustrate how a Njem partnership may affect not only quarrels between affines but also the maintenance of peace within and between kin groups.

Jang Lo Bi has been arguing with his wife's brother Chuang Zong for some time over a patch of garden about one-sixth acre in size. How the argument was started is unknown. Both men claim ownership of the farm, with Jang arguing that Chuang gave it to his (Jang's) father in lieu of cash as part of the *goro* paid to get his wife (Jang's sister) some twenty or so years before. Chuang denies this, stating merely that he loaned it to the old man for quite a different reason.

Recently, Chuang engaged Jang to build a house for him for one pound, five shillings. When it was partly finished, there was another argument between the two men. Chuang had agreed to pay Jang five shillings as a down payment, and when Jang went to get it, Chuang claimed he did not have the money. The hard feelings began to build up on both sides with the earlier and deeper conflict over the farm coming to fore. Men of both houses who were not contestants soon became involved.

However, Chuang has as a *bwa-njem* the wife of Choji Lo Bi, a younger man who has always apparently gotten along well with Chuang. They have done each other a number of favors; they worked in the tin mines together, they go drinking in Bukuru, and so forth. Choji refused at first to take sides in the argument, but he evidently had a few words with Jang. (He had said was that he did not see why Jang could not be patient and wait for his money.) The outcome was that Choji gave Jang four shillings for Chuang with the understanding that the latter would repay him.

Months later, when the house had been built and the incident was over with, Choji revealed that it was his wife, Bus, who had given him the money (for her *rwas-njem* Chuang), which she had saved from the sale of beer. He did not object to her use of the money in this manner. Her reason for doing so was that she felt the conflict between Jang and his "brother" Choji would divide the house (Lo Bi) and that this was bad.

Institutionalized Friendship: *Bwong Sa*

Of the 190 men who farmed and shared crops with one or more other persons, forty-two did so with men whom they called "big friends." One man farmed and shared individually with three friends, although he had available to him all degrees of male consanguines and affines. Four other men farmed and shared with two friends each, and two men cultivated farms with friends of their fathers. There are several Birom words for what I have translated as "friend" with distinctions according to the sex of the person speaking and according to the presumed closeness of the relationship. This latter distinction is perhaps analogous to that made in English between "friend" and "acquaintance." But there is no English equivalent to the term *bwong sa*, most frequently expressed as just *sa*. The relationship expressed by this term is recognized in ethnographic writing on Africa as "institutionalized friendship."

A *sa* to a Birom man is an unrelated male of his own generation with whom he shares a pact of inviolate companionship, love, and mutual aid. Since it is always preferable that the *bwong sa* should not live nearby, he is never or rarely a neighbor but rather lives in a distant ward or even a nearby village. Many men of

Du have *sa* (plural, *bisa*) who are from Shen or Zawang but none from more remote areas. A man shares with his *bwong sa* most of the varied events and features of his life. Today, one of the common expressions of this friendship is the frequent sharing of articles of clothing. These young men are "best buddies" in a very real sense, one that is recognizable in other cultural settings. They help each other with farm chores, usually the harvesting and threshing of grain, which require great strength and stamina. They come to each other's aid in all disputes, especially those that may involve physical violence. In older times, they raced horses together and raided together off the plateau. It is said that a man preferred to tether his horses with this friend, for the latter will take the best care of them.[2] One of the most important of all indigenous customs for a young man was the service of the *bwong sa* to intercede in love affairs. It was he who approached the girls, spoke for his friend, and tried to win the girls over. According to informants, the only thing that a young man would not share with his *bwong sa* were the secrets of the circumcision/puberty ritual "Ngasang," a ceremony performed every seven years in precolonial times by the Bi-Gabong.

It is the Birom belief that a young man should have only one *bwong sa*. To share the secrets of one's life with too many young men was not considered proper, and young men who flit from one friend to another were considered (and still are) somewhat fickle. In the past, fathers used to warn their sons against extending their loyalty to too many friends. And even today, when there is much mobility and there are more complex relationships with unrelated men, especially in the towns and mining camps, I have heard fathers advising their sons that it is best to have just one trusted friend. Some men engage in heated arguments with their not quite mature sons about their associations with too many young men. They are particularly cautious when their sons spend time with young men who are not Birom. The *bwong sa* is distinguished from the *sa jogo*, a playing or joking friend. A young man or unmarried girl would have several or many "playing" friends. The only requirements were that they be unrelated and of the same sex and age. Such friends stay together mostly for recreational purposes. In the evenings, young girls and boys with their *sa jogo* can be seen and heard dancing and singing together. The friendship continues as they grow to maturity but remains superficial and lighthearted. They have no understood obligations of economic aid. Playing friends may sleep and eat together and are usually members of the same neighborhood or contiguous areas. The *bwong sa*, on the other hand, has specific economic and social obligations of the sort already described.

Notes

1. Customs of this sort may have been much more widespread than ethnographic data recognize. Robert F. Spencer (1959) points out that among the North Alaskan Eskimos, men

and their wives' lovers have a special relationship to one another and that "sexual relations . . . [serve] to cement the ties of friendship and mutual aid" (85). Wife lending and exchange of wives is also found in the Far East among peoples like the Todas of India (first discovered by W. H. R. Rivers). See Walker (1986).

2. In a personal note, Dr. Paul Baxter has suggested that tethering a horse with a distant friend also probably preserved it from claims by kin for loan or for brideprice.

Summary and Theoretical Implications I I

THIS WORK APPROACHES the understanding of sex roles from a different perspective that is reflected in a small but growing body of anthropological literature. Central to this perspective are certain premises suggested by studies in human and cultural ecology. One is that sex roles and certain social differences based in gender so widely manifest in many cultures may have developed because of their adaptive value. At least we have to allow for the possibility that certain customs and practices, while today they may appear detrimental to women's interests, may reflect an underlying reality of their once critical ecological function(s). A second premise sets aside the idea of universal oppression and antagonism (which has yet to be proved) and raises the question whether women may have been as instrumental in the origination and preservation of their customs as were men. It suggests the possibility that, under certain ecological circumstances, some customs, including many now denigrated in the West, may have been developed by women in furtherance of their interests as they perceived them. A third premise is that patrilineal systems are heterogeneous; they are not all the same, and we should study each such society separately to reach conclusions about the roles of women. We may well find that there are large differences in the ways differing patrilineal systems handle sex and gender roles, although superficially certain features may appear very similar.

There is a fundamental reality to patriliny that has rarely been expressed in the literature. At bottom, patriliny is a set of principles, an ideology, and a body of social practices that bind males together within and over generations. Patriliny integrates a man into the mother–child dyad by connecting his identity with a women's children, and it does a better job of this than matriliny. My own suspicion is that women understand this and that is why they support and promote patrilineal ideology. Women may in fact have helped create these values somewhere in the early stages of human history because by making men feel responsible and conditioning them to care for their children, even in their absence, women and their children derived significant benefits. A male who provides a woman with goods and services is more likely to care for her children if he has a vested interest in them, if he believes, as patrilineal values always portray, that his sons are part of him and his conduit to immortality. That is why mothers always teach their sons to love, respect, obey, and honor their fathers. In Africa, such conditioning starts early in the first years of a boy's life. Long before boys grow up, their mothers have helped forge an emotional link between them and their fathers. Their sons grow up wanting to be fathers, to have sons, and to pass on something of their own identity and cultural knowledge to their sons. Paternity, or the concept of social fatherhood, was undoubtedly an invention of women; men had to be taught that it also benefits them. Males who have the ability to bond with a woman's offspring would have been preferred over those males who showed no emotional interest in their children. While this is clearly a speculative hypothesis, I suspect that many features of early human cultures, when fully analyzed, would reveal this principle.

The Ecological Perspective

In this study, I have developed several approaches to the analysis of gender roles. The most fundamental is an ecological one that demonstrates connections between social institutions and processes and features of the plateau habitat. I pointed out that those characteristics of kin group organization most directly related to ecological or environmental factors were its small size, the low level of genealogical segmentation, the flexibility of its composition, the ease with which agnatic kinship ties could be manipulated, and the longer-range tendency to segment under pressure of population on land. These characteristics were developed as responses to the variable fertility of the soil, the topography of the land, population distribution, intervillage hostilities, the dangers of slave raiding, the diversity of cultivable crops available to the Birom, and their exploitative techniques. The small, independent kin group, easily maneuverable at certain genealogical levels, has been seen to bear a consistent relationship with all important features of the Birom ecological niche at their specific points of interaction. Because of its size, its predictable friability, and the manner in which it operates, the kin group is easily adapted to a wide range of socioecological conditions such as have characterized both precolonial and modern times.

Of the various factors affecting Birom activities and adaptive decisions, warfare is a complex phenomenon that had great ecological significance. It can be postulated as the variable most determinative of the human landscape. It is the single most important cause of the distribution and specific locations of villages throughout the plateau. Patterns of warfare can be viewed as the outcome of competition among migrating groups for the most valued lands. At the same time, it was the mechanism by which these groups were effectively spread out and kept apart to maintain a thrust toward maximal or efficient use of the productive resources in land. The even more potent factor of fear (and threat) of warfare and slave raiding also affected the human exploitation of wild animal resources. Indirectly, it served to regulate and control hunting behavior because it restricted the opportunities for hunting to designated safe periods during the year.

The sociogeographic landscape, associating varying degrees of safety and danger to different zones of land, was a product of different types of hostilities and the fears relating to them and the variable fertility of the land. One of the consequences was that certain lands, those depicted as most dangerous, were protected from permanent intrusion and modification by human groups. By what might be considered negative feedback, these areas were maintained as hunting preserves and as reservations for sylvan products. Thus, it can be argued that the fear of warfare was perhaps a major ecological device that served to strike and to maintain a balance between human groups as predators on the one hand and the wild game population and natural forest resources on the other. The alternative surely would have been more intensive use of animal, land, and plant resources, possibly a decline in animal population and hunting areas with subsequent loss of animal protein, increased conflict over strategic resources, and ultimately a drastic decline in and maladaption of the human population.

Ecological realities also provided the basis for the rigid sexual division of labor and were correspondingly instrumental to the emergence of a distinction between the "public" and "domestic" domains. These analytic categories prove useful for delineating the distinctive realities of gender roles in many African societies. These domains are defined as interactional spheres that have a grounding in the fact that the gender division of labor assigns different tasks to men and women, separates the sexes spatially, and establishes different rules or norms for how individuals function within these spheres. The theoretical positing of separate spheres can be an excellent tool for analyzing gender asymmetry, but one must be careful not to presume that the spheres are always reflective of opposition or hierarchy unless there is clear evidence of such.

The public domain can be viewed through a separate model pertaining to the structure of society and how its male figures are related to the resources of the land. What constitutes the structural elements of this social system are the agnatic and jural relationships among men and groups of men who are more bound by customary laws than are women. The system provides the rules and guidelines that govern relationships among men within and between different generations. Male relationships are predicated on property rights—rights to inherit, use, and allocate land and livestock. This also includes rights to one another's services with respect to the cultivation of land, rights to share in the produce of the land under certain circumstances, and rights to the support of the kin group in all interactions in the public domain. There are privileges, immunities, and responsibilities attached to agnatic group membership that are abrogated only under those circumstances when kin connections are severed.

I analyzed kin groups in terms of certain diagnostic functions and processes that constitute the dynamic aspects of group membership. I demonstrated that competition among men for scarce resources and for women leads to conflict within the agnatic unit. Frequent quarrels and disagreements heighten the stresses and strains of agnatic relationships. The potentiality for open conflict is sufficiently great that it operates as a constraint on any man's ability to maneuver within the system. I note, for example, that men cannot borrow farms or even personal items easily from one another for fear of instigating a quarrel, nor do they consistently work and share with close agnates, although this is the ideal.

Men are bound to one another in a complex system of formal ties of structured kinship, characterized by fairly rigid status relationships, of authority and subordination, as well as by competitiveness. Moreover, men's decision making is restricted in scope by structural concerns; it is group bound and limited because they must function to maintain the separateness of both landholding units (kin groups) and the estates to which they are bound. This has important implications for women's roles.

The Domestic Unit: Female Roles within the Structure of Patrilyny

Anthropologists have long recognized the domestic unit or household as a separable arena of activities in human societies (Netting, Wilk, and Arnould 1984). Studies have drawn attention to the critical themes or activities that differentiate the household from larger social units, such as the lineage and clan, that have a more public presence. Women are the core figures in the domestic unit; without them, no household can long survive. They have de facto control over access to sex and food, and this provides much of the basis for their social power and influence. Women begin to realize this in the early years of marriage and particularly after the births of children. Women socialize all the children in their early years and have tremendous influence over the values that are inculcated in them. Younger women also learn from older women how to deal with men, to influence their behavior, and to restrain the exercise of power over men that their affective ties bring them. As women grow older, both their social power and their autonomy increase. Women past menopause are no longer subject to the demands of their husbands and act quite independently. A striking characteristic of social interaction everywhere is the respect paid to older women by both women and men and especially younger men. Many older women can and do exercise enormous influence in both the domestic and the public domain.

Because of the age difference at marriage, most women become widows at some time in their lives, and a number of alternatives become available to them, including the levirate, remarriage, or remaining single in their husbands' home. It also includes having lovers in the cicisbeian relationship, whether or not formal remarriage takes place. Widows also maintain themselves with the support of sons, sons-in-law, brother's sons, sister's children, and other relatives. These options are not all available to men as widowers.

The Significance of the Cicisbeian Relationship

The significance of Njem is that it expands the number of men to whom a woman is linked by ties of affection and economic obligations. The cicisbeo (or lover) provides certain basic economic benefits for his mistress (and her husband) in exchange for sexual access and a loving and relatively egalitarian relationship with a woman. In addition, there was a trade-off: Traditionally, the husband also gained prestige and eminence, and an enlarged number of supporters comprised of men who were lovers of his wives and husband's of his mistresses. Thus, marriage and Njem linked together various individual men in strategically significant alliances.

In the postcolonial period, the institution of Njem has a much reduced importance in the lives of men. But women seek to retain the practices because of the benefits derived from them. To the extent that they are able to do so, they are also modifying the custom in ways that appear to make it more adaptable to modern circumstances. Young women, for example, seek to establish Njem with men who have cash income from regular jobs, such as truck drivers, tributers, and other mine workers with long-established positions. The only exceptions are a few young Christian women who are torn between what was and still is a valuable tradition for women and the need to appear to adhere to modern Christian values of monogamy.

Women and Property

Although men are the "owners" of property, I have shown that there are practical and structural limitations to the implementation of their claims to ownership. Some limitations derive in part from the rigidity of the structuring of male roles. I have also pointed out that rights to the holding and use of farmlands vary in the different zones. The most valuable farms are the garden farms worked by women, yet they produce the foods most identified as low status. These farms are subject to the strictest tenure, use, and inheritance rights, and most of the conflicts among men over land have to do with the garden farms. Yet the reality is that the majority of women come to work these farms independently of their men and to control the food supply that they also process.

In addition, women are given garden farms to use by their fathers, brothers, and other men that are designated as "women's gardens." They have acknowledged absolute control over these farms. Moreover, women are able to borrow farms with greater ease than their husbands as well as to command the services and gifts of a larger number of persons than are available to their husbands. In chapter 7, I referred to a number of land transactions that took place during the period of this fieldwork. Although men frequently informed me that they borrowed from or lent a farm to another man, I soon learned that it was very often their wives who actually initiated and set into operation these transactions. Women did not seem to mind that such maneuvers over land were expressed in terms of male ownership. Moreover, it became clear that they had more choices than did men in determining from whom to borrow or rent a farm or with whom they would cultivate and share farm produce. These options are made possible by their involvement in cicisbeian relationships as well as by their broader cognatic ties that do not terminate at the genealogical boundaries of the agnatic kin group, as is the case with their husbands. A man cannot control the goods and services that his wife acquires through such ties.

Women and Decision Making

The data reveal that women influence much public decision making in a myriad of ways. Women have expert knowledge of all issues and events in the public domain, although they do not openly participate in formal judicial affairs, moot courts, or public rituals, such as the Great Ceremonies. We have seen that the Bi-Gwom Kwit, or ritual leaders, can determine the propitious time for various farming activities only after their wives dream special dreams. Does this reflect collaboration between the ritual leader and his wife, or is this to be seen primarily as a decision made by a woman? It clearly shows that women are able to, indeed expected to, successfully influence men in their public roles.

Wives and mothers do not hesitate to voice opinions about public matters to their men. Women continue to employ traditional methods of social control, including the use of gossip, scandal, and ridicule for both sexes. Women influence the outcomes of public issues by virtue of their relationships to the men involved, through customs that affect them indirectly, and through their persuasive powers. With verbal accusations and public scandal, they put pressure on men in order to protect what they perceive as their interests. The most vocal women are senior women who have passed menopause and have the freedom to do literally whatever they desire within the context of village life.

In this connection, women claim special rights that are distinct from those that men enjoy, and they are very jealous of these rights. Any man who infringes on these rights or on the domain of women, regardless of age, would suffer the condemnation of all women. Such collective actions and sentiments impose powerful sanctions. There are fines if a man lets his goats damage a woman's fields. Stealing is a major and most heinous crime among the Birom. But there is one form of stealing that is legitimate and acceptable. A woman with small children who are hungry can take yams or other tubers from any garden, especially during the preharvest hunger season, and she does so with impunity. A young man who steals, especially something valuable like meat, would be subject to severe punishment by his older kinsmen.

It is in decisions about food, particularly, that we see the exercise of women's decision making. Women operate with great authority and autonomy in planning ways to feed their families and in other areas of social life, such as decisions about the marriages of their daughters. Women borrow farms with great facility from men in the village and are not limited by the issues, conflicts, and restrictions that apply to men. They control the food supply and use various strategies to maximize their acquisitions of foods and other goods. Moreover, they can call on the services of unrelated men as well as related men in a manner that supersedes any of the choices that men can make. When asked about any of these activities of women, men plead ignorance; they inevitably respond that they do not know about the affairs of women. They simply blot from view the realities of women's lives and the centrality of women's ultimate power, which is also a direct recognition of the separate spheres in which women operate.

It is the long-existing and traditional independence of Birom women that has made it possible for them to utilize various strategies for supporting their households in the modern context. When some women decades earlier began to prepare food or beer to sell to mine workers, their husbands often complained or attempted to prevent them from doing so. But the women persisted, and such entrepreneurial activities eventually became accepted by men, although some very old men continue to argue that the practice is wrong or unacceptable. The benefits to women of having additional income can hardly be denied when children go hungry or when everyone suffers during the preharvest hunger period.

The question of why food crops produced by male labor have higher status and are considered more valuable than those produced by women can best be answered within the framework of women's decision making. The high valorization accorded to *acha* may have been the critical factor that operated to induce or stimulate production. Why else would a man risk danger and possibly death to grow crops on the open plains? Any culture must have internal forces that inspire and energize its carriers to thrust into domains where caution would be the better part of valor. The Birom reward those men who produce superior *acha* crops with the praises of other men, the promise of high social standing and esteem, and, most important, the praise, attention, and favors of women. In time, the *acha* crop itself became transmuted into a symbol of manly qualities, particularly those associated with the critical male role of guardian and protector of women and children. These values are very suggestive that they originated with women, whose objective was the survival of their children.

Women are related to men and to one another not as competitors but in terms of affective ties. They operate outside the system of structured positions of men and are able to relate to and interact with persons of other kin groups without the constraints imposed on men. There are no spheres of social action in which women are expected to be bound by the rules that govern men in their relationships. Because women function in a separate cognitive sphere of social interaction and by virtue of the multiple and expandable ties that women have with other women and men, they are enabled to make a wider range of decisions than are men, and their decisions are drawn from a greater number of alternatives. Women's strengths in this patrilineal system derive from the fact that they have more room to maneuver within the system than do men. They can and do manipulate the system itself and thus act as agents for effecting social, economic, and political changes. The consequences of the introduction of cash, or general-purpose money, is a good example of this latter point within the modern context. Women perceive any increments of cash obtained from external sources as analogous to the gifts and services that they traditionally received from lovers, brothers, fathers, and any other person outside the kin group or household. They assert exclusive control over these resources, a fact that has become a source of friction with their men who have tried unsuccessfully to interpret money as if it were, like land, a male form of property.

For many women, especially widows, reliance on cash, much of which they earn themselves, has enhanced their sense of security, at least in the immediate postcolonial period. Thus, while they preserve forms of deference behavior with their husbands that are traditional to the culture, they may simultaneously also control the household purse strings. In any case, they are able to maintain economic autonomy and viability within the context of the patrilineal-cum-patriarchal system despite the ideology and overt forms of male dominance.

In sum, the strategies for successful exploitation of the plateau environment came to require separate and specialized gender spheres. Perhaps it was an inadvertent outcome, but male roles evolved in such a manner that men are bound by fairly rigid rules governing the holding and use of strategic resources in land and customs regarding the relationships among independent agnatic kin groups in regard to the land. Women were and still are excluded from this system of agnation—the structured positions and roles. Their actions and independent decisions still provide flexibility to the system, and this is one source of their power.

This study suggests the need for rethinking our conceptualizations of patrilyny. Not all patrilineal systems are the same; that is, they do not all equally give scope to the realization of women's goals and interests. But it is inaccurate and misleading to presume that all patrilineal systems are oppressive to women or that most of their significant features are detrimental to women. Patrilyny is an ideological theme comprised of numerous components, customs, beliefs, institutions, practices, rules, privileges, taboos, and so forth. Of the several systems of descent recognized in human societies as organizational principles, patrilyny is the most prevalent. A partial explanation for this fact may be that many of the components of patrilyny were developed because they were perceived by women as benefiting them and the households of which they were the center.

Economic Realities of the Colonial Era

Appendix A

COMPARATIVELY LITTLE has been written about the economic welfare of the plateau peoples despite the fact that it has long been recognized that the general conditions of farming areas, particularly those closest to mining, have deteriorated markedly. In 1910, the colonial administration made a preliminary survey of landholding that included some few data on the indigenous crops of the plateau. The main purpose was to describe what was thought to be the native systems of land tenure. From time to time, in subsequent years, touring officers made notes about farming among the Birom people. Much of this material is superficial and confined to statements about subsistence farming, enumerations of the various types of crops, and estimates of areas under cultivation. All the early ethnographic reports plus the existing published literature expressed the belief that the plateau peoples were and still are dependent on certain native staples for their basic diet.

In 1934–1944, a survey was made of Birom farming at Gyel, a large village area southwest of Jos. This was the first and only survey concerned exclusively with an indigenous plateau community. It was also conducted at a time when there was growing resentment of and opposition to mining in the area. The results of this report led to the demarcation of a large area south of Jos as a "congested area" and the subsequent closing of this part of the high plateau to further mining leases. The 1944 survey found that "60% of Gyel was arable, 20% was not farmable (rocky outcrops, etc.) and 14% was lost to the farmer (10% being due to mining and 4% to stranger settlements)."[1] It was noted that farmlands in use were rapidly deteriorating because of overcultivation. Land was "farmed without manuring for 6 or 8 years in the areas of better soil and then left fallow for 2 to 3 years" when, in order to recuperate, the land should have been left fallow for a period three to four times as long as the cultivation period. Furthermore, "of the arable land at Gyel it was found that 72% had been cultivated and 28% was fallow. In unprofitable areas . . . 19% was cultivated and 81% was fallow. By agricultural standards at least half the land should be under fallow" (loose notes from Gyel Survey).

The report specifically pointed out that mining took place in alluvial river and streambeds, which contain the best soil in the area. Four-fifths of Gyel was found to be under lease to mining operations, either by mining lease, exclusive prospecting licenses, or certificates of occupancy, and 86 percent of all arable lands was under lease in June 1944. One-eighth of the original arable land had been lost to the farmer because of tin mining. Of the land so destroyed, none of it had been returned to agricultural use, as it consisted chiefly of infertile dumpings and tailings that would require leveling and rejuvenation of the topsoil. At that time, approximately 150 to 200 acres of land in Gyel were being alienated to mining operations each year, and "there is no vacant land for the use of the expanding populations" (loose notes from Gyel Survey). The report added that the Birom have no cash crop, as there was no surplus, and evidence indicated that they were becoming more dependent on casual work in the mines for cash income with which to buy extra food and other necessities.

Economic Survey of Du Village

Almost twenty years later, my similar study in Du village indicated the presence of virtually the same problems of land shortage and low soil fertility. The most frequent complaint of farmers was the meagerness of the crops. Elders were very much aware that the land had progressively become worse since the white men came, and the more cynical men concluded that the "poor *acha*" was part of a plot to exterminate the indigenous peoples.

Like all farmers who are faced with precariously low production of food supplies, the Birom farmer well knows the peculiarities, requirements, and growth habits of individual crops. Most Du villagers recognize, for example, eight to ten different types of *acha* according to their growth patterns, color, leaf and head sizes, taste, and yields; a farmer can describe their characteristics no matter how minute. Farmers plan in advance the rotation of crops so that a new field is opened with the most nutritionally demanding crops and each subsequent year is alternated between these and the least demanding until the soil is exhausted. At the same time, cultivators must consider other factors in the cycle, such as the best time to ridge for yams. Should he level the ridges the next year for finger millet and then reridge them again for yams? Or should he rotate with *acha*, the crop that least depletes the soil, so that the farm can be opened again with guinea corn? Through these numerous decisions, the farmer ekes out the last drop of productivity from his farms. Should he or she make an unwise decision, it might be disastrous. Many times I have come across a farmer carefully going over every foot of a farm wondering whether it will support one more year of *acha* or should it be left to lie fallow. And there are other, less crucial decisions regarding the intercropping of *choro*, *makaya*, or some other native vegetable not as central to the diet. For each farm plot, farmers analyze the overgrowth and the height and strength of the wild grasses and weeds to get a careful assessment of its potential for the coming years.

Even so, crop yields are still unpredictable, and this is a harsh reality to be faced. There are the unusual disasters. In one household (the only one so affected in this survey), goats got into the yam beds and killed all the young shoots. In another household, the first heavy rains washed all the millet beds away. Even more important are the normal ranges of variation for each crop planted over which the farmer has little control. Such a variation can be judged from our survey of one common variety of *acha*, *were chun*. We had information from nineteen different farms dispersed throughout the village and owned by sixteen different farmers. The farms varied in size from one-tenth of an acre to the largest, which was approximately two acres. The variation in output was from a low of 160 pounds per acre to a high of 600 pounds, which was achieved by one farmer on a small farm that he fertilized even though it was considered good land at the outset. (The next-highest rate of productivity was 480 pounds on what was known as "good" land.) The average crop of *were chun* produced 266 pounds per acre. One farmer who got three bags (180 pounds) from a full acre of land stated that he used to get twelve bags (800 pounds) each year from this same farm but now never gets more than four. By way of comparison and in confirmation of the farmer's experiences, crop yield statistics dating from 1926 (the earliest date available in the archives) showed that in this same general area, the average yield of *acha* was 900 pounds per acre. Statistics on *dankali* (sweet potatoes), guinea corn, finger millet, *tamba*, and yams evince a similar pattern of decreasing yields from those obtained in the early decades of the century.

The holding and use of farms was too fluid and imprecise to provide really significant quantitative information. Many if not most men do know the extent of lands actually belonging to their *lo* groups, but farms were so frequently lent and borrowed or else pawned that accurate statements of what lands a man *may* exploit and what he *does* cultivate over a period of time was impossible. Men frequently showed me farms that they claimed belonged to their kin group and were rightfully available to them but that were being farmed by outsiders often unknown to them. "This is our land but I do not know to whom these yam ridges belong." Or, conversely, a man may point out the farms held by his kin group, but he himself may have borrowed or "rented" several farms for his own use. Adding to this complexity is the fact that men and women often farm and share the produce with persons who are not of their own kin group. Many women, particularly widows, shared farmwork with a variety of kinsmen and friends. The amounts of foodstuffs that women obtained were independent of the actual productivity of their husband's lands.

A simple recording, then, of the acreage held and worked by a man within his own kin group is not and perhaps never can be an accurate statement of what is available to him and his household in terms of the resources of the village lands. Farm plots are small, averaging, in my survey of over 100 farms of all types, about five-eighths of an acre each. Further subdivisions called *gandu* are recognized within each plot, and men will sometimes divide *gandu* among themselves so that every man of a kin group will be able to share satisfactorily in the division of the fertile and less fertile areas. Each year, there may be modifications of existing divisions of land within the group and accretions or recombinations as men and women die or leave to live elsewhere or as families are enlarged. This, and the fact that much farming was previously done in the hills and the sheltered rocky areas, accounts in large part for the smallness of plot sizes and the attention to minute subdivisions, particularly of the more fertile areas.

Foodstuffs Consumed

In a study of 221 domestic units in six wards of Du, I had as one important goal obtaining information on the amount of food produced compared with the amount of food purchased. While it was possible to observe several families throughout the day and to note the amounts of food prepared and eaten, there was difficulty in eliciting answers to questions regarding quantity. The Birom attention to and interest in matters of food is not reflected in precision of measurement (compare Richards 1939, 204). The family head does not think in terms of weight, for he well knows that women can stretch a meager supply of grain. He does know how many bags (standardized[2] Birom measurement) of grain he got from his farms, and he will know roughly how many months his family had to eat yams last year.

One of the best measures of foods consumed was the counting of how many *mudus* (bowls) of grain are utilized by women daily during certain periods of the year. Since yams and other tubers are dug from the gardens and eaten as needed, most women will remember how many months they fed their families only yams. A man will not usually know or remember how much foodstuffs were bought for his family in the market or from other Birom during the year, and most times he will not even know how much was spent during the preceding week on food. Most food purchases are made by women, and always the outlay is as haphazard and unpredictable as the income. Records of this kind are not usually kept even by the few literate adults, such as the schoolteacher or pastor. Any sort of planning with foresight with regard to cash income and outlay is rare, and this usually takes the form of aiming at some brief, unusual advantage. Nevertheless, people do think in terms of a day's supply, a week's supply, or a month's supply of normal foods, and women attempt to space the use of grains and tubers to spread them as far as possible over the year.

In 1960, 215 of the 221 domestic units with a total of 1,119 people grew 1,243 bags of *acha* (threshed), a total of 74,580 pounds. Approximately 25 percent of this amount was stored to be used as seed in the following year. Of the remainder, an estimated 70 percent is edible after drying and removal of the pericarp.[3] Thus, some 39,155 pounds of *acha* were consumed, averaging slightly under 35 pounds per person. (No allowance has been made for the difference in consumption of children and adults here or for the inevitable amount of waste.)

Some thirty-seven households grew guinea corn during the year, harvesting just under a bag apiece, adding another 2,400 pounds of grain to the *acha* supply. Sixty-four households grew 111½ bags of *gei* (bulrush millet), adding 7,248 pounds of grain, and 123 households grew small amounts of *pana* (finger millet), averaging approximately 90 pounds each. Thus the total grain additional to acha was about 20,700 pounds. Allowing 15 percent for seed[4] and another 20–25 percent for waste (a conservative estimate), then approximately 60 percent of the grain was consumed, or 12,320 pounds.

Maize was grown by eight households, two of which regularly grew it for sale in the local market. The six other households grew very small amounts (less than one-sixth of an acre) of maize, always in home gardens close to the compound, where the soil is enriched by waste from the household. Most farmers do not grow maize for the very practical reason that it depletes the soil of nutrients more so than any of the other grains and is more vulnerable to insect pests. In addition, although it ripens quickly and has the highest yield of all grains, it is difficult to store.

Every household, with one exception, grew at the minimum three of the major types of yams, the one exception being the victim of a disaster that destroyed all its small yam gardens. Other tubers, such as sweet potatoes (145 households) and cassava (54 households), were grown in quantities that only lasted for several weeks. Most of the cassava was sold in nearby market areas. The quantities of other types of yams were too small for calculation and thus insignificant as basic sources of food. Every household that grew yams indicated a surprisingly high degree of dependency on yams for the basic foodstuff during the greater part of the year. The average household ate yams eight and one-half months out of the year, and in the months of severe hunger, even half-rotted yams would be consumed. The wealthiest households in the village depended on yams to a much lesser extent and had them only as supplementary meals during five months of the year. The poorest family in Du village was composed of three people who relied primarily on yams for more than ten months.

Along with these ordinary staple crops, all households grew minor crops of assorted native vegetables: various greens, several varieties of Indian Rosselle, beans, squash, cowpeas, marigold, and sugarcane. Most of these were intercropped with the millets or yams and consumed only as needed. In addition, all households made use of wild plants of many different types (eighteen by one count) that are gathered by women from time to time. A major source of wild vegetables used to be the banks of riverbeds and copses of trees near well-watered areas. But nearly all these more fertile areas in and around Du village have been destroyed by mining. In any case, the minor crops, domestic or wild, are not important sources of food, for they are never eaten in large quantities. All vegetables are considered supplementary to the grain–yam diet, and many are used primarily for seasoning and for varying the texture of the main porridge dish. Beliefs about the curative, laxative, or restorative qualities of certain vegetables lead to their consumption in regular but small amounts. Wild vegetables, insects, rodents, and snakes constitute a meal only in extreme cases.

One of the more surprising discoveries about the village, brought out in the economic survey, was the large amount of foods now actually purchased for daily consumption and the number of domestic units that depend to a great extent on these externally produced foods. One hundred and ninety-nine domestic units purchased 651 bags of guinea corn in the Jos and Bukuru markets during the year. Each bag has a standard weight of 200 pounds and cost, in 1959–1960, £2. Thus, some 130,200 pounds of guinea corn, more than twice the total amount of all grains grown in the village, were purchased, all presumably for consumption. Moreover, though Birom protest that *acha* is not bought in the market, and it is true that it is not an important market item, some thirteen households bought small amounts of *acha* during the year (from 2s. to 26s. worth). Ten domestic units bought some maize, five bought millet, and twelve purchased yams—and in nearly all these cases, the amount constituted full meals for only a few days or weeks.

European vegetables are much sought after today, particularly by those who consider themselves modern or enlightened. The most common ones bought, such as tomatoes, potatoes, carrots, and cucumber, are occasional treats that are frequently shared. Native vegetables, such as various kinds of squash, spinach, melons, yams from the south, beniseed, and so forth, are also bought in the market in greater quantities, being less expensive than European counterparts. Salt, oil, pepper, and other condiments are stable needs purchased by nearly all households.

Livestock within the village is not a reliable source of meat and, in any case, amounts to very little considering the total population at the time of this survey. Livestock is not easy to keep because of the requirements for fodder and water. There were, early in 1961, 263 goats in the village. However, these are never killed for their meat but are kept for the observance of specific rituals, the most notable of which are the funeral rites. Goats may also constitute part of the exchanges involved in marriages, although today nearly all exchanges take the form of cash. The number of sheep was negligible (27), and along with the 756 chickens reported, they are generally kept to be sold to outsiders whenever ready cash is needed. Animals or livestock thus are a kind of savings. Dogs (202) and chickens are eaten on occasion, however, although the small number suggest that this is very rare. There were also 96 pigs, 103 rabbits, and 7 cows in the village. A breakdown by domestic unit is even more suggestive of the distribution of domestic animals in Du. Eighty-three bi-*lalla* (domestic units or households) shared the 263 goats; only 6 bi-*lalla* had the sheep, 149 had chickens, 147 owned dogs, 26 had pigs, 15 had rabbits, and only 2 owned the 7 cows. Six of the cows were owned by one householder, the chief of the district.

Meat is rarely eaten in the village. By far the greatest amount of meat consumed is bought in the market, in small pieces varying in value from a few pence to several shillings. Most informants did not know how much they had spent for meat in the previous year; of those who did know, the range varied from "over £10" as reported by a relatively wealthy mining contractor to four pence. This latter was the total purchase of meat by an old woman who said she usually begged for her food. My estimate is that the average household spent less than £4 on meat annually. Only three of the 221 household heads bought no meat or fish during the year, and these were among the poorest people in the village, with all the members of the households being elderly and unemployable. One hundred and twenty-two householders also purchased small amounts of fish in addition to meat in the market.

The survey showed that a small number of Du people buy a fairly wide variety of market goods, from simple furniture (native-made tables and chairs) and clothing to foods and household utensils. While all households do buy some sorts of foodstuffs, these other items are luxury goods restricted to the wealthier few. Bicycles, for example, are bought only by a few younger men who have jobs and by schoolteachers; my estimate is that there are no more than a dozen in the village. All the younger men and women wear cloth clothing based on the general patterns found in Nigeria.

Many families have kitchen utensils of European pattern, such as aluminum and enamel pans of various sizes, a few spoons, knives, and so forth. The possession of these items is often used as a criterion of social standing. For some people, they have become prized personal items with a significance beyond their utilitarian value. However, the most important index to any man's social and economic status in Du is how he feeds: what he eats, when he eats, how much he eats, and from where he obtained it. A poor man eats perhaps one meal a day and sometimes goes for several days without eating. If he is somewhat better off, he has two basic meals, the morning *bwirik* (a kind of watery gruel of pounded grain) and the late afternoon or evening meal, *tuk npolo*, which is a porridge or stew of grain and vegetables. For most people, however, at least one of these meals will be composed entirely of roasted yams or supplemented with them. Wealthy families may have meat once or twice a week, and they may also be served three meals a day, with an afternoon soup called *leng* being consumed at midday. Poor families have little or no meat but at times resort to lizards, rodents, grasshoppers, birds' eggs, and a few wild birds infrequently caught. A few wealthy families supplement the morning *bwirik* with milk purchased from local Fulani herders for their children, and fresh fruits bought in the market are eaten during the day. They also have a greater variety of dishes, including pounded yam with meat sauces that they have learned from southerners.

The diet of the Birom thus shows a fair amount of diversity in types of food consumed. But there is an acknowledged deficiency of protein, particularly meat protein, and of fat. The low calorie intake of families in this survey is demonstrated by the data given on foodstuffs consumed. On the basis of total grain products produced and purchased, we can roughly estimate an intake of three pounds of grain per week per person or seven to ten ounces of grain per day per adult with similar amounts for children. This is consistent with my personal observations in three families, based on a count of the number of *mudus* (approximately one and one-half pounds per bowl) that each woman prepared daily for her family.

According to Davies, *acha*, millet, and *tamba* are nutritionally similar grains. An ounce of each provides 2 grams of protein, 0.4 grams of fat, 20.5 grams of carbohydrates, and 94 calories. The average adult in our survey thus gets less than 1,000 calories from grains per day. Yams provide 34 calories per ounce, little protein, and virtually no fat. If there is no shortage, adults will consume several yams per day weighing from 4 to about 20 ounces each. Adding the small caloric content of relishes, peas, beans, green leafy vegetables, and cucurbits, an adult in a household well supplied with regular food may achieve an intake of 2,000 to 2,400 calories per day during good periods. Normally, however, it is much less, although the daily intake varies tremendously with the seasons and the economic situation of the kin group. For several months during the rainy season, adults may average as little as 700 or 800 calories per day, most of which would be from yams if there were any left. It is not uncommon for one or more adults in a single household to go without food for a day or so in order that the children can be fed.

Sources of Income

That the village of Du is now an integral part of a larger cash economy is indisputable although not always obvious. There is no household in Du without some form of cash income. All families must buy, at the minimum, salt and oil in the market or beg from other family members, and all households with an able-bodied male must pay taxes.

A survey, taken in the later part of 1960 and early 1961, of all adults in six wards of Du showed that two-thirds of the men (206 of a total of 312) had some cash earnings during 1960 and that almost 45 percent (175 of 385) of the women also earned some cash by their own efforts. And this is not the complete picture. Only fifty-nine men (18.9 percent) have never had any sort of employment or earned any cash, and 18.4 percent of the women (seventy-one) have never had cash earnings. The male labor force in Du consists of a vast majority of unskilled individuals and a limited variety of semiskilled (see tables A.1 and A.2). The sources of cash income are 1) earnings or wages from the minefields, 2) wages from other unskilled work in the government or private companies (mostly construction work, clearing land, digging wells, and so forth), 3) skilled and semiskilled specialized occupations, 4) commercial and trading activities, 5) land compensation from mining, 6) bridewealth, 7) gifts, and 8) illegal tin mining. Each of these is discussed next.

1. The largest amounts of income from employment are from work on the minefields. Of the 312 men who were interviewed for their work histories, 68, or 21.8 percent, were currently working as unskilled labor in the mining industry. This represents 33 percent of the total working force of 206 men. Of these 68 men, 45 worked as casual labor, and 23, or 11 percent, of the total workforce worked year-round as laborers, headmen, tributors,[5] or independent contractors (only 2 men, members of the same family). Another 8 men worked in skilled or semiskilled jobs as drivers, mechanics, carpenters, or bricklayers, and 2 others worked in white-collar jobs as clerks, making a total of 78 men currently employed in the mining industry, of whom 33 worked throughout the year. According to the tax returns, there are 82 men in Du village who work permanently in the mines.

Table A.1   Marital Status, Education, and Occupations of Birom Men by Age-Group

	Age-group					
	15–25	26–35	36–45	46–55	Over 55	Total
Number in each age-group	83	56	76	47	50	312
Marital status						
Married	12	46	70	42	39	209
Single	68	5	1	3	—	77
Widowed	—	—	—	1	11	12
Divorced	3	5	5	1	—	14
Education						
Junior primary	31	12	14	4	1	62
Senior primary	37	3	—	1	—	41
Still in school	38	—	2[a]	1[a]	—	41
All grades						
Present occupation						
Trained in some skill or trade but not working in the same	3	4	2	—	—	9
Working skilled or semiskilled jobs	4	6	7	2	—	19
Unskilled mine labor, year-round (noncasual)	5	8	9	1	—	23
Unskilled mine labor (casual)	7	21	16	1	—	47
Unskilled labor (non-mines, government, and private)	11	15	16	3	—	45
Domestic service	2	1	—	—	—	3
Commerce and trading	—	1	5	2	7	15
Miscellaneous native crafts	2	—	1	2	—	5
White collar	6	2	5	2	—	15
Farming only	4	3	16	28	9	60
No occupation and no longer farming	5[b]	—	1	5	35	46
Never employed for wages	32	1	5	5	16	59
Past occupations						
Mines	11	14	38	34	31	128
Army, native police, other government job	2	6	17	7	1	33

[a] Attending local trade school.
[b] All young men attending secondary school at Riyom during most of the year but legal residents of Du village. All perform minor farming task when at home.

Table A.2   Marital Status, Education, and Occupations of Birom Women by Age-Group

	Age-group					
	15–25	*26–35*	*36–45*	*46–55*	*Over 55*	*Total*
Number in each age-group	91	105	88	64	36	384
Marital status						
Married	58	101	70	38	11	278
Single	30	—	—	—	—	30
Widowed	—	1	17	25	25	68
Divorced	3	3	1	1	—	8
Education						
Primary school[a]	15	1	1	—	—	17
Present occupations						
Casual labor—mines	26	36	19	2	—	83
Selling food, wood, or cactus	5	3	5	4	1	18
Sells or has sold native beer	5	23	39	14	2	87
Miscellaneous	3	1	4	4	—	12
Past occupations						
Casual labor—mines	26	56	58	46	21	207

[a] Only two girls had gone past senior primary grades. Both were in secondary school at Gindiri.

This emphasizes the fact that few men work steadily in year-round jobs and still reside in the nuclear village wards. About ten years before the end of the colonial period, a Birom Training Center was established at Bukuru that was administered by the Chamber of Mines. The purpose was to produce skilled and semiskilled local labor for the mining companies. Since 1952, there have been an annual average of about sixteen Birom boys trained at the center. Once trained, the boys leave the village and go where the jobs are and prefer to live in better houses in Bukuru or in the mining camps or satellite wards of the village that are closer to the mines' offices. By estimates taken from genealogical records for three generations, there are approximately 120 men from Du living and working elsewhere, most of whom also have their wives with them. A fairly large number of these men are in the military or in civilian government posts in Jos and other towns.

The most important source of income (particularly in terms of its distribution) from the minefields is from casual labor. Almost every man, woman, boy, and girl over fifteen has at some time in his or her life worked in this capacity, some for only a few days or weeks. Both men and women take a job for a specific reason: men usually to pay taxes and men and women to buy beer, clothing, or blankets. The survey shows that male casual laborers have a total lifetime work pattern quite different from that of women. Men usually work as diggers with pick and shovel; the women transport the ore-bearing subsoil in head pans. These casual laborers work so sporadically that it is almost impossible to estimate their earnings, and very few of them keep an account of how much was earned. All of them demonstrate a common but highly variable pattern of work. Sometime during the dry season, men sign on as part of a gang, consisting of a headman and six to ten more laborers. They work for a few days or a week or maybe two and then quit for various reasons, the more usual of which is to rest. The rest period also varies according to individual whims; it may be a week or two or a month or more. One common variation is to work several weeks out of every month for three months, skipping a day here and there. Some men work in this manner six or seven months of the year, all of the dry season, stopping only to begin the farming cycle.

Women work no more than a total of a few weeks a year, and many women stated that they had worked only one season for several weeks, whereas all men, except for a few young ones just starting, returned to the mines year after year. Quite a few women have worked only a short time in a single season. The tendency for girls and young women is to work a few weeks a year for several seasons prior to marriage, after which only a few said they continued to work.

The income of those men who work year-round varies according to their occupation. Tributors and contractors have the greatest variation. All indicated that there are some weeks during which they earn nothing at all. Commonly, the average range is £2 to £5 per week, but a few men (such as the two contractors) earn more, occasionally up to £55. The largest income in the village was that of a contractor who earned £300 one year and now averages £30 per annum. The average wage earnings of skilled and semiskilled laborers working year-round was 23s. per week. (A number of younger men had not worked a full year at the time of this survey.) Average earnings for the men are rarely over a pound a week for a full week's work, and usually they are much less. Women working a full week may earn 6s. or 8s. with the range being 2s. to 16s. last year. Thus, women have very insignificant earnings from working in the mines, and they soon turn to other income-producing activities (discussed later).

The Birom are not now and never have been a reliable source of minefield labor although living quite close to and frequently only a few hundred feet from an open paddock. They first started coming to seek jobs in the 1920s and since that decade have constituted only a minor portion of the entire workforce. In addition to those men presently employed in the mines, another 128 men have worked in the mines in the past and are now either employed elsewhere or doing no work at all. This means that two-thirds of the adult males in the six inner wards of Du have worked in the minefields. Of the 385 women in the survey, 83, or slightly less than 22 percent, worked in the minefields in 1960–1961. Another 207 have worked in the mines in the past, meaning that 75 percent of the women have had some experience in the mines. What has facilitated these work patterns is the fact that no one has to emigrate to find mine work and that daily distances to and from work are relatively short.

2. In Du, there are a number of men who work irregularly as laborers for various departments of government, such as the Health Department, Public Works Department, Survey Department, and Forestry Department. There are also a few private employers other than the mines, such as several long-established trading firms and particularly the missions. During my stay in the village, the Sudan United Mission started the construction of a large center near Bukuru, and many laborers who ordinarily would be working in the mines were recruited from the surrounding districts. Most of this work tends to be temporary, lasting only until a specific project is finished, and fits the patterns of working short periods for cash that most of the men prefer. In my survey, forty-five men, or 14 percent of the total (21.8 percent of the workforce), were working in nonmining employment during 1960. Of these, twenty-two worked at the new Sudan United Mission theological training center, and of these twenty-two, none had worked over nine months; most had worked six months or less. Out of twenty who reported that they worked for government departments, only six had worked more than one year on the same job. Earnings in these laboring jobs were comparable to that of laborers on the minefields (21s. per week), but the overall income was steadier. These facts again underscore the temporary and insecure character of Birom labor.

3. Skilled labor in private or government employment is exceedingly rare in Du. There is one bricklayer who has worked for the Sudan United Mission for twenty-four years (an unusual case), a carpenter who had worked for the Forestry Department for three months, and a man who has repaired bicycles at Bukuru for fourteen months. The bricklayer's earnings varied from £2 to £10 per month, the carpenter earned £5 per month, and the bicycle repairman earned from £2.4 to £4 per month.

The nineteen men in Du working in some skilled or semiskilled manual labor earn very little more than their fellow Birom in the unskilled jobs. Of the eight skilled men working in the mining industry, many are still at the apprentice level, earning an average of £1 per week. Caterpillar drivers earn about 25s. per week. The rest of the skilled men—four carpenters, three tailors, and a barber in Bukuru—work for themselves and have varying earnings.

4. Commercial and training activities involve a number of people in very small-scale business. Two men in Du specialized in and made a living growing European-type vegetables for the market at Bukuru. One of these men sold mostly corn (maize), some of which he purchased from Bauchi. In the previous year, he made a profit of £12.15. The second man was much more sophisticated: He spent several years in the army and learned how to grow and care for such foods as tomatoes, cabbage, peppers, and potatoes, all of which he now cultivates. Even with manuring, his yield is poor, and he rarely gained as much as £1 a week in season from the sale of his produce. His total gross income from sales in 1960 was £38. Of the other thirteen men who reported that they earn cash only through their selling activities, seven were old men, over fifty-five years old, who during several days a month in the dry season gather and sell firewood and dried prickly pear cactus for a few shillings. One man sells salt within the village, in the mining camps, and in Fulani settlements, and the rest sold firewood and occasionally some cassava in nearby marketing areas. Their earnings amount to only a few shillings a week during a portion of the year.

By far the largest amount of petty trading is carried on by the women of the village. But they are not the typical market women of the southern areas. The majority of women sell native beer sporadically or on a regular basis. While most of their sales are within the village, almost all of them at some time have sold beer to mining camp personnel who come to a weekly open market spot (*bauda*) for drinking and eating only. This *bauda* is an informal gathering with no special name that takes place only during the dry season, when most of the beer is made. A few outsiders (Hausa and Igbo) also come to the more private beer-drinking festivities, particularly if they are acquainted with anyone of the family holding the beer session. In any case, it is difficult to estimate the amount of outside money coming into the village from the sale of beer.

In addition to the eighty-three women who sell beer on occasion, there are another eighteen who regularly sell wood, cactus, or food. Food is sold at the *bauda* on Saturday afternoons and at the courthouse when it is in session every Monday. The income from the sale of beer and/or food is extremely variable. An industrious woman may earn up to 15s. in one day from her oil tin of beer and her penny cakes of food. But she would rarely do this more than twice a month if that. Most of the women who sell beer prepare it no more than four or five times in the season because corn is expensive to buy and *acha* is even dearer because of its scarcity.

In the survey by households of the domestic economy, fifty-three householders out of the total 221 domestic units stated that during the year they had sold some food crops. Another 113 householders had sold firewood, cactus, or some other fuel material (corn stalks, dried grasses, tree roots, or cassava stalks) during the year, and seventy-one had sold some animal meat (either whole animals or in parts). Such sales usually occurred only once or twice, and in almost all cases there was another form of more regular cash income available to the domestic unit. The total value of such individual sales varied from 1s. for a single sale of dried cactus by an old man to the £38 received by another householder for the sale of twenty pigs in Bukuru market. (He is one of three or four men who have started regularly raising pigs for sale.) In nearly all the cases, the householder remembers what the amount of the sales was, so the figures on this are fairly complete.

Cassava accounted for almost all the food crops sold. Virtually everyone who grows cassava at all sells some if not all of it in the market. Cassava is a late arrival on the plateau, and the Birom have other tubers that they prefer. Sixteen households out of the fifty-three involved in these sales sold yams also, and one person sold sweet potatoes, while another sold a small amount of *acha* and millet to a villager who lives outside the inner wards. These sales were small, varying from 2s. to £3; the average sale realized 17s.2d., and the total value of such sales was £45lls.2d.

Fuel material is a ready source of petty cash when there is almost no other way of obtaining it. It entails no outlay other than the physical labor of collecting the dried cactus or cutting the trees and is most often the source of income for older men and women who desire a few shillings for drinking beer. In only ten cases was the income £1 or more, and these were usually cases where an entire tree was felled and cut into several loads of firewood. In almost all other cases, the amounts received were 2s. to 5s. Thus, the total income for 113 persons was only £53 with an average per person of 9s.4d. All these products were sold outside the village and represented cash coming into the village area.

The sale of meat and live animals provides a larger income at a single instance, but the net income, which is not easily computed, tends to be comparatively small. In some instances, for example, men have bought several animals for £5 or £6 for the specific purpose of selling them as meat. Gross income from the sales may be £8 or £9 or in some cases less than that. If the animals had been bought many months or several years previously, the men frequently fail to realize or to take into consideration the original outlay plus whatever maintenance has been provided. Animals, more than any other commodity, are frequently sold and resold within the village. This is particularly true of goats, nearly all of which are used in burial rituals and never killed and consumed merely as meat. This adds to the difficulties of assessing the income from such sales. Chickens are sold within the village, but most go outside into local marketing areas (in labor and

mining camps). Pigs almost always are eventually sold out, especially to southerners, as many Birom are not fond of pork and the Muslin Hausa do not eat it. In
two cases that I know of, the same pigs were sold twice in the year, once to
another man in the village and then to some traders outside the village. One horse
and a donkey were bought during the year, and the meat was sold after the skins
were used in reburial rituals. In both cases, the net income was less than £2. These
sales of meat do not include the cooked meat that women frequently sell at the
courthouse and several other areas in and around the village. The total value of
meat sales was £354.12s.5d., with an average of about £5 per householder to the
sellers. However, as indicated previously, the actual or net realization in many
cases would be much less.

5. Land compensation may have been the largest single source of cash income
during the previous fifteen years by volume alone. This is a payment made by the
mining companies for their destruction of farmlands. As I have already indicated,
it is now regulated by law and is intended to be reimbursement for ten years' loss
of crops. In 1961, the demarcation and destruction rate for good farmland in this
area was about £28 per acre. For poor lands, it may get as low as £5 or £6, and
most of this land is poor.

Theoretically, the land reverts back to the farmer on completion of the mining operations, but no farmer can do much with dumps, tailings, and masses of
clay. Since 1957, an attempt has been made by the government to reclaim some
of the land (in fact, most mining leases today contain a rather ineffectual reclama-
tions clause), but it takes an estimated three years before anything will grow on
these areas and another fifteen or more years to make them even minimally productive. The cash representing ten years' cropping value is never enough to last
until the land is productive again; in every case, as the Birom view it, the land is
lost to the farmer forever.

Land compensation is paid out in lump sums, usually to the chief, to be
divided among the heads of the families claiming ownership of the land. In nearly
all cases, it is again further subdivided as many as five to six times until almost
every man in a *lo* or a group of related *lo* (*yere*) has a share. This may amount to
as little as a few shillings or several pounds per man. Such money is quickly spent
by these individuals, but not always for the purpose for which it is intended, to
purchase grain as a replacement for the crops lost. Among the 221 domestic units
in this survey, only three failed to receive any land compensation during the year.
In six other cases (all related men), land compensation is due, but the amount is
under dispute, the farmers claiming more than the company is willing to pay. The
heads of all other domestic units admitted receiving anywhere from 5s. to three
cases where sums of £50 per person were received. The total amounted to

£990.8s. Most of these families have had land compensation several times over a period of twenty years. There are a few families that have never received land compensation either through sharing as a member of a larger land-claiming unit or as monies directly paid to them as specific owners of the land. The average income to each family was thus about £4.14 from land compensation. Whatever the amount, compensation is an irregular and unpredictable type of income.

6. Bridewealth and cash from the transfer of a female child (in Pyomo exchange) are from a sociological standpoint the considerations of two distinct types of transactions. But from an income standpoint, they can be considered the same and are treated together in this section. Almost always, the amount involved is fairly large by Birom standards; I know of few cases where the amount was under £10. The standard bridewealth for a girl's first marriage is 16 (£10 = horse, £6 = six goats), and while this sum is normally what is expected and received, there are many occasions when a young man has paid much more. The largest paid in Du village to my knowledge was £56 for a girl who had been educated to standard V in a mission elementary school. The exchange of a pre-nubile girl usually brings considerably less in actual cash, £10 to £12 being quite common. Like land compensation, it is a single-occasion windfall.

However, in many instances, the bridewealth is paid in installments, along with the additional emoluments due to various members of the bride's family. In some cases, the final payments are not made until after the birth of one or several children. However, the recipient (the father or brother of the bride) cannot depend on regular payments, and promises to pay are often not kept. It should be understood that bridewealth does not for the most part represent new cash income to the village but merely the circulation of already existing cash supplies from one group to another. Where, however, the bridegroom is a man outside the village area (or the inner wards, which are the subject of this study), from a nearby town, or from another village area, we must consider this as proper income. In a study of marriages for three generations, it was found that 19 percent of the Du women are married out, that is, to men of nearby villages, Forum, Shen, and Zawang being the most common.

More important as a source of real new income and so treated by the Birom was the wealth acquired by exchanging a young girl for food with Buji, Jerawa, and Anaguta peoples, known to the Birom as "Pyomo." Because such transactions are now illegal, it is very difficult to obtain information about them. Informants readily admitted to the practice in older generations, although few would admit to it in recent times. The customarily established consideration in precolonial times was a *bwan* (storeroom of grain, the equivalent of twenty-four bags of grain) or a horse. During the colonial period, it was from £8 to £12, depending on the kin group's needs.

That the Pyomo exchanges were widely practiced in the past is demonstrated through a study of genealogies. Of more than 120 genealogies collected, sixty-one, or approximately every second group, were selected for study. All Pyomo exchanges were recorded and divided into two generational units: (A) older generation, which included all known marriages of women who would be about thirty-five years of age and older, and (B) all known marriages of the two youngest generations, that is, women less than thirty-five years of age. Forty-five of the *lo* groups (73 percent) had at least one Pyomo transaction, while sixteen (27 percent) had none. The total number of girls involved was 104, or slightly over two girls per group, with only fifty-four of these being in the older generation. Seventeen houses had transactions in both generations. The variation was from a *lo* group with a single exchange to one house that had seven and another with six, all of which were in the younger generational group. The total of Pyomo transactions represented about 6 percent of all marriages. The Birom viewed such arrangements primarily as a source of sustenance when a kin group had reached desperate straits.[6]

7. Like Pyomo transactions, gift-giving represents an almost unknowable and unmeasurable amount. It is impossible to ascertain how many people depend on gifts and to what degree or, for that matter, the total volume of gifts coming into the village. On the one hand, it is an important means of redistribution within the village; on the other, it is a source (and no doubt an important one) of new, "real" income to the village. Gift giving is the common form of demonstrating the relatedness of kinship, and even where there is no direct need, it goes on very frequently. There are, in fact, few (if any) domestic units whose numbers do not at some time receive gifts from a source external to the village. Gifts vary in value from a penny to a £2 bag of guinea corn. Generally, outside of cash, they come under three categories: food, clothing, and trinkets, with food being by far the most important.

In some cases, gifts from kinsmen who live and work away from Du mean the difference between starvation and the bare minimum of subsistence. Generally, these cases involve older parents or a widow or (rarely) a widower who has no sons or at the most one or two grown sons, none of whom live in the village. The recipients of such gifts are almost always women. Sons (and daughters) have the primary responsibility for caring for elderly parents, and in Du this takes the form of periodically sending foods to them and sometimes money. The most common food crops received are bags of guinea corn. Every widow reported that she received help in the form of foods from sons and daughters as well as daughter's husbands. The help varies considerably from a few shillings' worth in the summer months (a time of periodic starvation) to two bags of grain plus meats, fruits, some modern canned goods, sugar, salt, and oils. There were three cases of widows who had no sons but were being helped by their sons-in-law. In my survey, there were at least nineteen domestic units that were quite largely dependent on such gifts. In four of these cases, there were no close kinsmen (close in the sense of under strong obligation such as sons, daughters, and sons-in-law), but the members were being fed by other more distantly related persons. Generally, such extreme dependency carries some risks, as few will feed an old person all the time. But an occasional meal from a large number of persons throughout the year, plus food from "begging," often suffices.

8. The stealing of tin and illegal tin mining are understandably sources of income about which it is difficult to get information. One hears about them only through gossip. Informants know that they occur in Du, and some of them know the names of participants. They are fairly regular occupations for a few men, but no one admits to this or is willing to reveal how much income is gained. Some of the younger men justify these activities by arguing that the land was stolen from the Birom and that the tin rightfully belongs to them.

The actual stealing is done by men who know the land areas well. Most men engage in stealing tin ore during the night, and if they are not themselves tributors or contractors, they act as a kind of "hired help" for the Hausa or Igbo man who makes a business of illegal mining. The tin is sold at 6d. or 8d. per cigarette tin, usually to a small operator who does not question its source. During a strike at A.T.M.N. in December 1960, one miner estimated that from three to five tons of tin were stolen in the Bukuru area (Du, Gyel) alone.

These are the economic activities from which the Du people enjoy somewhat more foodstuffs and material goods than what they can produce from the land. Nearly all these are avenues through which goods and money may be and are brought in from the outside world. There is, of course, a great deal of internal barter and trade, exchanging of goods, pawning, and renting of consumable or movable goods as well as of farmlands. By these means, goods and cash are circulated throughout the village. All this means that the Du Birom are dependent on outside markets and sources of income to a surprisingly high degree.

During any specific period of time, all families do not have the benefits deriving from all eight sources of income. Dependence on different resources varies from one family to another and is correlated to a high degree with the number of able-bodied men in the group and with their ages. There are numerous other factors that dictate the nature of income-producing activities. It is important also to note that there is no one stable, permanent source of income for any Birom family in Du village. The only families who could afford to depend on one major source of cash income are the chief, a truck driver, and possibly the two independent mining contractors. But they and their kinsmen also engage in some small trade and have had land compensation. The varieties of incomes are largely sporadic and often indeterminable. Women particularly have become increasingly accustomed to the fragmentary nature of income sources and for most their individual efforts are aimed at expanding their involvement in as many of these activities as possible.

Sharing and gift giving are grounded in the multiplication of personal ties of household members with outsiders. The many ties that households have, especially the critical ties through women, were part of the adaptive strategies utilized by the Birom in the precolonial past and extended into the colonial present. Such ties were essential for the survival of the village and contributed much to the apparent cohesiveness of village life throughout the colonial experience.

Finally, it should be observed that none of the sources of income identified here are predicated on activities that require fundamental change in a person's lifestyle or cultural values. The absence of demand for labor migration meant that the home lives of indigenous peoples employed by the mines were left intact, except for perhaps the daily absence of young women who were only temporarily engaged. Even the acquisition of a skill may be affected through periodic trips (daily or weekly) to the nearby towns or training centers. Only land compensation disrupts some families, namely, those who have been forced to relocate their compounds. Native communities were not required to open up their villages to strangers, nor were their communities altered by government intervention. For all people, cash income enhances their awareness of and interests in the outside world, but the Birom do not view it as basically altering their way of life.

Notes

1. The last survey before the period of this field research was made during 1956–1957 with a goal of identifying the principal crops and land usage on the plateau. It was part of the larger agricultural survey of the Northern Region and provided little detailed data on the plateau peoples. Data are available in Riyom Government Farm Notes, PLA-CRO-15, at the Department of Agriculture.

2. The Birom make standard-size bags for carrying and storing grain. The average bag of *acha* weighs sixty pounds, guinea corn sixty-five, finger millet sixty-five, and bulrush millet seventy.

3. Riyom Government Farm Notes.

4. A greater proportion of *acha* is kept for seed than other grains, although I do not have information about the reason for this practice. It is likely that during the hunger months, even some of this seed is consumed. Davies reports in the Gyel Farm Survey that approximately forty pounds of seed is sown per acre.

5. Tributors are laborers, usually registered with a mining company or operator, who

choose their own areas to work and are paid according to the amount of mineral they produce. Contractors are hired by the mining company to provide laborers for removing the over-burden. They produce no mineral and are paid by the hour or piecemeal by the amount of soil removed.

6. Needless to say, Birom parents love their children as much as any other peoples, and the anguish at the loss of a child is almost unbearable, as I myself witnessed. Their ancient choice was between watching all their children, perhaps the entire kin group, starve to death and vanish or sending one child away to grow up and marry in another society in exchange for food.

The situation of the Birom with respect to their daughters is hardly unique to the human condition. Records from ancient times on and from the British Isles to China show that in extreme deprivation, people throughout the world have resorted at times to the sale or exchange of their children for food. The girls sent to Pyomo lands were no worse off, perhaps better off, than their sisters who remained at home.

Appendix BI
(*Lo Shom Dong* = "*Old Name*")

Lo Gong Jing

Lo Rwang Shom

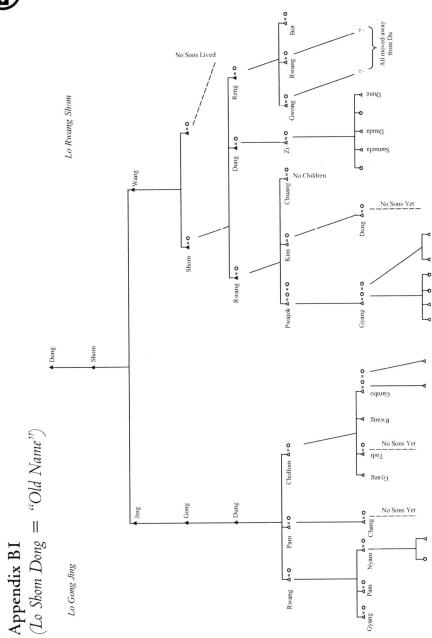

Appendix B2
Lo Gyang Pwara
or
Lo Kwon

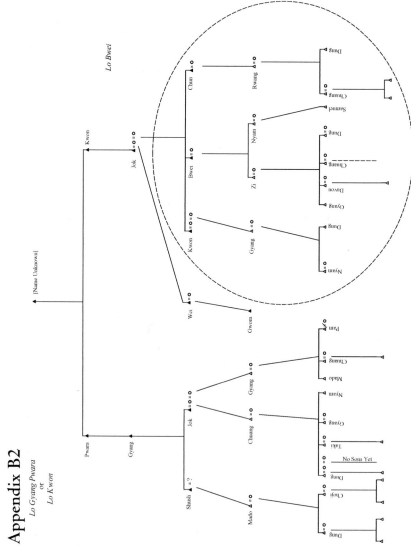

Appendix B3

Lo Chang

(Lo Tok Chang)

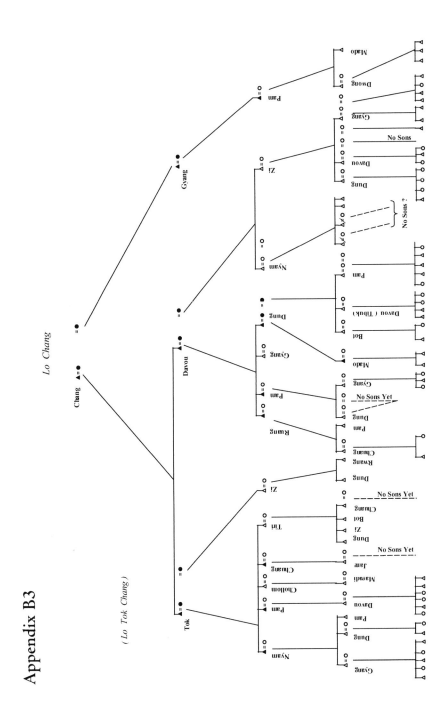

Appendix B4

Lo Gyang Bagei

Lo Dam

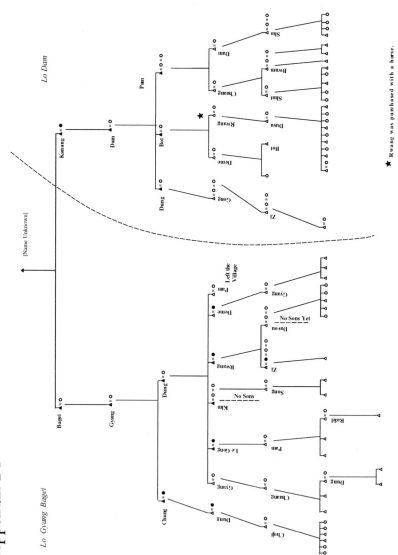

★ Rwang was purchased with a horse.

Appendix B5

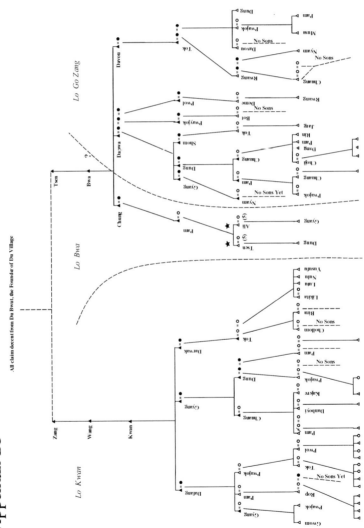

All claim decent from Du Bwai, the Founder of Du Village

Lo Kwan

Lo Bwa

Lo Go Zang

★ At one time, Lo Bwa was a large kin-group, but many deaths have reduced its numbers.
Both Tsen and Ali have had five wives, and most of their sons are dead.

REFERENCES

These are some of the works that have influenced my thinking or provided data that have been called on in this book. I refer often to older literature that provide a gold mine of ethnographic data often unknown to many younger anthropologists. The list is not exhaustive, as numerous other works could have been included.

Adepoju, A., and Christine Oppong, eds. 1994. *Gender, Work and Population in Sub-Saharan Africa.* Portsmouth, N.H.: Heinemann.

Amadiume, I. 1987. *Male Daughters, Female Husbands.* London: Zed.

Ames, C. G. 1934. *Gazetteer of Plateau Province.* Jos: Government Printer.

Archbold, R. A. 1942. "When Pagans Battled on the Bauchi Plateau." *The Crown Colonist,* September, 575–76.

Ardener, Shirley, ed. 1975. *Perceiving Women.* London: Malaby.

Baker, Paul. 1962. "The Application of Ecological Theory to Anthropology." *American Anthropologist* 64, no. 1: 14–21.

Baker, Tanya M. 1954. "The Social Organization of the Birom." Ph.D. diss., University of London.

Barnes, J. A. 1949. "Measures of Divorce Frequency in Simple Societies." *Journal of the Royal Anthropological Institute* 79, nos. 1–2: 37–62.

———. 1955. *Seven Types of Segmentation.* Rhodes-Livingstone Journal, no. 17. Manchester: Manchester University Press.

———. 1959. *Marriage in a Changing Society.* Rhodes-Livingstone Papers, no. 21. London: Oxford University Press.

Barth, Frederick. 1956. "Ecological Relationships of Ethnic Groups in Swat, North Pakistan." *American Anthropologist* 58, no. 4: 1079–89.

———. 1966. *Models of Social Organization.* Royal Anthropological Institute of Great Britain and Ireland Occasional Paper, no. 23. London: Royal Anthropological Institute.

Bates, Daniel G. 1998. *Human Adaptive Strategies.* Needham Heights, Mass.: Allyn & Bacon.

Bauchi Province Reports. 1904. Letter from Assistant Resident, November 24, File S.N.P. 10/3.

Birom Tribal Notebook. 1954, 1959.

Bohannan, Laura. 1952. "A Genealogical Charter." *Africa* 22, no. 4: 301–15.

Bohannan, Laura, and Paul Bohannan. 1953. *The Tiv of Central Nigeria*. Ethnographic Survey of Africa. London: International African Institute.

Bohannan, Paul. 1963. *Social Anthropology*. 1963. New York: Holt, Rinehart and Winston.

———, ed. 1967. *Law and Warfare: Studies in the Anthropology of Conflict*. Garden City, N.Y.: Natural History Press.

Boserup, Ester. 1970. *Woman's Role in Economic Development*. New York: St. Martin's.

Bouquiaux, Luc. 1970. *La Langue Birom*. Bibliotheque de la Faculte de Philosophie et Lettres de l'Univesite de Liege. Paris: Societe d'Edition Les Belles Lettres.

———. 2001. *Dictionnaire Birom*. Paris: Edition Peeters.

Brown, Judith. 1970. "A Note on the Division of Labor by Sex." *American Anthropologist* 72, no. 3: 1072–1978.

Burns, Sir Alan. 1958. *History of Nigeria*. 5th ed. London: George Allen and Unwin.

Cohen, Ronald. 1961. "Marriage Instability among the Kanuri of Northern Nigeria." *American Anthropologist* 63, no. 6: 1231–49.

Cohen, Yehudi. 1968. "Culture as Adaptation." In *Man in Adaptation*. Edited by Y. Cohen. Chicago: Aldine, 45–68.

Colson, Elizabeth. 1958. *Marriage and the Family among the Plateau Tonga of Northern Rhodesia*. Manchester: Manchester University Press.

———. 1960. *Social Organization of the Gwembe Tonga*. Manchester: Manchester University Press.

———. 1974. *Tradition and Contract: The Problem of Order*. Chicago: Aldine.

Cunnison, Ian G. 1956. "Perpetual Kinship: A Political Institution of the Luapula Peoples." *Journal of the Rhodes Livingston Institute*, no. 20: 28–48.

Curtin, Philip D. 1964. *The Image of Africa: British Ideas and Action, 1780–1850*. Madison: University of Wisconsin Press.

Davies, J. G. (A. D. O.). 1944. "Birom Lands: Report of the 1943–44 Gyel Farm Surve." Unpublished manuscript, Northern Nigeria Government Files.

———. 1949. "The Birom." Unpublished manuscript.

———. N.d. "A Note on Birom Land Tenure." Unpublished reports, Northern Nigeria, Government Files, D. C. J. 1403.

Di Leonardo, Micaela. 1991. *Gender at the Crossroads of Knowledge: Feminist Anthropology in the Postmodern Era*. Berkeley: University of California Press.

Epstein, A. L. 1952. *Divorce Law and the Stability of Marriage among the Lunda of Kazembe*. Rhodes-Livingstone Journal, no. 14. Livingstone: Rhodes-Livingstone Institute.

Evans-Pritchard, E. E. 1945. *Some Aspects of Marriage and the Family among the Nuer*. Rhodes-Livingstone Papers, no. 11. Livingstone: Rhodes-Livingstone Institute.

———. 1951. *Kinship and Marriage among the Nuer*. Oxford: Oxford University Press.

———. 1965. *The Position of Women in Primitive Society*. New York: Free Press.

Fallers, L. A. 1957. "Some Determinants of Marriage Stability in Busoga: A Reformulation of Gluckman's Hypothesis." *Africa* 27: 106–21.

Fortes, Meyer. 1945. *The Dynamics of Clanship among the Tallensi*. London: Oxford University Press.

———. 1949. *The Web of Kinship among the Tallensi*. London: Oxford University Press for the International African Institute.

―――. 1953. "The Structure of Unilineal Descent Groups." *American Anthropologist* 55, no. 1: 17–41.

―――. 1959. "Descent, Filiation and Affinity." *Man* 59, no. 309: 193–97; no. 331: 206–12.

―――. 1969. *Kinship and the Social Order*. Chicago: Aldine.

Fortes, M., and E. E. Evans-Pritchard. 1949. *African Political Systems*. London: Oxford University Press.

Frake, Charles O. 1962. "Culture, Ecology and Ethnography." *American Anthropologist* 64, no. 1: 53–59.

Fried, M. H. 1967. *The Evolution of Political Society*. New York: Random House.

Fried, M., M. Harris, and R. Murphy, eds. 1967. *War: The Anthropology of Armed Conflict and Aggression*. New York: Natural History Press.

Friedl, Ernestine. 1975. *Women and Men: An Anthropologist's View*. New York: Holt, Rinehart and Winston.

Gleave, M. B., and R. M. Prothero. 1971. "Population Density and Slave Raiding—A Comment." *Journal of African History* 12, no. 2.

Gleave, M. B., and H. P. White. 1969. "The West African Middle Belt: Environmental Fact or Geographers' Fiction." *Geographical Review* 59.

Gluckman, Max. 1950. "Kinship and Marriage among the Lozi of Northern Rhodesia and the Zulu of Natal." In *African Systems of Kinship and Marriage*. Edited by A. R. Radcliffe-Brown and Daryll Forde. London: Oxford University Press, 166–206.

―――. 1953. "Bridewealth and the Stability of Marriage." *Man* 53 (September): 141–43.

―――. 1955a. *Custom and Conflict in Africa*. Oxford: Basil Blackwell.

―――. 1955b. *The Judicial Process among the Barotse of Northern Rhodesia*. Glencoe, Ill.: Free Press.

―――, ed. 1962. *Essays on the Ritual of Social Relations*. Manchester: Manchester University Press.

―――. 1963. "Gossip and Scandal" [Essays in Honor of Melville J. Herskovits]. *Current Anthropology* 4, no. 3: 307–15.

―――. 1965a. *The Ideas in Barotse Jurisprudence*. New Haven, Conn.: Yale University Press.

―――. 1965b. *Politics, Law and Ritual in Tribal Society*. Chicago Aldine.

Goldschmidt, Walter. 1965. "Theory and Strategy in the Study of Cultural Adaptability." *American Anthropologist* 67, no. 3: 402–7.

Goodenough, Ward. 1955. "A Problem in Malayo-Polynesian Social Organization." *American Anthropologist* 57, no. 1: 71–83.

Goody, Ester N. 1962. "Conjugal Separation and Divorce among the Gonja of Northern Ghana." In *Marriage in Tribal Societies*. Edited by Meyer Fortes. Cambridge: Cambridge University Press.

Goody, Jack. 1959. "The Mother's Brother and the Sister's Son in West Africa." *Journal of the Royal Anthropological Institute* 89, no. 1: 61–89.

―――. 1962. "Fission of Domestic Groups among the LoDagaba." In *The Development Cycle in Domestic Groups*. Edited by Jack Goody. Cambridge: Cambridge University Press, 53–91.

Gough, Kathleen. 1959. "The Nayars and the Definition of Marriage." *Journal of the Royal Anthropological Institute* 89, no. 1: 23–34.

Gray, Robert. 1969. "Sonjo Bride-Price and the Question of African 'Wife Purchase.'" *American Anthropologist* 42, no. 1: 34–57.

Greenberg, J. H. 1956. "The Measurement of Linguistic Diversity." *Language* 32, no. 1: 109–15.

———. 1963. *The Languages of Africa*. La Haye: Mouton.

Grove, A. T. 1952. "Land Use and Soil Conservation on the Jos Plateau." Bulletin 22. *Geological Survey of Nigeria*. Kaduna: Nigerian Government Printer.

Gulliver, P. H. 1963. *Social Control in an African Society*. London: Routledge and Kegan Paul.

Gunn, Harold D. 1953. *Peoples of the Plateau Area of Northern Nigeria, Part VII*. Ethnographic Survey of Africa. London: International African Institute.

———. 1956. *Pagan People of the Central Area of Northern Nigeria*. Ethnographic Survey of Africa. London: International African Institute.

Hafkin, Nancy J., and E. G. Bay, eds. 1976. *Women in Africa: Studies in Social and Economic Change*. Stanford, Calif.: Stanford University Press.

Hallpike, C. R. 1970. "The Principles of Alliance Formation between Konso Towns." *Man* 5, no. 2: 258–80.

Hammond, D., and A. Jablow. 1970. *The Africa That Never Was*. New York: Twayne.

Hardesty, Donald L. 1972. "The Human Ecological Niche." *American Anthropologist* 74, no. 3: 458–66.

Hay, Margaret J., and Sharon Stichter, eds. 1995. *African Women South of the Sahara*. 2d ed. London: Longman.

Helm, June. 1962. "The Ecological Approach in Anthropology." *American Journal of Sociology* 67: 630–39.

Hodgson, Dorothy L. 2000. *Rethinking Pastoralism in Africa: Gender, Culture and the Myth of the Patriarchal Pastoralists*. Oxford: James Curry; Athens: Ohio University Press.

Howard, Alan. 1963. "Land, Activity Systems and Decision-Making Models in Rotuma." *Ethnology* 2: 407–40.

Isichei, Elizabeth. 1982. *Studies in the History of Plateau State, Nigeria*. London: Macmillan.

Johnston, Bruce F. 1958. *The Staple Food Economies of Western Tropical Africa*. Stanford, Calif.: Stanford University Press.

Kaberry, Phyllis M. 1952. *Women of the Grassfields*. London: Her Majesty's Stationery Office.

Keesing, Robert M. 1967. "Statistical Models and Decision Models of Social Structure: A Kwaio Case." *Ethnology* 6: 1–16.

Laws, Col. H. W. 1954. "Some Reminiscences of Colonel H. W. Laws of His Arrival on the Plateau in 1903." *The Nigerian Field* 19, no. 3: 105–17.

Leach, E. R. 1959. "Aspects of Bridewealth and Marriage Stability among the Kachin and Lakher." *Man* 57 (April): 50–55.

Leacock, Eleanor. 1978. "Women's Status in Egalitarian Society." *Current Anthropology* 19, no. 2: 247–75 (with comments and reply).

Lebeuf, Annie M. D. 1960. "The Role of Women in the Political Organization of African Societies." In *Women of Tropical Africa*. Edited by D. Paulme. Berkeley: University of California Press, 93–119.

Lerner, Gerda. 1986. *The Creation of Patriarchy*. New York: Oxford University Press.

Lévi-Strauss, Claude. 1967. *Structural Anthropology*. New York: Doubleday.

———. 1971. "The Family." In *Man, Culture and Society*. Rev. ed. Edited by Harry L. Shapiro. London: Oxford University Press, 261–85.

Mair, Lucy. 1962. *Primitive Government*. Baltimore: Penguin.

Malinowski, B. 1927. *The Father in Primitive Psychology*. London: Kegan Paul.

———. 1930. "Kinship." *Man* 30, no. 17: 19–20.

Maquet, Jacques. 1971. *Power and Society in Africa*. London: Weidenfeld and Nicolson.

Mascia-Lees, F. E., and N. J. Black. 2000. *Gender and Anthropology*. Prospect Heights, Ill.: Waveland.

Mason, Michael. 1969. "Population Density and 'Slave Raiding'—The Case of the Middle Belt of Nigeria." *Journal of African History* 10, no. 4: 551–60.

Mauss, Marcel. 1954 [1923]. *The Gift*. Translated by I. Cunnison. New York: Free Press.

Meek, C. K. 1925. *The Northern Tribes of Nigeria*. London: Oxford University Press.

———. 1950 [1931]. *Tribal Studies in Northern Nigeria*. Vols. 1 and 2. New York: Humanities Press; London: Oxford University Press.

———. 1957. *Land Tenure and Land Administration in Nigeria and Cameroons*. London: Her Majesty's Stationery Office.

———. 1969. *A Sudanese Kingdom*. London: Kegan Paul.

Middleton, John. 1965. *The Lugbara of Uganda*. Case Studies in Cultural Anthropology. New York: Holt, Rinehart and Winston.

Middleton, J., and D. Tait. 1958. *Tribes without Rulers*. London: Routledge and Kegan Paul.

Mikell, Gwendolyn. 1997. "Introduction." In *African Feminism: The Politics of Survival in Sub-Saharan Africa*. Edited by Gwendolyn Mikell. Philadelphia: University of Pennsylvania Press, 1–50.

Milton, K. 1979. "Male Bias in Anthropology." *Man* 14: 40–54.

Mitchell, J. Clyde. 1956. *The Yao Village*. Manchester: Manchester University Press.

Monckton, G. C. 1929. "Report on Land Tenure Customs of Jos Division." Unpublished papers, Government Files, Kaduna.

Muller, Jean-Claude. 1969. "Preferential Marriage among the Rukuba of Benue-Plateau State, Nigeria." *American Anthropologist* 71, no. 6: 1057–61.

Netting, Robert. 1968. *Hill Farmers of Nigeria*. Seattle: University of Washington Press.

———. 1969. "Women's Weapons: The Politics of Domesticity among the Kofyar." *American Anthropologist* 71, no. 6: 1037–46.

Netting, Robert, R. R. Wilk, and E. J. Arnould, eds. 1984. *Households: Comparative and Historical Studies of the Domestic Group*. Berkeley: University of California Press.

Obbo, Christine. 1976. "Dominant Male Ideology and Female Options: Three East African Case Studies." *Africa* 46, no. 2: 371–89.

———. 1980. *African Women*. London: Zed.

Oboler, R. S. 1985. *Women, Power and Economic Change: The Nandi of Kenya*. Stanford, Calif.: Stanford University Press.

Okonjo, Kamene. 1976. "The Dual-Sex Political System in Operation: Igbo Women and Community Politics in Midwestern Nigeria." In *Women in Africa: Studies in Economic and Social Change*. Edited by N. Hafkin and E. Bay. Palo Alto, Calif.: Stanford University Press, 45–58.

Oppong, Christine. 1981. *Female Power and Male Dominance: On the Origins of Sexual Inequality*. Cambridge: Cambridge University Press.

———, ed. 1983. *Female and Male in West Africa*. London: Allyn and Unwin.

Ortner, S., and H. Whitehead. 1981. "Introduction: Accounting for Sexual Meanings." In *Sexual Meanings: The Cultural Construction of Gender and Sexuality*. Cambridge: Cambridge University Press, 1–27.

Paulme, Denise, ed. 1960. *Women of Tropical Africa*. Berkeley: University of California Press.

Peacock, Nadine R. 1991. "Rethinking the Sexual Division of Labor." In *Gender at the Crossroads of Knowledge*. Edited by Michelle di Leonardo. Berkeley: University of California Press, 339–60.

Peters, Emrys. 1960. "The Proliferation of Segments in the Lineage of the Bedouin in Cyrenaica." *Journal of the Royal African Institute* 90, no. 1: 29–53.

Provincial Annual Reports. 1903, 1905, 1906, 1911, 1912, 1921, 1922, 1923, 1924, 1932. Kaduna: Government Printing Office.

Radcliffe-Brown, A. R., and Daryll Forde. 1950. *African Systems of Kinship and Marriage*. London: Oxford University Press for the International African Institute.

Rapport, Roy A. 1967. "Ritual Regulation of Environmental Relations among a New Guinea People." *Ethnology* 6: 17–30.

Reiter, Rayna. 1975. *Toward an Anthropology of Women*. London: Monthly Review Press.

Richards, Audrey. 1939. *Land, Labour and Diet in Northern Rhodesia*. London: Oxford University Press for the International African Institute.

———. 1948. *Hunger and Work in a Savage Tribe*. Glencoe, Ill.: Free Press.

Riyom Government Farm Notes, PLA-CRO—15. "Farm Survey." Department of Agriculture, Northern Nigeria.

Rogers, Susan C. 1975. "Female Forms of Power and the Myth of Male Dominance." *American Ethnologist* 2, no. 4: 727–56.

Rosaldo, M., and L. Lamphere, eds. 1974. *Women, Culture and Society*. Stanford, Calif.: Stanford University Press.

Rowling, C. W. 1940. "Report on Land Tenure, Plateau Province." Kaduna: Government Printer. Manuscript.

Sanday, Peggy R. 1981. *Female Power and Male Dominance*. Cambridge: Cambridge University Press.

Sangree, Walter H. 1969. "Going Home to Mother: Traditional Marriage among the Irigwe of Benue Plateau State, Nigeria." *American Anthropologist* 71, no. 6: 1037–61.

———. 1972. "Secondary Marriage and Tribal Solidarity in Irigwe, Nigeria." *American Anthropologist* 74, no. 5: 1234–43.

Schapera, Isaac. 1963. *Studies in Kinship and Marriage*. Occasional paper, no. 16. London: Royal Anthropological Institute.

———. 1967. *Government and Politics in Tribal Societies*. New York: Schocken.

Schlegel, Alice. 1972. *Male Dominance and Female Autonomy*. New Haven, Conn.: Human Relations Area Files.

Schneider, David. 1953. "A Note on Bridewealth and the Stability of Marriage." *Man* 53 (April): 55–57.

Service, Elman R. 1971 [1962]. *Primitive Social Organization*. New York: Random House.

Skinner, Elliott P. 1961. "Intergenerational Conflict among the Mossi: Father and Son." *Journal of Conflict Resolution* 5, no. 1: 55–60.

Slocum, Sally. 1975. "Women the Gatherer: Male Bias in Anthropology." In *Toward an Anthropology of Women*. Edited by Rayna R. Reiter. New York: Monthly Review Press, 36–50.

Smedley, Audrey. 1974. "Women of Udu: Survival in a Harsh Land." In *Many Sisters: Women in Cross-Cultural Perspective*. Edited by C. Matthiesson. Glencoe, Ill.: Free Press, 205–28.

———. 1980. "The Implications of Birom Cicisbeism." In *Women with Many Husbands: Polyandrous Alliance and Marital Flexibility in Africa and Asia*. Special issue of the *Journal of Comparative Family Studies* 11, no. 3: 345–57.

Smith, M. G. 1953. "Secondary Marriage in Northern Nigeria." *Africa* 23: 298–323.

Spencer, Robert F. 1959. *The North Alaskan Eskimo*. Bulletin 71. Smithsonian Institution, Bureau of American Ethnology. Washington, D.C.: U.S. Government Printing Office.

Sudan United Mission. 1910, 1913, 1914, 1918, 1919. *The Lightbearer*.

Sudarkasa, Niara. 1974. *Where Women Work: A Study of Yoruba Women in the Marketplace and in the Home*. Paper 53. Ann Arbor: University of Michigan, Museum of Anthropology.

Sweet, Louise. 1965a. "Camel Pastoralism in North Arabia and the Minimal Camping Unit." In *Man, Culture and Animals*. Edited by Anthony Leeds and A. P. Vayda. Publication 78. Washington, D.C.: American Association for the Advancement of Science.

———. 1965b. "Camel Raiding of North Arabian Bedouin." *American Anthropologist* 67, no. 5: 1132–50.

Tait, David. 1953. "The Political System of the Konkomba." *Africa* 23.

———. 1956. "The Family, Household and Minor Lineage of the Konkomba." *Africa* 26: 219–49, 332–42.

Temple, O., and C. Temple, eds. 1919. *Notes on the Tribes, etc. of the Northern Provinces of Nigeria*. Capetown: Government Printing Office.

Tremearne, A. J. N. 1912. *Tailed Headhunters of Nigeria*. London: N.p.

Turner, V. W. 1957. *Schism and Continuity in an African Society*. Manchester: Manchester University Press.

Vayda, Andrew P. 1961. "Expansion and Warfare among Swidden Agriculturalists," *American Anthropologist* 63, no. 2, pt. 1: 346–58.

———, ed. 1969. *Environment and Cultural Behaviour*. New York: Natural History Press.

Vogt, Evon Z. 1960. "On the Concepts of Structure and Process in Cultural Anthropology." *American Anthropologist* 62, no. 1: 18–33.

Walker, Anthony. 1986. *The Toda of South India: A New Look*. Delhi: Hindustan Publishers.

Weiner, Annette. 1976. *Women of Value, Men of Renown*. Austin: University of Texas Press.

Wolfe, Alvin. 1959. "The Dynamics of the Ngombe Segmentary System." In *Continuity and Change in African Cultures*. Edited by William R. Bascom and M. J. Herskovits. Chicago: University of Chicago Press, 168–86.

Worsley, Peter. 1956 "The Kinship System of the Tallensi: A Revaluation." *Journal of the Royal Anthropological Institute* 86, no. 1: 37–75.

Wright, Quincy. 1965. *A Study of War*. 2d ed. Chicago: University of Chicago Press.

Yanagisako, Sylvia. 1979. "Family and Household: The Analysis of Domestic Groups." *Annual Review of Anthropology* 8: 161–205.

INDEX

acha (*digitaria exilis*), 34, 35, 45, 68–69, 73, 139–41. *See also* farming
adaptation, 7, 227, 228–35; strategies of adaption, 32–41
affines, affinal, 213–17
agnatic collaterality, 85
agnatic kin groups, 53–58, 65, 75, 84–99; agnation, 196–207; conflict among, 197–201
alluvial mining, 21
Amalgamated Tin Mines, 49
avunculate, 207–13

Baker, Tonya, 5, 7, 28, 40, 41–43, 102
Barton, Rev. Charles, 28. *See also* missionaries
Bauchi Province Reports, 20, 21, 47
Birom Tribal Notebook, 21
brideprice, bridewealth (*dwa*), 38, 92, 131, 136–43; in cash, 157
Bukuru, 17, 18

Christians, 15, 19, 27
cicisbeism, (*njem*), 134, 138, 179, 217–24, 231
colonialism, 16, 17–30
congested areas, 49
core groups, 58–63

divorce, 132, 139, 169
domestic domain, 9, 229, 231–35
domestic unit, 163–94
Du (Udu), 49–63

ecology, 8, 31–48, 65–81, 227–35
exchange value of women, 134–43

farming, 32, 144, 240–45; cereal crops, 34; horticulture, 32
forests, deforestation, 20–21

gender division of labor, 65, 129–31, 143–53, 229
gender and property, 173–88
Great Ceremonies, 103

Hausa, 17, 18, 24–27, 37
horses (*dwa*), 36, 38. *See also* brideprice
hunger, as cultural theme, 45–48

institutionalized enmity, 44–45
intervillage relationships, 41, 44
Islam, Muslim, 15, 19, 28

Jos plateau, 15
Jos, town of, 15–19

kin groups. *See* agnatic kin groups; structured kinship

labor, 24
land alienation, 21; land compensation, 22, 23–24, 79–81
Laws, William Henry, 17
Levirate, 148, 166
life cycle of kin group, 83–89

markets, 19
marriage, 129–61; function of, 131; life
    cycle of, 163; stability of, 132–33
mining, alluvial, 21. *See also* tin-mining
missionaries, 27–30
multicentric economy, 38

Naraguta Tin Mines, Ltd., 18
Native Administration, 18
Netting, Robert, 33
Nigeria, 15, 16, 35
Njem. *See* cicisbeism

old age, 147–49, 230–31

paternity, 137, 138, 157
patrilineal ideology, 4–5, 53–55
politicojural domain, 9, 53–63, 105–11. *See
    also* wards, 113–27
polygyny, 149–52
population, 52
Pyomo marriages, 135–36

rituals, 101–11; intervillage, 103–5

segmentation, definitive, 78, 88–89, 94–99
slavery, slave raiding, 17, 38, 65
social organization, 53–63
sodalities, 58–63, 101, 103
structured kinship, 153–58, 195
Sudan Interior Mission, 29–30
Sudan United Mission, 28. *See also* mission-
    aries

theory of patriliny, 227–28
tin mining, 17–30; brothels/prostitution in,
    26; influence of mining camps, 24; mar-
    kets in, 25; mine labor, 24, 245–49
types of farms, 66–69

wanderers, 76
wards (manjei), 51–52, 113–27
warfare, 38–45
women's rights to land, 175–79

ABOUT THE AUTHOR

Audrey Smedley has a B.A. in history and an M.A. in anthropology and history from the University of Michigan. She received her Ph.D. in social anthropology from the University of Manchester, England. She has taught at Wayne State University, Oakland University, Tufts University, the State University of New York at Binghamton, and Virginia Commonwealth University. Her most significant work so far has been on the development of the idea of race with two editions of her book *Race in North America: Origin and Evolution of a Worldview* (1993, 1999). Along with numerous articles and book chapters, she has also prepared major items for *Encyclopaedia Britannica* on race and on African societies. Since her two years of field research in northern Nigeria, Smedley has traveled and lectured widely. Her interests continue to be on how human societies structure their social relationships.